TIPS FOR PSYCHIC SELF-DEVELOPMENT

In *The Complete Book of Psychic Arts*, experienced psychics and channelers offer several suggestions on how you can develop your psychic abilities. Among them are:

- Experiment with different forms of divination. You may start out with tarot cards, but get better results with remote viewing or psychometry. Search and you will find the methods that work best for you.

- Practice regularly. When beginning, keep your sessions short—twenty to thirty minutes. If you practice on a routine basis, the psi action will eventually become automatic.

- Learn from a teacher. A teacher does not have to be a famous seer, just someone who knows the ropes better than you and who can help you along until you gain experience.

- Attend workshops and developing circles. In these groups the psi energy of many is pooled and the student tends to make more rapid progress than when starting out solo.

- Go slowly. Accept the visions you receive; don't force results.

About the Author

Morwyn (Colorado) first became fascinated with psychic phenomena as a child and resolved, at age ten, to devote her life to developing her own psychic potential. Since then, Morwyn has studied the American Pagan Movement; Ceremonial Magick; Witchcraft in England, Wales, and Scotland; Meiga magick in Galicia; and Afro-Brazilian magical traditions in Brazil. She also owns a mail-order metaphysical supplies company, Dunraven House.

To Contact the Author

If you wish to contact the author or would like more information about this book, please write to the author in care of Llewellyn Worldwide and we will forward your request. Both the author and the publisher appreciate hearing from you and learning of your enjoyment of this book and how it has helped you. Llewellyn Worldwide cannot guarantee that every letter to the author can be answered, but all will be forwarded. Please write to:

Morwyn
℅ Llewellyn Worldwide
P.O. Box 64383, Dept. K236-4
St. Paul, MN 55164-0383

Please enclose a self-addressed, stamped envelope for reply, or $1.00 to cover costs.
If outside U.S.A., enclose postal reply coupon.

DIVINATION PRACTICES FROM AROUND THE WORLD

THE COMPLETE BOOK OF PSYCHIC ARTS

MORWYN

1999
Llewellyn Publications
St. Paul, Minnesota 55164-0383

FIRST EDITION
First Printing, 1999

Cover design by Lisa Novak
Editing and interior design by Astrid Sandell

Library of Congress Cataloging-in-Publication Data
Morwyn.
    The complete book of psychic arts : divination practices from around the world /
Morwyn.—1st ed.
        p. cm.
    Includes bibliographical references and index.
    ISBN 1-56718-236-4
      1. Divination—History. 2. Spiritualism—History. 3. Psychic ability—History. I. Title.
BF1750 .M67 1999
133—dc21   99-045050

Llewellyn Publications
A Division of Llewellyn Worldwide, Ltd.
P.O. Box 64383, Dept. K236-4
St. Paul, MN 55164-0383
www.llewellyn.com

Printed in the United States of America

DEDICATION

For my husband, John, the scientist, who has served as editor, devil's advocate, coach, and inspiration for all my books over the years.

Special thanks to Tom Csere for providing me with many important respondents' names.

And to all of the survey respondents who wrote their hearts out in service of their field.

Contents

PREFACE

The atmosphere of the exhibition hall resonates with energy and expectancy. Even a person relatively not tuned in psychically can tell the merchants have slaved for two days to make their booths as attractive as possible to entice the public to buy their wares. Some sellers, decked out in Renaissance-style flowing robes, put the final touches to their displays, arranging a set of incenses just so, adjusting the lighting on the crystal display, placing medicine pouches next to books on shaman visioning.

Around the perimeter, psychics, channelers, and astrologers sit at card tables, some preparing themselves for the day's readings by meditating or silently chanting a mantra. Others, spying old friends, gather in clusters of two or three and chat quietly, catching up on each other's recent activities.

Once in a while, an exhibitor glances at the long line of customers forming inside the entrance and extending into the parking lot beyond the field of vision.

"Looks like it's going to be a pretty good turnout," someone comments, referring to the throng of people of all ages, shapes, and ethnic groups almost visibly palpitating with repressed excitement. Others nod in agreement.

This is the Colorado Metaphysical Fair, the largest and most successful event of its kind in the region. The fair has thrived for a number of years under the able direction of Shanti and Coreen Toll, becoming something of an institution regularly attended by thousands.

Somewhere a gong sounds and a hush falls over the hall. Shanti steps up to a podium to go over the "dos and don'ts" of the fair, and leads the group in a short meditation. Then he says, "Thank you all for participating today. We have a great fair planned, with many events and speakers from all over the country. Let us remember that our main purpose is to serve the community by providing high quality merchandise and insightful readings. May we offer to the public gifts of Spirit, and provide seekers with what they need to help improve their lives, find happiness, and attain higher knowledge, in the spirit of true community and fellowship, Love and Light. Let the fair begin!"

With that, the doors burst open, and the public streams in, moving rapidly past the merchandise booths to the perimeters, hardly glancing at the wares so carefully set on display. They are racing to sign up for sessions with their favorite psychic and intuitive readers, channelers, or aura portraitists and don't want to be disappointed by filled appointment cards, since some readers command a wide following. The merchandise can wait. The most important goal is to get a good psychic reading from a reputable practitioner.

Veteran vendors stand, smiling greetings at the faces in the crowd. They understand that they probably won't do much business for a couple of hours, but their time will come. After a while, customers riding high on their readings will filter back from the psychics' tables. The fairgoers, feeling they now can spend time leisurely browsing through the merchandise on display, will buy books, tarot cards, tapes, incense, rain sticks—all the goods associated with psychic phenomena, natural healing, and the Occult.

As the day goes along, trade picks up. Customers leave satisfied with the items they have purchased and with their readings, which have given them fresh insights and new directions to pursue. Readers and merchants close down their booths, feeling fulfilled in that they have provided needed services to the public, and that they, too have learned more about life and humanity.

Everyone, it seems, wants to know what the future will bring. Psychic fairs, like the one described above, are tremendously popular, attracting thousands every year. Practically every newspaper contains a horoscope column that loyal readers avidly scan this art consciously attempt to foresee the future and communicate it to others. Precognition differs in that it may be spontaneous, triggered by a personal crisis, or perceived in a dream.

Retrocognition, precognition's opposite, concentrates on acquiring knowledge of past events and circumstances by paranormal means. For example, by touching or holding an artifact from an archaeological dig, a type of clairvoyant called a psychometrist can relay information about the object—where it came from, how it was made, its purpose, who possessed it. Retrocognition also enters into past-life readings, in which a psychic, who believes that people are reborn—that is, reincarnated on Earth over many lifetimes—tells people about their former existences.

You may have read about or seen stage performers who, through the power of concentration and force of will, cause objects to move and may even bend spoons. Or perhaps you've heard tales of houses where the contents move around all by themselves with no apparent physical agent involved, sometimes flying through the air and dashing against walls and ceilings. These are examples of two different kinds of psychokinesis, or PK. Both phenomena exercise the conscious or unconscious influence of mind over matter without resorting to the senses or any physical means.

Together, ESP and PK are known as *psi,* a term coined by psychologist Robert Thouless from a letter of the Greek alphabet. Psi encompasses a whole range of paranormal phenomena, including everything mentioned so far as well as intuition, dreams, and hallucinations.

WHERE DOES PSI COME FROM?

Parapsychology is the study of paranormal events. The researchers who apply scientific means to experiment with these activities and analyze findings are called psychical researchers or parapsychologists. Many psychical researchers believe that psi talents actually are inherent faculties that everyone possesses. They have found that people can enhance and refine these facilities with concentration and practice. Often, they liken psi skills to the ability to singing: everyone who can speak can sing. The talent can be improved by taking voice lessons, but some people are naturally better at it than others. In the paranormal field, those who are "better at it" either by nature, or by practice, are known as psychics or clairvoyants.

Louisa E. Rhine, one of the first modern parapsychologists, once commented that over several years of observation and experimentation, she came to the conclusion that some people are especially gifted. For the rest of us, the faculty "operates unconsciously; it only breaks through a little now and then, like flecks of sunshine on a rainy day."2

Some psychics are convinced that Divinity has invested them with this gift, and that it is their responsibility to use it to help other people sort out life issues. Some of these seers assert that their occult knowledge of such matters derives from communion with spirits of the dead. These people call themselves Spiritualist mediums because they mediate between spirits and humans. They hold that spirits inhabit another world, sometimes called the astral plane, which coincides with the physical world in space, if not necessarily in time. If a medium falls into an altered state of consciousness, called a trance, in order to communicate with spirits, this person is referred to as a trance medium. If, in the presence of the medium, objects like bouquets of flowers, small stones, or musical instruments suddenly appear out of nowhere, or a milky substance condenses and shapes up into a likeness of the spirit, the person is called a physical medium. Object materializations are known as apports, and the milky, etheric substance is named ectoplasm.

These days, most mediums are called channelers, and channeling has become popular with people who are searching to expand their spiritual horizons. Channelers may or may not believe that they commune with spirits of the dead. Many indicate that they contact other nonphysical entities such as angels, demons, aliens, and evolved beings from higher planes of existence, known as the inner planes. Channelers do exactly what their name implies—they open a channel, or a line of communication through their physical bodies between individuals of this world and essences from other realms. You will meet many channelers and mediums in this book, as well as those who practice other psychic arts.

Is This Stuff for Real?

The visions are in the mind or soul of the seer and nowhere else.
—Sepharial, *Second Sight*3

That is the $64,000 question! In this age, the physical sciences reign supreme. Our modern societies have progressed on the material plane quite a bit since the days before the Industrial Revolution. Thanks go to scientists who developed theories about how the universe operates and originated a scientific method to prove or disprove new findings according to these theories. In many cases their ideas have worked. But not in every case. For these scientists, psi is troublesome because it steps outside the boundaries of current scientific knowledge and defies the rules. And when the carefully elaborated rules are broken, the sovereigns of science are not amused.

Precognition is viewed as a prime miscreant because it presupposes that a person can know about an event that will take place sometime in the future without resorting to the normal five senses. Telepathy commits a similar sort of offense because the perpetrators, otherwise known as telepaths, also bypass the normal sensory channels and transmit information by using the mind alone. A telepath often knows what is happening to another person in a faraway place at the moment the event is occurring. This ability defies the laws of physics as they are understood today that states that nothing can travel faster than the speed of light and that no matter the type of signal, its potency weakens over distance. And the telepath doesn't even feel remorse!

According to physics, psi misbehaves in a number of ways. It is difficult to measure by current scientific methods because it often occurs spontaneously or at times of personal crisis. It may rely on an emotional bond—called rapport—that is established between the experimenter and the psychic subject. Emotions have no place in a rigidly scientific worldview. Psi events are also notoriously difficult to repeat under environmentally unfriendly conditions, such as the sterile world of the laboratory. After all, psi relates to the psychic realm, and the word *psychic* is derived from a Greek term that involves the soul, the unconscious, and the life force. How can any traditional scientist worth his salt be expected to quantify such things?

The worst part is that psi raises questions about the nature of reality and implies that an aspect of human nature exists that is deeper than the conveniently measurable physical shell we all walk around in. Renegade parapsychological notions challenge the neatly compartmentalized universe that traditional science has so meticulously constructed. If what the parapsychologists claim is true, the traditional scientists might have to change their opinions or eventually be transcended. So what can the opposing camps do but fight?

Luckily, it seems that a branch of science called quantum mechanics is on the threshold of discovering at least a partial solution to this quandary. Maybe no blood will be shed in the fight, after all! Quantum mechanics, by studying the behavior of subatomic particles, has come up with the theory that the universe is connected in hidden ways. These recondite connections may account for different forms of awareness in the human mind such as clairvoyance. In the Time-Life Books series *Mysteries of the Unknown,* the editors offer a famous example that shows how subatomic particles follow rules that run counter to the laws of physics:

> In this thought experiment, two particles—say, an electron and its antimatter equivalent, a positron—collide, annihilating each other and creating two photons, which speed off in different directions. By the strange laws of quantum mechanics, photon A does not possess properties such as spin or velocity until it is noted by an observer; the very act of measurement is said to "collapse its wave function" and assign it values at random. At the moment that observers do measure photon A, causing it to acquire a certain spin, photon B will acquire the opposite spin, no matter how far away it is, and despite having no connection with the first particle. Photon B somehow seems to "know" instantaneously what photon A is doing.[4]

It would seem that the capacity and function of memory is far more complex than anybody realizes. If such occurrences take place at a subatomic level, why not also inside a clairvoyant's head? Perhaps the psychics are tuning into memories they don't consciously know they have.

People of all ages and conditions from cultures around the world have been fascinated by psychic phenomena, including divination, for centuries. Each group of "psi explorers" has made some contribution to the understanding of the big picture, and this is why the history of the field is included in the first part of the book. Part II of this book offers more about the nature of psi and how it works discussed from the point of view of those who practice it. Part II also visits with current-day "explorers," fielding their opinions on the subject.

THE PSYCHICS SURVEY

In my quest to find out more about the paranormal, I decided to go straight to the "oracle's mouth," as it were, and directly contact psychics around the country and the world. Who better than the practitioners themselves to shed light on the subject?

I drew up a list of professionals culled from personal contacts, media advertisements, and published listings of names. I didn't want to exclusively interview professionals because I was also interested to see how the population at large handles their psychic faculties, and if these amateurs' opinions differed from the professionals'. To this end, I added to the list names of individuals who divine for themselves, family,

The Egyptians also developed a system of astrology/astronomy, in part to forecast the time of the annual flooding of the Nile. They called the star upon which they based their calculations the heralding "Sothis" star, or "dog star."

These fatalistic people who lived along the Nile held that a person's future was pre-ordained by the position of the stars and planets in the sky at the moment of birth. Consequently, parents had horoscopes cast for newborns and also consulted the Hathors. These women, who took their name from the goddess Hathor, also known as the Queen of Heaven, were endowed with remarkable psychic gifts.

If a person wanted to uncover more details about mundane aspects of their lives, they could consult a priest, who produced a talisman and a piece of black cloth and instructed the inquirer to wrap them together and wind them around the left hand and wrist before retiring for the night. The priest also gave the sleeper certain names of power or magickal formulas to recite before sleeping in order to induce a prophetic dream about the question. One of the formulas, written on a papyrus in the British Museum in London, reads:

> Sachmu . . . epaema that Ligotereench, the Aeon, the Thunderer, Thou that hast swallowed the snake and dost exhaust the moon, and dost raise up the orb of the sun in his season, Chthetho is the name; I require, O lords of the gods, Seth, Chreps, give me the information that I desire!

Officially sanctioned dream interpreters held office and recorded many prophetic dreams for posterity.

ANCIENT GREECE AND ROME

Two basic divisions within the art of divination have been distinguished since early times. The first is direct vision, such as the Egyptian priests' dreams and interpretations, or any information gleaned clairvoyantly by entering an altered state of consciousness, through crystal gazing, pyromancy, or by experiencing premonitions. In the second category is divination by analogy, where the chance arrangements of objects (like cowrie shells, runestones, bones), statements overheard, observations of the behavior of animals, patterns of smoke rising from burning incense, and cloud movements are interpreted in light of a specific question.

Aristotle, while exploring some Egyptian ruins, discovered a document on palmistry, which was later translated, and today forms part of the basis for Western palmistry.

The great mathematician Pythagoras (582–497 B.C.) consulted a magick mirror that he held up to the light of the moon in order to divine the future.

Apollonius of Tyana, a Pythagorean scholar and mystic of the early Christian era, learned divination techniques on his travels to Babylon, India, and Asia. He was also attributed with the ability to communicate with the dead, and is credited with having raised the ghost of Achilles.

Even Cicero (106–43 B.C.), the renowned Roman orator and author, while somewhat skeptical about astrology and fortunetelling techniques, believed that dreams could foretell the future.

Greek mythology reveals how predominant the divinatory arts were in that culture. For example, a Spindle of Fate of human destiny was turned by the goddesses known as the Three Fates. Clotho spun out birth and the thread of life; Lachesis wove the length of life; and Atropos, when the time was nigh, snipped the life thread with her shears. The lunar goddess, Hecate, with snakes coiling from her hair and attended by howling dogs, was another who could foretell the destiny of all human beings. This dark goddess reminds me of Exu in the Afro-Brazilian pantheon. In the same way that Exu is not an orixá (god), Hecate is not considered an Olympian. As with Exu, the traveler is likely to run across her on a lonely road or at a crossroads, as one of her titles, *antaia,* "she who meets," suggests. Most people were terrified of her, as they are of Exu, because of her bizarre appearance. Nonetheless, it is Hecate for the ancient Greeks, and Exu for the Brazilians, who is able to tell the future.

In spite of Hecate's formidable powers, both in Greece and Rome, the male god Apollo became the patron of prophecy and protector of the Muses, humankind's guiding geniuses. Originally this privilege belonged to Gaia, Mother Earth, but she was preempted by the sun god who nevertheless, retained the goddess's snakes as his symbol. Apollo's prophetic voice was considered universal, expanding beyond geographical barriers. Many sacred sites or oracles, from where the deity's voice was alleged to flow, existed throughout the ancient world. At the temple of Delphi, located at the foot of Mount Parnassus, the voice of Apollo most clearly resonated through his mediums, who were also called pythonesses.

Justinian, a Roman historian, describes the site before the temple was built:

> In a dark and narrow recess of a cliff at Delphi there was a little green glade, and in this hole, or cleft in the earth, out of which blew a strong draft of air straight up as if impelled by a wind, which filled the minds of poets with madness.[4]

ANCIENT AMERICANS

On the other side of the globe and presumably free from influence from both the Occident and the Orient, the Aztec empire of Mexico founded a college of augurs that offered courses in astrology and oracle interpretation (like observing the flights and songs of birds) as did the Romans. The goddess Toxi was the augurs' patroness.

Inca priests of South America made predictions by interpreting the patterns formed by coca leaves and grains of corn, as well as by examining the courses taken by spiders and the way fruit fell to the ground. Contemporary shamans from the Andean Highlands still divine with coca leaves.

Many U. S. American tribes seemed to follow similar traditions of interpreting oracles and dreams, and they practiced self-hypnosis by singing, sleep deprivation, dancing, prayer, and ingestion of psychedelic botanicals. After these preparations, the shaman entered the lodge alone and closed the opening. Soon a great clamoring arose from inside, and the tent shook as if being assaulted by demonic forces. Then the shaman asked questions and the spirits imparted predictions. The Spiritualist "cabinet" where the Spiritualists of the nineteenth century sat and produced physical manifestations of spirits, which will be described in the next chapter, is based on the Indian Shamanic lodges.

PAGAN EUROPE

Foremost among the many tribes that settled Northern Europe were the Celts and the Norse. They performed the same general kinds of divination as did the other cultures worldwide, and volumes are filled with the history and legends surrounding their practices. At the time they held power, Northern Europe was blanketed with vast forests, so tree oracles became a favorite mode of divination. Great store was also set by the snorting and gait of horses.

Since writing in any form was highly regarded, both the Celts and the Norse carved runic symbols into tree bark and rocks and scattered them on the ground to discover clues to the future. Only initiates known as runemasters and runemistresses could interpret the symbols. Stones, shells, and herbs were used in the same way. They also availed themselves of the ubiquitous cauldron for scrying.

These priests and priestesses lived lonely, nomadic existences, isolated from society. In spite of their hermitic ways, they were respected by all because when they appeared in villages or farmsteads, they foretold the residents' futures. These venerated shamans must have presented a mysterious sight to the simple farmers and villagers. They dressed in thick, dark blue cloaks and headdresses stitched from fur of badgers and other wild creatures. The women covered their hands with white catskin mittens and adorned their necks with gold torcs. After calling down the spirits with drums, rattles, and frenzied dancing, they read fortunes and healed the sick with snake bones, herbs, and sacred stones. Then they were regaled with a banquet and treated to the best accommodations the villagers could muster in a gesture of appreciation for their efforts.

PROPHETS OF THE RENAISSANCE

As European society evolved, so the science of divination became richer and more complex. By the time of the Renaissance, the world was starting to shrink and people, at least those of the privileged classes, began to travel beyond their boundaries to far-away places. They learned from other cultures and brought home the fruit of their accumulated knowledge to refine all fields of study, including prediction.

Many Renaissance magicians based their theories, in part, on the works of Hermes Trismegistus, a writer of the third century A.D., who, in turn, drew on Egyptian, Greek, Gnostic, and early Christian sources. His *Corpus Hermeticus* was translated in 1450 by Ficino. These voluminous writings dealing with astrology, magic, geography, medicine, education, and hymns to the gods were probably the work of several authors. The phrase now used by ceremonial magicians to explain the relationship between the macrocosm and the microcosm, "As above, so below," originates in Hermetic doctrine.

The material accumulated by Renaissance scholars marks the beginning of modern occultism, and the science of divination forms a part of this grand system. Chief among these Renaissance magicians was Paracelsus (1493–1524), Swiss naturopath physician, alchemist, and Hermetic philosopher, who among other things, wrote about crystal gazing.

Cornelius Agrippa von Nettesheim (1486–1535), like many of the figures of the time, was something of a character. This flamboyant, brilliant, but undisciplined true "Renaissance man" lived by his wits. His resumé looks like either a job counselor's nightmare or dream: he was everything, including a doctor, lawyer, financial advisor, historian, scholar, astrologer, alchemist, faith healer, exorcist, and secret agent. He treats modes of divination, including geomancy, astrology, and sieve divination in his masterpiece, *De occultis philosopha.*

Other contributors to the field include Jean Tibaulte, a French astrologer whose *La Physionomie des songes et visions fantastiques de personnes* (1530) forms the basis for modern dream interpretation, and Robert Fludd (1574–1637), an English alchemist and Rosicrucian thoroughly versed in geomancy. Around this time, the oldest existing tarot pack, the fifteenth-century Tarot of Charles VI surfaced. Rhabdomancy came into general use in sixteenth-century German mines as a way to help discover ore.

Colorful figures began to emerge in England. Even before the Renaissance, Roger Bacon (1214–1294), a monk and writer, was also an occultist. The good friar immersed himself in the study of astronomy/astrology, alchemy, mathematics, and herbal healing. He possessed a magickal glass through which he could peer and allegedly discern what his friends and relatives were doing within a fifty-mile radius. Since in those days most people rarely traveled far from home, this ability showed omniscient powers indeed.

Another Englishman, George Fox (1624–1691), became famous when he published a book in 1661 that predicted the London plague of 1665 and the fire of 1666. He claimed to have received the prophecies directly from God. Fox went on to found the Society of Friends (Quakers).

The paragon of seers and magicians of Elizabethan England was Dr. John Dee (1527–1608). This versatile personality was a graduate of Trinity College, Cambridge, geographer, philosopher, personal physician to the queen and her 007 secret agent in France, who also practiced astrology, rhabdomancy, crystal gazing, and necromancy. He owned several scrying balls—his famous smoky quartz crystal is displayed in the British Museum. With the help of medium Edward Kelley, he transcribed an angelic language called Enochian, still used by many ceremonial magicians to lend power to their rites.

Let it never be said that interest in astrology is merely an end-of-the-twentieth-century fad. Dr. Francis Moore (1656–1715), affectionately known as "Old Moore," for several years published *Old Moore's Almanack,* a potpourri of astrological information, predictions, herbal remedies, and medical advertisements. At the height of its popularity when most people only read the Bible, if they could read at all, the *Almanack* commanded an astounding circulation of more than a half-million copies.

Great Britain has always been an "equal opportunity nation" when it comes to divination, claiming as many female seers as males. Renowned during the Renaissance was Ursula Sontheil (1488–1561), better known as Mother Shipton. The daughter of the union between a psychic beggar accused of Witchcraft and a young aristocrat,

Sonthiel was raised in a convent and married Toby Shipton in Yorkshire at the age of twenty-four. She soon found that she possessed the uncanny ability to predict births, deaths, and marriages of those around her. Her infallible accuracy encouraged her to broaden her scope, and she began to foretell military and political events like the takeover of France by Henry VIII, Lady Jane Grey's death, and the fate of the Spanish Armada. Speaking in the symbolic language of poetry (a phenomenon more common to that era than this), she predicted discoveries far into the future like the telegraph and submarine, and the popularity of the tobacco and potato plants. In the end, she accurately foresaw the exact day and hour of her death.

The doyen of the era, however, was not an Englishman, but a New Christian (converted Jew) physician from St. Rémy, France, Michel de Notredame, better known as Nostradamus (1503–1566). He treated many patients, including his wife and children, who died horrible deaths from the plague. The sight of so much unnecessary suffering made the doctor question the meaning of life and death. In typical Renaissance fashion, he left his practice and traveled around Europe, studying alchemy and learning to predict the future by holding a forked rod over a bowl of water set on a brass tripod.

He published his first almanac of predictions in 1550, and in 1555 brought forth *The Centuries,* his most renowned predictive work, which has never yet gone out of print. He was sought after by those of noble birth and became Catherine de Medici's personal astrologer.

Nostradamus interpreters have found in his writings references to the French Revolution, the rise of Hitler and Mussolini, Hiroshima, East/West conflicts, AIDS, the Kennedy assassinations, and the advent of nuclear energy. While a heavy cloud of doom and gloom hovers over many of his prophecies, Nostradamus also foretells an environmental golden age, a time following the epoch of "acrid skies" (taken by some to mean environmental pollution) of spiritual renewal and peace on Earth with triumph of good over evil.

It is difficult to ascertain how much of what Nostradamus says represents actual predictions and how much can be chalked up to the inventiveness of his interpreters. In order to avoid persecution by the Inquisition, he purposely set forth his prognostications in a mixture of languages, including French, Provençal, and Latin. The almost 1,000 quatrain verses are replete with highly obfuscatory symbolism. No wonder there is so much room for interpretation.

DIVINATION IN THE AGE OF ENLIGHTENMENT

The eighteenth century is supposed to be the time when Westerners first turned toward a rational, experimental, and observational approach to science, which heralded the modern era. While members of the scientific community and the population at large took a skeptical view of the more outrageous claims of some prestidigitators, not all forms of divination fell into disrepute. Renewed fascination with all things Egyptian spurred interest in ancient methods of forecast, and ceremonial magicians still fervently sought to communicate with angels and other spirits.

Prominent scientists like physicist and mathematician Sir Isaac Newton and mining engineer, political economist, anatomist, and zoologist Emmanuel Swedenborg took their occult studies seriously. Newton (1642–1727) was a student of prophecy, especially of predictions found in the Bible. It is said that his interest in physics developed from his research into occult phenomena.

Swedenborg (1688–1772) also was a Biblical scholar. At the age of fifty-five he took up a monastic lifestyle, fell into deep trances, and communed with the dead. He predicted the future, one of the most startling events being the conflagration of his own home in Stockholm of which he had a vision while he was miles away in Göteborg. Swedenborg wrote sixteen books, including *Heaven and Hell, Divine Love and Wisdom,* and the *Arcana Coelesta.* The Church of the New Jerusalem was founded on his teachings and is still in existence.

Other contributors to the field in that century include Louis Claude de Saint-Martin (1743–1803) and Comte de St. Germain (supposedly active between 1710–1822, but more reasonably until around 1780, who purportedly discovered the elixir of life).

From this era, Qabalistic philosopher Pierre Mora presents a way to discover one's future bride or groom by dreaming: On a Saturday night, mix together powdered coral and lodestone with pigeon blood, place it inside a fresh fig, and wrap it all in blue taffeta. Deposit the bundles on top of a drawing of a pentagram and tuck everything under your pillow. According to Mora, you are sure to dream of your betrothed.

If you yearn to discover a mother lode of gold ore, but the idea of prospecting in deep, dank mine shafts is less than thrilling, try this method found in an anonymous magickal publication called *The Black Pullet* that began to circulate around 1740. It advises the operator to take a black hen and put it in a black box so that it will hatch an egg there. The progeny of this incubation is alleged to possess the unerring ability to seek out and discover gold. Alas, no results of this method, either positive or negative have been recorded.

Italian Comte Alessandro de Cagliostro (1743–1795) is possibly the most flamboyant figure of the era. The count was a genuine alchemist, crystal-gazer, psychic, ceremonial magician, and faith healer who promoted magickal studies through the establishment of Egyptian-style Masonic lodges. Cagliostro created a tarot deck that bears his name.

However, he was also an unprincipled adventurer who duped the ingenuous into handing over to him their wealth and worldly goods and who brought his wife to ruin. He met his downfall when he tried to establish Egyptian Freemasonry in the Papal States, thus challenging the power of the Roman Catholic Church. The Inquisition imprisoned him, and he died in jail.

Closing out the century was the advent of "animal magnetism," or mesmerism, as it came to be called after its main proponent, Franz Anton Mesmer. This Austrian doctor sought to cure patients by manipulating their minds and causing them to fall into trances. Mesmer's experiments, where subjects in an unconscious state transposed the senses, that is, heard with their eyes and saw with their noses, etc., were further developed by researchers like Dr. James Braid into a technique called hypnotism. You will learn more about Mesmer and Braid in the next chapter.

What hypnotism has to do with divination is that scryers and mediums often practice self-hypnosis and put themselves into light to deep trances in order to gain insights into the past, present, and future. Later in this book I will be introduce you to some methods of self-hypnosis that will help you hone your own psychic skills. Studies in hypnosis, in part, led to the Spiritualist movement of the nineteenth century, which is described in the next chapter. Before you read on, you might like to try the following mode of divination garnered from antiquity.

"ROMAN" OMENS

All cultures, including ancient Rome, have attempted to predict the future by observing accidents of nature and attributing significance to them. Hardly anything that moves or any human activity has escaped as a source of "fodder" for the "omen mill." In times gone by, when humanity moved more in harmony with the rhythms of nature, it made sense to appeal to this feeling of interconnectedness, or a way to make order out of the chaotic, often frightening future.

If we still the "noise" of our contemporary environment that insists on intruding on our ability to adjust to these natural rhythms, we can recuperate part of this inheritance and rediscover the oneness of life. I invite you to "do as the Romans did"— and the Celts and the Etruscans, and the Hebrews and the Egyptians—and bring yourself closer to nature by reading her omens.

Roman augurs prepared for these occasions with much ado. They dressed in white, carried a crooked staff like the kind that shepherds use, called a *lituus,* and pitched their tents at night on the hilltops overlooking the city. They mentally divided the sky into segments, and decided which omens appearing in which segment would be considered positive or negative. Then they settled back and scanned the skies for signs from the stars and harked to the calls of night-flying birds. From these indications they drew conclusions about the future.

In the following exercise, you will perform an enhanced version of Roman augury. You have the advantage over the Romans in that you have available to you information culled from sources other than Roman, including Celtic, Chinese, Amerindian, and Norse. The ancient Romans would be the first to admit that they adopted many customs and technologies from the cultures they conquered—if this data had been accessible to them they would have used it. In being eclectic, you are practicing divination in the spirit of ancient Rome.

This exercise also allows you flexibility because you can perform it by day or at night. Also, because aeromancy technically can be associated with any "signs from the sky," included is information on wind as well as something about capnomancy, divination by smoke. There is even a small section on interpreting movements of insects and other little critters that may cross your path while you are taking in the great outdoors.

Many of the specific meanings of bird calls, celestial formations, clouds, divisions of the sky, and the like have been lost in antiquity. After all, the seers of old were intelligent enough not to reveal all their secrets or else they could be deposed from their privileged positions! At the end of the exercise, many meanings for omens are listed, but interpreting their significance requires that you also use a good dollop of intuition.

DIVINATION EXERCISE

For this exercise, you will need the following items:

> white robe
> folding chair (or you can sit on a blanket on the ground)
> jacket or coat and more blankets to keep yourself warm,
>   especially if you are out at night
> incense burner
> quick-lighting coals
> matches
> Midnight Vision[5] incense (if you are divining by night) or
>   Psychic Vision incense (if you are divining by day)
> vial of Sibyl perfume anointing oil
> Apollo incense
> vial of Apollo perfume anointing oil
> notebook and pen
> black candle (the color black helps you sink into a trancelike state)
> candleholder

Gather together all the items, and perhaps some refreshments, and go to a deserted hilltop. If you live in the mountains or in the countryside, this is easy. If you live in a city, look for a park, botanical garden, or an institution—like a university—that has extensive grounds commanding a hilltop view. If you live in a very flat locale, set up in an open field with a wooded area at your back. The idea is to find a place with space around it to give you a good view of the sky and which is also in an area that attracts birds.

Put your robe on over your street clothes, set up the folding chair or spread a blanket on the ground, and position yourself so that you are facing south. The Romans considered the east to be a favorable direction when viewing the sky, and the west an unfavorable direction, and wanted the east to be to their left. This, even though birds flying from the left are considered negative omens in many cultures. Place the incense burner with the coal in it in front of you and the matches and incense within reach.

If it is nighttime, place the candle and holder close enough to you so you can light it to illuminate your notebook. If it is windy, a candle may not be practical. And since the Romans were great adapters of other cultures' technologies, it is perfectly acceptable "Roman" etiquette to use a flashlight.

Get comfortable in a seated position and relax. If it is cold outside, don your coat and wrap yourself in blankets so you feel cozy. Concentrate on the rhythmic sound of your breathing. If you hear traffic or neighborhood noise, do not try to block it out, just keep concentrating on your breathing. Soon the sounds of nature—rustling wind, faint movements made by small animals and insects in the underbrush, birds flying and calling in the sky—will take over. Let these sounds wash over you, lulling you into a hypnotic state. When you feel ready, light the candle and anoint your third eye with Sibyl oil. Say aloud the following invocation to the Sibyls:

> **Wise and wonderful women of the wyrd**
> **You, who open the path of communication**
> **Between this world and that of the Omniscient Ones,**
> **I call upon you to descend to this sacred space**
> **And aid me in my quest to know the future.**
> **Help me to interpret correctly the portents I am about to witness**
> **Both for myself and for the good of all humanity.**

Relax again, but this time remain alert to the signs of nature around you. Peruse the skies for cloud formations (if by day) or celestial phenomena (if by night). Study the Sun or the Moon, if one is visible. Watch for lightning and listen for thunder.

Do you see or hear birds? How many? From which direction are they flying? What do their calls sound like and where are they coming from? Write down your observations in the notebook without interpreting them. The only exception is to note if you experience a positive or negative impression about an individual omen.

Now, anoint your third eye with Apollo oil, light the Apollo incense, and render the following prayer to the Lord of Prophecy:

> **Great Lord of Divination! You who know the fates of all humankind,**
> **grant me a sign through this incense smoke that will give me the answer**
> **to a personal question that is important to me. Your response will help enable**
> **me to continue on my path of self-development and thus, fulfill the destiny**
> **I have planned for this lifetime of mine. So mote it be!**

Ask your personal question of Apollo. It can be anything as long as you deem that the answer will help clarify your lifepath. Do not make trivial inquiries, or you will dissipate the magickal force. Abuse Apollo's largesse, and he may never visit you again.

Light the coal in the incense burner and sprinkle some Apollo incense on it. Scrutinize the smoke rising from the burner for up to ten minutes and jot down details about the quality of the smoke and the direction it is blowing. Again, do not interpret the phenomena yet.

After writing down the information, extend a prayer of thanksgiving to Apollo and the Sibyls for the knowledge they have given you. Make sure the coal has cooled down, and bury the contents of the burner in Mother Earth by way of feeding her. Extinguish the candle, pack up your things, and go home directly.

Back home, prepare a cup of peppermint tea to which you add a pinch of mugwort.[6] Sit down at a table, and while you are sipping your tea, relight the candle, and set about interpreting the data you wrote down according to the guidelines at the end of this chapter and your own intuition. Omens with similar messages that occur close together are especially important. You may notice that the signs seem to cluster together in meaningful groups and that specific themes emerge. Proceed to "tell" the story presented by the omens on paper, cassette tape, or your computer. Work into the interpretations any intuitive feelings you experienced about any of the signs. Be careful not to make judgements about your findings.

Save everything you have written and check back a week later to see whether your omens came true. Since the kinds of omens you observed are ephemeral in nature, their predictive capabilities only can be considered valid for about a week. If you feel your intuitive faculties are behaving like a dead battery, turn to chapter 7 for hints on jumpstarting your psychic abilities.

LITTLE GUIDE TO ORINTHOMANCY

A little bird told me.

—Jonathan Swift, *Letter to Stella,* 1711

The ancients observed birds soar to the heavens, then swiftly and unpredictably drop from sight. They heard the birds' sometimes soothing coos, sometimes unnerving shrieks, sometimes uncanny, human-sounding cries, and they studied seemingly strange orinthological behaviors like courtship dances. In their minds, birds' erratic yet seemingly purposeful behavior must hold messages powerful for all living beings, including humans. Cultures worldwide have created legends about birds as guides, heralds of the seasons and the weather, messengers of births, deaths, and other important events.

In orinthomancy—divination by birds—the direction from which the bird is flying or calling is considered. Approach from the left traditionally bodes ill; from the right bodes well. The Celts believed that seeing a bird in the north presaged tragedy; in the south, good crops, in the west good luck, and in the east, good love.

White birds are a positive sign, unless the bird is an albatross, although occasionally they are taken as a premonition of unsettled times and melancholy. Black-colored birds usually are bad. These interpretations, of course, reflect folk superstitions about colors. People can't seem to make their minds up about piebald birds, though, so the magpie, for example, carries mixed messages. Here are some specific birds and their traditional meanings. If your personal opinions about certain birds differ, by all means, use your interpretations.

Bat. While the bat is a mammal, not a bird, orinthomancers take the movement of the bat into consideration in their divinatory practice. Once it was believed that when the Devil didn't have anything better to amuse himself, he took possession of a bat and flew around in its body—hence the negative press these mammals have received in the Western world. However, both the Chinese and Poles consider the bat a positive omen. The Chinese have decided that a bat must be very intelligent because its brain is so relatively heavy. They believe a bat sighting means long life and happiness. By tradition, bats flying on a summer evening mean clear, hot weather the next day. If the bat cries while flying, it is a portent of evil. Suspect either a false friend to plot against you, or alternatively, enjoy Batman-like protection from higher powers if you see a bat. For some South American Indian tribes, bats represent rebirth and introspection.

Cock. To hear a cock crow at dawn is a sign that the day will be untroubled because the cock, with his loud call and threatening strut, frightens devils away.

Crane. These elegant birds are believed to foreshadow thunder and rain, and enhance fertility of earth and body. If you sight a crane, it may mean that you are about to reexperience something or meet somebody from a past life, or perhaps reenact a karmic situation.

Crow. Generally a bad sign, yet sometimes sighting this bird bodes that a diligent old soul will soon enter your life and bring you an important message. To see one crow means bad luck, but two is a good omen; three are for good health; four for wealth; five for illness; six for death. The death does not have to be physical, it may refer to discarding an old, outworn belief, or a false friend. The meaning, as with all the omens, depends on what other signs are grouped with it.

Cuckoo. To hear the cry of a cuckoo, especially at the New Year, presages health and prosperity all year long.

Dove. A harbinger of peace, joy, purity, a happy marriage, and the blessings of Spirit. Doves can also foretell sadness and mourning.

Eagle. Longevity, power, fame, good news or—alternatively—danger. The eagle symbolizes longevity because it was believed by many cultures that its feathers are incorruptible, and that by placing them among feathers of other birds, it will consume them all in an effort to maintain life into perpetuity. In another legend, the eagle flies up to the sky, gets heated by the sun, then plunges into the water and arises again, renewed. In Scotland, it was believed that Adam and Eve retired to the Hebrides and still live there as eagles. Roman soldiers prized the eagle because to see one while on a march warned that the general or a hero among the troops might be in danger, and that the army should prepare for an enemy assault. If the troops spied an eyrie, they took it as a sign that they should set up winter quarters nearby, for they would be protected. If you should spot an eagle teaching its young to fly, it is a sign that you or your loved one is, or soon will be, in the family way. Eagles also signal opportunity and a change for the better.

Geese. It does not matter if you see one goose or many, sitting or flying. Geese mean that you will host an unexpected, but interesting guest. You may receive an invitation to a special event.

Gull. Indicates happiness; warning against gullibility. Beware if you are brushed by the wings of a gull in flight because by tradition, the gull foreshadows the death of a loved one. By the way, even if you live inland, you can still see gulls. While I do not pretend to be an orinthologist, I can tell you that here in the mountains of Colorado I have seen flocks of "land gulls" circling above the local shopping mall.

Hawk. Beware of powerful enemies if you see a hawk flying from the left.

Jay. These chatty fellows are alleged to get together with the Devil for gabfests every Friday. There they gossip about all the misdeeds humans have committed during the week. If you see a jay flying with a twig in its mouth, it is a sure sign you are about to land in the "hot seat" because the bird is taking fuel to stoke the fires of Hell.

Kingfisher. Scandal is afoot!

Loon. In Scotland, the loon is known as the "rain-goose" because to hear it cry forecasts wet weather. However, if you see them flying inland, it means good weather is on the way. When Norwegian seers hear a loon, they predict a death by drowning.

Magpie. As the folk saying about magpies goes, "One for sorrow, two for mirth, three for a wedding, four for a birth, five for silver, six for gold, and seven for a secret that's never been told."

Owl. In some cultures, the owl foreshadows evil, especially when it hoots three times. The owl probably got its reputation for malevolence from the fact that it hunts by night, makes a ghostly cry, and startles people with its enormous eyes. In ancient Athens, the owl was associated with Athena, patron goddess of the city, and it was a crime to kill one of these birds. European folklore is filled with tales of owls as familiars or companions to Witches and magicians. The owl is regarded as a symbol of wisdom, occult knowledge, and *meiga* (White Witch) magick for the Gallicians of the northwest of Spain, who still practice the Celtic religion of their ancestors. As an omen, it predicts a meeting with a night person or a significant event that will occur at night.

Peacock. This bird's call presages rain. It is considered unlucky to find a peacock feather on the ground, and particularly foolhardy to carry the feather into your home. On the other hand, to see a peacock is a sign of a fortunate marriage, riches, and good fortune in real estate. Beware of appearing vain to others.

Raven. Ravens bring messages. If you see a raven in flight, consider yourself blessed; you have the makings of a powerful magician. Ravens may indicate that a pessimistic person is hovering in the wings; don't let yourself be brought down by the negativity. Since ravens and crows look very much alike, I suggest you consult a book on orinthology with pictures to learn to distinguish these very "distinguished" birds.

Robin. These heralds of spring in northern climes also announce good luck and cheer. Make a wish when you see your first robin in the spring, and within a month your request may be granted.

Rook. When rooks cry out loudly, rain is soon to follow.

Sparrow. This ubiquitous little birdie allegedly foretells bad luck, especially for lovers.

Stone curlew. If you spot a stone curlew and happen to be affected with jaundice, or know of anyone who is, you can, by an act of will, transfer the disease to the bird, who will absorb the negative energy without feeling ill effects.

Swallow. A swallow sighting is a positive sign. If you spot one overhead, the weather will be clear. If they are flying near the ground, rain is on the way.

Swan. You will meet a mystic or a new lover soon. Swans are also a sign of tranquility and contentment.

Woodpecker. To hear a woodpecker knock wood bodes favorable news—unless, of course it is pecking a hole in your house!

Wren. The wren was sacred to the Picts and Celts. To see a wren is a very good omen, indeed. It means knowledge, power, and protection.

LITTLE GUIDE TO CELESTIAL PHENOMENA

New moon, true moon,
Star in the stream,
Pray tell my fortune
In my dreams.

—English folk saying

Clouds

Small, and broken and peppering the sky. Showers are on the way, but no heavy rain.

Blue-tinged. Success, especially in business.

Golden-tinged. A new or renewed romance is on the horizon.

Gray or black. Ill fortune; the blacker the cloud, the worse the luck.

Green or turquoise. A tornado is lurking in the vicinity; take cover.

Orange-tinged. Anger; disruption.

Pink-tinged. Tomorrow will be a beautiful day.

Red-tinged. A warning; destruction.

Silver-tinged. Good fortune after bad times (the proverbial "cloud with a silver lining").

White. Great, good fortune. Fortunately for all of us, most clouds are white!

Lightning

Forked lightning, if seen at night, foretells a clear, bright day ahead. In ancient times, lightning symbolized the gods' anger, and it was believed that you could protect yourself from divine wrath by carrying an acorn. People thought that certain trees, like the oak, attracted lightning, and that others, like the rowan, repelled it; hence the saying:

> Beware the oak,
> It counts the strokes,
> Avoid the ash,
> It counts the flash.

On both sides of my house, the original owners planted rowan trees, and in over one hundred years the house has not been hit by lightning. So there! I probably shouldn't mention that an enormous oak tree also graces the front yard, thus canceling out the rowans' protection. Seriously however, you shouldn't seek shelter under *any* tree during a storm, so be careful if you go "omening" in bad weather.

Moon

Pale moon or a ring or rings around it. Brings rain the following day.

Red moon. High wind warning. (By the way, although I live in one of the windiest areas in the world, I have never seen a red moon).

Sky

Green or pale yellow sky above the sunset. The next day will be nasty.

Dull in the morning with a small patch of blue. Fine weather by 11:00 A.M.

Red or rosy at night. The following day will bring fine weather.

Red or orange in the morning. The day will turn rainy.

Stars, Comets, Meteors

Throughout history, much has been made of comets as signs of cataclysmic events on Earth. Comets were observed to precede both the birth and death of Julius Caesar. A large comet was sighted just prior to the Norman Conquest of Britain in 1066. Sometimes it has been thought that comets foretell plagues and natural disasters, or in a positive sense, that a dream is about to come true or that a child will be born. Lest you think that the modern world has left these superstitions behind, recall the suicides of the Heaven's Gate cult in 1997, following the appearance of Haley's comet.

Sun

A halo around the Sun means snow or rain are on the way.

Will-o'-the-Wisp (also known as foxfire, fairy fire, or jack-o'-lantern)

Although this phenomenon does not come from the sky, it has to do with atmospheric conditions, and is therefore included here. These mysterious lights are sometimes seen hovering or moving around marshes, fens, and churchyards. Scientists think they result from the ignition of gases that emanate from decaying plants or animals. In folklore, they have acquired many meanings. One is that they are wandering souls passed over to the Other Side, but who, for some reason, are returning to Earth. Some tribes considered them positive signs and thought that following the blinking lights would lead one to discover a great treasure. Others thought the lights could draw the foolhardy to a hideous death in quicksand. Still others maintained that following the flashing lights would lead a traveler lost in the marsh to safety. I suppose your point of view depends on whether you are the kind of person who sees a cup half-empty or half-full and believes that the wandering soul will guide you to either Heaven or Purgatory.

Rainbow

Undoubtedly you have heard about the ephemeral pot of gold at the end of the rainbow. When you were a child, you may have frantically run around the neighborhood as I did, trying to catch up with it. Rainbows have represented great fortune ever since God flashed one before Noah's eyes to signal the end of the Great Flood. In Normandy, on the day that heralded the end of World War II in Europe, with the dawn came a gigantic rainbow that arched over the entire battlefield. Double and triple rainbows are doubly and triply good. But wouldn't you know, those pesky "half-empty cup" folks have taken a hand in the following rhyme:

> Rainbow at night, sailor's delight;
> Rainbow in the morning, sailor take warning;
> Rainbow to windward, foul all day;
> Rainbow to leeward, damp runs away.

Thunder

If you hear thunder, Thor, the Norse god of thunder, and Xangô, his Brazilian counterpart, are on the warpath. If you hear it while you are out "collecting" omens, I suggest you put a quick end to your session and seek shelter. Thunder forewarns rough times ahead for the next day or so.

Critters

When you are out in nature waiting for omens to happen, you are not immune to flying and crawling critters. Nature does not distinguish between you and a rock, and a spider or an ant will just as soon crawl up your leg as a tree trunk, especially if you are sitting still. Here are a few "critter meanings" to keep you occupied while you're swatting at whatever is "bugging" you.

Ant. Busy days ahead; avoid stressing out over work. Time to get away from dull routine and give yourself an outlet for your creativity. Advisement to become more thrifty.

Bee. Messenger of the gods that brings good news; a swarm of bees (unless you are allergic to them) means prosperity, a busy social agenda, and public recognition.

Butterfly. Pleasurable, if frivolous pursuits are on the agenda. You may be disappointed in another's fickleness. You may be scattering your forces; try to concentrate on a more limited number of activities to get ahead.

Crickets. You now have more than an environmental reason to take the household bug spray to your local hazardous items disposal unit because crickets are considered good luck to have around the house. If for any reason they should decide to pick up stakes, they take their luck with them. Besides bringing good fortune, there is a very good practical reason to keep crickets around or to pay attention to them when you are outdoors: they can tell you the temperature. Count the number of chirps you hear for fifteen seconds, and add 37 to get the degrees in Fahrenheit.

Firefly. They once were called "the eyes of god," which translated into "omenese" means you'd better behave because someone is watching you!

Frog. Frogs croak when the barometer drops. These cute critters stand for fertility of body and mind. A pregnancy may be announced. Success comes through changing your job or residence.

Grasshopper. You will receive a letter, phone call, or e-mail from someone who is traveling abroad.

Ladybug. Count yourself lucky if a ladybug deigns to land on you; your roses will be aphid-free in the bargain! If this little critter stays on you long enough, count the numbers of spots on its back. One is for luck; two takes it away; three augurs ill health. Any more than three tells the number of months you will remain happy. If you are on the lookout for a significant other, note the direction the lady bug flew from; this is the direction from which your prince or princess charming will appear.

Spider. Success is yours after persistence, determination, and hard work. Spiders also indicate an unexpected monetary windfall. Keep buying those lottery tickets!

Smoke Patterns

When you light incense, not only do you open your mind's eye to psychic vision, you can also practice the art of capnomancy and find omens in the patterns made by the smoke rising from the burner.

Silently ask a "yes-no" question and throw a bit of incense on the burning coal. If it sparks, the answer is "yes," if not, or if it does not catch on, the answer is "no," or "not now," If the smoke blows left and right, the answer is no; if it blows to and fro in front of you, you will get your wish. If it rises in billowy, dark clouds, or the coal fails to catch on at all, it is a bad omen. When asking about the weather, if the smoke blows to the west, rain is on the way, and if it streams to the south, the storm will be ferocious. On the other hand, if the smoke blows to the east or north, fair weather is in store. Finally, if the smoke puffs around in a circle, beware of enemies.

Wind

The direction the wind is blowing from on a certain date is particularly significant in Scotland. Some canny Scots go outside on New Year's Eve to forecast the next year's weather by observing the wind. If it blows from the south, the year will be warm and productive; if from the north, cold and blustery with a poor harvest. Wind blowing from the west means a warm year with plenty of milk; from the east presages the most bountiful year of all. Who says the Scots in their inhospitable climate don't look on the bright side of things?

The Scots are not the only ones to forecast weather on certain dates by harking to the wind. In Germany, by tradition, if high winds wail between Christmas and the New Year, it is a good sign because it means the trees are "copulating" and they will bring on a bountiful harvest.

While you are figuring out the wind direction so that this factor can enter into your omen interpretations (wind from the east is bad; from the west, good; from the north, expect a surprise; from the south, you will have either a positive or negative confrontation), pause for a few minutes and listen to the sound it makes. Remember the adage: "The answer is written on the wind."

A final thought: if you set up camp in a field of dandelions in the morning and the flowers are closed up you might think of taking a "raincheck" on omen hunting for the day because rainy weather is imminent. Happy "omening!"

Notes

1. Joel II: 28–29.

2. The conclusion that the Ghanaian spirits offered was that small families were better than large ones for modern times.

3. Lewis Spence, *An Encyclopedia of Occultism* (1960; reprint, Secaucus: Citadel Press, 1977), p. 134.

4. Fodor Nandor, *An Encyclopedia of Psychic Science* (Secaucus: Citadel Press, 1966), p. 86.

5. Formulas for the incenses and oils referred to in this chapter (more psychic development formulas are in chapter 7).

   Midnight Vision incense: ¼ cup black incense base, 1 tablespoon blue incense base, 1 tablespoon cut sandalwood, 1 crushed bay leaf, ½ teaspoon anise seeds, 1 tablespoon Indian tobacco, a pinch each of thyme and cinnamon, 8 drops fir oil, 7 drops myrrh oil, 1 teaspoon narcissus oil, ½ teaspoon carnation oil.

   Psychic Vision incense: ¼ cup white incense base, 1 tablespoon frankincense peas, 1 teaspoon benzoin powder, a pinch each of wormwood, marigold flowers, and cut beth root, 1 teaspoon honeysuckle oil, 1 teaspoon sandalwood oil.

   Sibyl perfume anointing oil: 6 drops fougère oil, 1 teaspoon dark musk oil, ½ teaspoon spice oil or eugenol oil.

   Apollo perfume anointing oil: 1 teaspoon heliotrope oil, ½ teaspoon narcissus oil, 3 drops lime oil, 6 drops cinnamon oil, 3 drops citronella oil, 3 drops geranium rose oil, 1 drop lavender oil.

   Apollo incense: ¼ cup gold incense base, 1 tablespoon frankincense peas, 2 teaspoons cut bayberry bark, ½ teaspoon mistletoe leaves, 1 teaspoon crushed chamomile flowers, ¼ teaspoon cinnamon. Add the same oils as in the perfume oil and include ½ teaspoon bayberry oil. For more complete directions on how to make incenses, see my book, *Witch's Brew: Secrets of Scents* (Atglen, PA: Whitford Press, 1994).

6. Mugwort, like all artemisias, can be poisonous if ingested in large quantities, so use only the smallest pinch as a psychic aid. Peppermint is also alleged to help increase psychic awareness. It is said that if you drink a cup of peppermint tea before bedtime you will experience prophetic dreams. If that night you dream about anything that relates to the omens you saw, add it to your notes.

CHAPTER TWO

THE SPIRITUALIST PHENOMENA

A Nineteenth-Century Movement

We concluded to go to bed early and not permit ourselves to be disturbed by the noises, but try and get a night's rest . . . I had just lain down. It commenced as usual. I knew it from all other noises I had ever heard before . . . My youngest child, Cathie, said, "Mr. Splitfoot, do as I do," clapping her hands. The sound instantly followed her with the same number of raps. When she stopped, the sound ceased for a short time. Then Margaretta said, in sport, "Now do just as I do. Count one, two, three, four," striking one hand against the other at the same time; and the raps came as before.

—Mother of Katie and Margaretta Fox[1]

By far, the most influential trend of thought on the study of psychic phenomena and practice of divination in modern times has been Spiritualism. Part religion, part socio-politico-philosophical doctrine, this nineteenth-century movement brought about the science of parapsychology and in one way or the other, continues to affect how many people view the field.

Although Spiritualism was "born in the U.S.A.," its roots stretch back to the oracles of antiquity discussed in the last chapter. Those traditions, coupled with scientific experiments of the eighteenth century that culminated in mesmerism and hypnotism, form the basis of Spiritualist doctrine.

PRECURSORS

Franz Anton Mesmer (1733–1815), whom you met in the last chapter, believed that a universal magnetic fluid exists that flows through and links all forms of life within the universe. He theorized that illness results when a person's magnetic fluids fall out of balance, and that application of magnetic forces, which he called "animal magnetism," can redress the imbalance and heal the body. He applied these healing forces by having patients sit in "magnetized" water. While they lounged around in an eighteenth-century version of a hot tub in a darkened, strongly perfumed room, they were lulled by soft music playing in the background. As they relaxed, Mesmer stroked them with the magnetized healing energy contained in his hands. In essence, the patients became entranced.

Among others who pursued Mesmer's lead was Scottish surgeon Dr. James Braid. He also induced trances to help cure patients of psychological ills and in this way anaesthetized them so they could withstand the pain of surgery. With Braid, the science of hypnosis had found a name.

It was a short step from "magnetic" or "hypnotic" trances to the self-induced "mediumistic" trances of Spiritualism, when mediums would, for a brief period, give their wills over to "controls" and receive and transmit messages from the spirit world.

One precursor who practiced this sort of self-hypnosis was the German Frau Frederica Hauffe (1801–1829), also known as the Seer of Prevorst. Hauffe was bedridden with a host of diseases almost her entire short life. As she lay in bed day after day, she came to believe that spirits hovered in her room. She conversed with them, sometimes in a language that sounded like Hebrew. Thus, she became one of the first documented trance voice cases of the modern era. She also produced poltergeist phenomena, practiced divination with a rod, and was able to trace perfect geometrical shapes in the dark.

Another trance medium who heralded the Spiritualist movement was American mystic Andrew Jackson Davis (1826–1910), also known as the "Poughkeepsie Seer." He came from what we might nowadays call a dysfunctional family with an alcoholic father and a visionary mother, and received very little formal education. Yet he overcame his environment and by the age of twenty made his fame as a psychic healer. He also wrote erudite tracts on mystical philosophy, the evolution of the universe and humankind, and systems of government and economy, which he claimed to have channeled in part from Swedenborg and Galen. His extraordinary work, *Principles of Nature,* was published in 1847. As Davis explained, he developed the ability to see through the human body as if it were transparent, and so, he identified the diseased organs. In his book, Davis also predicts the dawning of the Spiritualist era, a prophecy that would be fulfilled within a year by two young girls from his home state, as you shall see.

DAWNING OF A NEW AGE: THE FOX SISTERS

It was a case of being in the right place at the right time. Two children, daughters of a poor farmer in Hydesville, New York, galvanized the Spiritualist movement. Kate (1841–1892) and Margaretta (1838–1893) Fox first manifested spirit rappings at home in the way described in the quote at the beginning of this chapter. The "rapper" identified himself as a murdered peddler whose body lay buried in the cellar.

When investigators later searched the house, a man's bones were indeed found in the basement. Soon the girls were giving demonstrations around the state—and eventually throughout the country—to a captivated public. Others followed their lead, and the Spiritualist movement took off.

Although the Fox sisters' "spirit rappings" eventually were proved to result from cracking their knee and toe joints, the trickery did not deter many people from believing in spirit communication and embracing the new movement. Although both women confessed to fraud, Margaretta later withdrew her confession, averring that it had been coerced. The retraction left an opening for true believers.

Automatic writing, planchettes, and direct communication from spirits quickly replaced the tedious and limited rappings. All sorts of phenomena soon adorned the Spiritualists' repertoire including séances, table-tipping, floating trumpets, materializations, and spirit photography. (See below for a description of spirit photography.)

In a typical séance, an even number of males and females, skeptics and believers gathered in a room swathed in total darkness at a round table, presided over by the "sensitive," or medium. The medium fell into a trance and the control, or guiding spirit, took over his or her personality, often speaking in a different, often heavily accented voice. Departed spirits communicated through the control, using the medium's vocal cords and body. A cone called a trumpet encircled with luminous bands—to prove it was not being held by anybody—might float through the room, pause by certain sitters and transmit messages from the dead that sounded even more eerie when filtered through the device. Bouquets of flowers, photographs, and small live birds might suddenly appear "out of thin air" and be offered to a sitter. Ectoplasm, the ethereal matter from which spirits were thought to manifest, sometimes emitted from mediums' mouths, noses, ears, and other parts of their bodies. If you are interested in holding your own seance, turn to the end of this chapter for hints on how to conduct a sitting.

Prominent citizens, both in America and abroad, became converts. Among their ranks, Spiritualists counted authors including Harriet Beecher Stowe; Arthur Conan Doyle, who founded the Spiritualist Association of Great Britain; publisher Horace Greely; business tycoon Cornelius Vanderbilt; former Supreme Court Judge J. W. Edmonds; Queen Victoria; and President Abraham Lincoln—who if not a practitioner, at least attended séances in the White House.

THE POWER OF "RAPPOMANIA"

What drew followers to this movement, which at the height of its popularity attracted millions of adherents worldwide? Science holds part of the key. On one hand, Spiritualists reacted against the mechanistic view of body, soul, and spirit espoused by scientists of the Age of Enlightenment. The possibility of communication with spirits of the dead offered hope that there is more to life than the bag of bones that composes the human body, and that when our physical forms are commended to the ground, some part of us survives.

On the other hand, the physical wonders produced by science led many people, who had no idea of how these feats were achieved, to accept that anything was possible. If people could now receive and transmit messages over invisible telegraph wires, why not also communicate through a spirit telegraph?

Spirit photography became all the rage for awhile in Spiritualist circles. The technique was invented by professional photographer William H. Mumler, who happened to take a self-portrait and inadvertently made a double exposure. In the background appeared an image of his cousin who had died twelve years earlier. Capitalizing on his discovery, Mumler set up as a spirit photographer, and people flocked to him to have their photos taken with deceased loved ones hovering protectively in the background. Mary Todd Lincoln, Abraham's wife, was among Mumler's distinguished clients. Other photographers jumped on the bandwagon, and soon spirit photographers pervaded the Western world like today's paparazzi.

Many distinguished leaders in nineteenth-century society, such as the names mentioned above, seemed to believe in, or at least did not discount the possibility of spirit communication. If it was good enough for them, why not for the average person on the street? After all, philosopher Allan Kardec (1804–1869) had outlined many basic Spiritualist principles, and even founded a new religion that seemed both spiritually and scientifically sound.

Kardec (born Hypolyte Léon Denizard Rivail) was a French doctor, phrenologist, and philosopher who created a religion similar to Spiritualism, which he named Spiritism. Kardec opined that spirits of the dead and masters on the inner planes exist who return to Earth to communicate messages of solace and wisdom. He was convinced that contact could be made with these entities through mediums. Kardec favored automatic writing because it was more reliable than trance voice. He did not trust the veracity of information produced when the medium lost consciousness during a session, and he felt that visions and voices were subject to personal interpretation. For Kardec, automatic writing offered the most tangible proof of survival.

Spiritism is distinguished from Spiritualism principally in that Kardec's followers believe in reincarnation, whereas a Spiritualist may not; also, Spiritists accept no one but their founder and his works as the definitive authority.

Another reason why Spiritualism enjoyed such sudden, widespread popularity was that it promised much—including, if not necessarily reincarnation, some form of eternal life—and asked little in return. Spiritualists were not required to tithe, nor did they subscribe to "hellfire and damnation." The tenets of the religion generally did not interfere with the dogmas of other faiths, and the religion was convenient— it could be practiced virtually anywhere at any time. In short, Spiritualism represented the ultimate in "gain without pain."

Many readers may not realize that despite the legacy of our Puritan forefathers, the pre-Civil War United States was not a nation of churchgoers. Only 25 to 35% of the population at that time belonged to a major religion, and many small sects like Mormons, Quakers, and Seventh Day Adventists vied for each other's business. Spiritualism may have succeeded, in part, because it appealed to people who did not follow organized religion, but wanted the comfort and assurance that life continued beyond the grave. In those harsher times, almost all families had experienced the death of an infant or child, and the situation only got worse during and after the Civil War, when the male population was decimated.

Not to be underestimated was the fact that Spiritualism offered equal opportunity in religion. A person's age, race, sex, and level of education made absolutely no difference in the world of mediumship. Women were especially attracted because the so-called "feminine virtues" of the era, like passivity, mildness, and lack of formal education suddenly counted as characteristics of the consummate medium. Women stood up in front of large audiences, and people actually listened.

THE GREAT PRETENDERS

With all this going for Spiritualism, no wonder "rappomania," as it was called in the popular press, sometimes ranged out of control. Charlatans saw a way to turn an easy buck, and many medium wannabes didn't have the wherewithal to discipline themselves to a true medium's life. (More on how mediums train and prepare in Part II.)

Along with the icons of the era came the great fakes.

For instance, Henry Slade holds the dubious honor of inventing slate writing. In this form of automatic writing, the mental medium sat on one side of a table and the sitter on the other. Under the table between them they held two slates pressed together with a bit of chalk wedged in between. Soon after Slade fell into a trance, the chalk was heard scratching on the slate. At the sound of three raps, the medium came to, and the session was over. Examination of the slates revealed "spirit" messages. Although Slade was never caught cheating outright, he was convicted of obtaining money under false pretenses, and left the country.

Slade's place was taken by William Eglinton, who was caught writing on the slate. Eglinton also produced so-called ectoplasm that was found to be fabric dipped in phosphorous and suspended on thin, telescoping rods.

Physical mediums, that is, those who allegedly produce physical phenomena from the spirit world like floating trumpets, ectoplasm, trembling tables, and the inexplicable sounding of musical instruments, were most often caught in deception. Infamous tricksters included Ira and William Davenport, who manifested sounds from a cabinet while their hands supposedly remained firmly bound. They were aided by dim lighting, sleight-of-hand tricks, and the public's fervent desire to believe in spirits. Another physical medium, Italian Nino Pecorio, who manifested some of the same phenomena was proved to be nothing more than an escape artist. When Houdini bound Pecorio's body and swathed him in cloth, the escape artist was only able to produce faint rappings.

MEDIUMS OF THE SPIRITUALIST ERA

Not all mediums were charlatans, as skeptics may have us believe, and several remarkable names stand head and shoulders above the rest of the practicing Spiritualists of the era. One was Andrew Jackson Davis, whom you met earlier, and who wrote defining literature in the field. British psychic medium, Emily Hardinge Britten (1823–1899) also contributed to the understanding of the field with *History of Modern American Spiritualism* and *Nineteenth Century Miracles.*

Mrs. W. R. Hayden, a well-educated, erudite American, introduced the modern movement to Britain. On her trip to England, she was first ridiculed because she only managed to relay minimal information by way of spirit rappings that spelled out words. However, people soon realized that the information was quite accurate and that she could not have known it otherwise. On her return to the United States, Hayden graduated with a degree in medicine and spent the rest of her days practicing as a physician.

Born to an upper-class family in Scotland, Daniel Dunglas Home (1833–1886) traveled the other way across the Atlantic from Britain to America. His parents died young, and he was adopted by a childless aunt who moved him across the Atlantic. From an early age, the handsome lad manifested acts of telekinesis and levitation. In his most phenomenal levitation feat, observed by three witnesses, he floated out one window of a third-floor room and into the window of an adjoining room.

Home traveled throughout Europe and performed before English royalty, the Russian Czar, Napoleon, and the Kaiser. Some loved him (he married the Czar's niece); others hated him (Charles Dickens and Robert Browning penned scathing criticisms of his performances). Home was never caught cheating, and even held séances in full daylight, which was practically unheard of in his era. He never took money for his work. He was tested by respected researcher Sir William Crookes, and declared genuine. Crookes may have been right, or at least the Roman Catholic Church must have thought so, because they excommunicated Home in 1864.

Other famous mediums in America were brothers William and Horatio Eddy, clairaudient psychics who claimed to be descended from Salem witches, and who during the 1850s helped turn Chittendon, Vermont, into the Spiritualist capital of the world. They exhibited all the usual marks of mediumship of the era including spirit rappings and full materializations. Although the physical manifestations were considered fake, the brothers possessed undeniably true psychic abilities.

THE FRENZY ABATES

Perhaps the very success of Spiritualism held the seeds of its own destruction. As we have seen, its wild popularity led to rampant mountbankery in some sectors, which in turn, gave skeptics and clerics plenty of fodder for their defamation campaign. The relative lack of organization and ritual, amorphous doctrine, and few places of worship eventually caused much of the public to lose interest.

Spiritualism never died out completely, and in fact, it can be said to be enjoying a modest rebirth. More than 10,000 Spiritualist trance mediums are registered in the United States as members of the Spiritualist Association of Churches. Several survey respondents indicate an association with the Spiritualist Church.

The hub of Spiritualism today at Lily Dale, New York, is thriving. The tiny, gated community in the far western corner of New York state was founded in 1879 by Spiritualists and Free Thinkers. Although the Fox sisters never even visited there, after they died, their Hydesville farmhouse was moved to Lily Dale where it remained as a shrine until it burned in the 1950s. Spiritualist psychics hang colorful, wooden shingles from their cottage doors, and a lighthearted sign in the lobby of the Maplewood Hotel reads, "I can read your mind and you should be ashamed of yourself." Thousands of believers, New Agers, and the curious visit Lily Dale every summer to hear noted speakers like Deepak Chopra, attend workshops, and receive readings and healings. These days, Spiritualist mediums are as likely to channel messages from aliens and evolved entities from other worlds as they are to relay messages from the dead.

In London, Conan Doyle's Spiritualist Association of Great Britain, housed in an elegant old building in the heart of the embassy district in Belgrave Square, draws scores of people to nightly lectures, workshops, demonstrations, and séances. One needs to book an appointment early to see the best mediums for a personal consultation.

Kardec's Spiritism flourishes in the lush tropical soil of Brazil, where Spiritist centers all around the country attract tens of thousands of adherents. It is said that during the years of the last military regime (1964–1985) many of the commanders of the armed forces embraced the Spiritist faith. Speaking from personal experience, when I lived in Rio de Janeiro, I stayed for a time in a home where the head of the household, an army colonel, and his sons regularly attended Spiritist sessions every Saturday afternoon. LAKE, a large publisher of Kardec's books in São Paulo, prints millions of copies of Spiritist literature every year.

SCIENCE AND THE PARANORMAL

Some people are at the table who expect tricks—in fact, they want them. I am in a trance. Nothing happens. They get impatient. They think of the tricks—nothing but tricks. They put their minds on the tricks, and—I—and I automatically respond.

—Eusapia Palladino, Italian trance medium[2]

As to telepathy, just what . . . you think might be expected to come through telepathy—emotional experiences you are only too anxious to hear of again . . . these are just what you do not get. All through, you have the feeling that the person on the other side is trying to find something that isn't obvious to your own mind, and even where it is fairly clear to your mind it comes as a surprise to you and often only becomes really clear later . . .

—Dr. William Brown, psychic researcher[3]

Because of the commercialization of Spiritualism and ensuing rash of fraud, a group of skeptics, mostly scientists, evolved who specialized in detecting deception. These men of science fulfilled their mission so assiduously that by 1880, many mediums felt bound to spend more time supplying proof that they were not cheating than actually communicating spirit messages.

In order to prove that they were not charlatans, many mediums subjected themselves to severe tests. A cabinet, based on the concept of the Indian shaman's lodge, and large enough to accommodate one or more persons, was procured because it was thought that spirits manifested more readily in this "protected" environment. Experimenters then tied the medium hand-and-foot to the walls of the cabinet, and the bindings were sealed with wax. Almost as soon as the cabinet door was closed, loud rappings, sounds of musical instruments, singing, and other noisy manifestations commenced. When the experimenters opened the cubicle door, the medium was found still securely tied up and sitting in the same place. Many mediums, like the Davenport brothers and Pecorio, were actually escape artists who incorporated mediumship as part of their repertoire, just like any other vaudeville act. Unfortunately, the opportunists did not do much to enhance the reputations of those mediums who genuinely sought spirit contact.

Not all scientists were dead set against the Spiritualist movement and its manifestations. For example, physicist Michael Faraday (1791–1867) and philosopher and psychologist William James (1842–1910) both studied the Ouija board and other forms of spirit communication in order to better understand the psychology of the mind.

In the early 1870s, a few scientists began publishing scholarly papers on the nature of paranormal phenomena, thereby confirming that at least some portion of the scientific community was beginning to take the subject seriously. Sir William Crookes (1852–1909) identified mediumship as a manifestation of a "new force" that needed to be researched in a classically scientific way. Sir William Barret (1844–1925), professor of physics at the Royal College of Science in Dublin, experimented with hypnosis and published a paper on some of the more spectacular physical phenomena, like levitation and the ectoplasmic manifestations associated with mediumship.

After a few false starts, the Society for Psychical Research (SPR) was founded in 1882 in Great Britain, followed by the American Society for Psychical Research (ASPR) (1885), and the Boston Society for Psychical Research (BSPR) (1925). SPR founders included outstanding figures of the era in both science and Spiritualism. Chief among the Spiritualists was the Reverend William Stainton Moses (1839–1892). Moses was a graduate of Exeter College, Oxford, a university master, and curate. He also wrote highly literate tracts on Spiritualism that are still read today.

F. W. H. Myers (1843–1901) was another distinguished founder, who hailed from Trinity College, Cambridge. A classics scholar, lecturer, and promoter of higher education for women, he founded a precursor of the SPR, called The Cambridge Ghost Society.

Myer's tutor Henry Sidgwick (1830–1900), also helped create the SPR. Sidgwick became a prominent Spiritualist researcher in the areas of automatic writing and mediumship. Fellow Ghost Society member, classics, medicine, music, and law scholar

Edmund Gurney (1847–1898) joined the group. Frank Podmore (1856–1910) rounded out the Cambridge contingent. Later he wrote an important book on the era, *Modern Spiritualism* (1902). All of these men, through research, experimentation, or practice made worthy contributions to the birth and development of the science that was later to become known as parapsychology.

The Society aimed "to investigate the large body of debatable phenomena designated by such terms as mesmerism, psychical and spiritualistic, without prejudice or prepossession of any kind."[4] They classified their efforts into six categories, overseen by committees whose members produced reports so useful that they are still pondered today. The areas included: telepathy (which they called thought-reading); hypnotism and clairvoyance (the committee on mesmerism); Reichenbach extra-sensory research;[5] apparitions of the living and the dead, and hauntings; the physical phenomena produced by Spiritualists; the literature, which consisted of collected and collated materials already existing on these subjects.

The only committee that did not fare well was the physical phenomena committee, whose members fell out among each other because of the split between scientific researchers and Spiritualists. This difference of opinion infected the entire organization so that by 1887 only a quarter of the remaining members were declared Spiritualists.

Researchers submitted mediums to the grueling trials described earlier and uncovered many frauds. If you wish to read more about these probes and how the tricksters produced their illusions I recommend you read *The Physical Phenomena of Spiritualism* by Hereward Carrington.[6]

Just because sharp practices were unmasked does not mean that all the mediums were dishonest or that those who were caught always cheated. The reasons why even a genuine medium might occasionally go astray even today are complex. According to the respondents in the psychics survey conducted for this book, although greed and the ability to play on the emotions of the vulnerable and gullible still play a part, other variables enter into the equation. Some, like Eusapia Palladino, who was quoted at the beginning of this section, strive to please, and so fall under tremendous pressure to perform quickly and accurately every time, even though the psi faculty does not always cooperate in this way. Survey respondent Libby Henits comments that "This 'craft' is just that—it's not an on-demand phenomenon, so especially the famous would be tempted to fraud."

Respondents remark that the need to maintain a certain visibility in the profession by holding to exhausting schedules can quickly drain a psychic's ability.

Some cite that a few psychics, exhibiting all-too-human foibles, may lack humility and not want to admit that they do not know something. Selena, who is a reader, softens this criticism by pointing out that some psychics may, in this way, be working through their own karmic issues. Darryl Anka, a channeler, feels that part of the answer may lie in an individual psychic's lack of clarity about the balance of life. Sketchy training, immaturity, and extremism are all mentioned.

Cyndi Dale offers the unique slant that some psychics may be tempted to deceive because they get tired of using their faculties to benefit others rather than themselves.

On the other hand, many respondents comment that fraud is occurring less frequently these days because the public is becoming better educated.

OTHER EXPERIMENTS

Besides uncovering deception, the SPR and ASPR pursued other paths to discovering the nature of telepathy and clairvoyance, partly because these subjects interested them, and partly because the phenomena lent themselves readily to controlled studies. Moreover, some researchers sought to accumulate enough "hard data" to overcome the objections of Victorian materialists and refute the then-stylish mechanistic theories of the mind.

To Myers, the classics scholar and a founder of the SPR, we owe the term *telepathy*, which he coined from a Greek word meaning "feeling at a distance." In his opinion, telepathy entails communication between individual minds of impressions that involves some kind of "action at a distance," as he puts it, without resorting to the recognized sensory channels.

Researchers became curious about telepathy through studying the findings of the mesmerists who recorded that some of their subjects, while in trance, read the thoughts of their hypnotists. In order to test this phenomenon, Sidgwick devised an experiment whereby he sat in a closed room and chose two digits at random and concentrated on them. The subject, seated in another room, wrote down impressions of Sidgwick's numbers.

Sir Oliver S. Lodge (1851–1940), another SPR member, followed the same procedure by asking a sender to draw a picture and having the receiver attempt to reproduce it. This general concept was expanded by Gilbert Murray (1866–1957) of Oxford, who had his subjects concentrate on vivid historical scenes.

Soon hypnotized subjects were asked to perceive a real scene that was actually occurring at a distance and tell the experimenter what was happening. Roger Bacon's "magick ball" of medieval times was finally getting confirmation. The term *clairvoyance* was invented during the time of the SPR and ASPR to describe a perception, visual or otherwise, of events or objects without using the physical senses.

FAMOUS SPIRITUALIST MEDIUMS

The SPR and the ASPR also recorded many interesting cases, some of which follow.

Reverend William Stainton Moses (1839–1892), whom you met as a founder of the SPR, was an Anglican clergyman who converted to Spiritualism after attending a séance. He began to investigate trance mediums and the phenomenon of automatic writing as a member of the SPR. He also believed that he was surrounded by a group of spirits who communicated knowledge to him. After his death, the medium Leonora Piper allegedly communicated with him and his spirit group.

Florence Cook (1856–1904) caused a stir because she nearly discredited the SPR. She was a beautiful English trance medium who, during séances, took on the personality of "Katie King," a buccaneer's daughter. Sir William Crookes thoroughly investigated her and found her to be genuine, but it is said that his affection for Cook may have clouded his judgment because she was caught on film disguising herself as Katie during manifestations.

A "horse of the same stripe" was Elizabeth Hope Reed (1855–1919), an English psychic medium, automatic writer, and Spiritualist, who professionally called herself "Madame Elizabeth D'Esperance." At one séance, she allegedly dematerialized the bottom half of her body. Reed also materialized on several occasions the spirit of Yolande, an Arab girl, but the "spirit" was discovered to be none other than Madame D'Esperance herself. In spite of the deception, it seems she experienced dissociation during these episodes because she felt considerable physical pain when her alter ego was "mistreated."

A case that falls into the "gray area" between genuine and fake was that of Eusapia Palladino (1854–1918), an Italian physical medium who was studied in depth by many researchers. Among her feats were the abilities to levitate and to manifest ectoplasmic hands during séances. Although a genuine medium, it appears that she felt pressured to perform, so sometimes resorted to trickery as she explains in the quote at the beginning of the section on "Science and the Paranormal" (see page 39).

On the other side of the coin was Geraldine Cummins (1890–1979), an Irish automatic writer, who became known as the "medium with integrity." She studied automatic writing from noted French medium Helen Dowden and dictated works at incredible speed. Although she never visited the Middle East, Cummins was able to produce strikingly accurate and vivid details about the early Christian era. Among her books are: *They Survive, The Scripts of Cleophas Unseen Adventures, Swan on a Black Sea,* and *Mind in Life and Death.*

A strange case was that of Pearl Curran (d. 1936), a St. Louis housewife with no prior unusual interest in books, who became an automatic writer of literary works. One evening while playing with the Ouija board, her principal guide revealed herself as Patience Worth, a Quaker immigrant of centuries gone by, who had died prematurely in an Indian raid. Under the auspices of Patience and other guiding spirits, Curran dictated more than three million words (this, before the days of personal computers), including novels, epic poems, and dramas. She was investigated extensively by the ASPR, but no deception was ever detected. It has been postulated that by unconsciously practicing self-hypnosis, Curran was able to tap creative reserves embedded deep in her unconscious mind.

One of the most acclaimed mediums of the era was Leonora Piper (1859–1950). Piper discovered her faculty while consulting a psychic healer about a tumor. She was studied by William James, Richard Hodgson, and other members of the ASPR and declared genuine. On a good day, through her control, a deceased French doctor, Piper poured forth copious information about the deceased friends and relatives of those who came to her for a sitting. Since she could not have had prior access to much of this information, it is assumed that she was an adept telepath.

OTHER BRANCHES OF DIVINATION

Mediumship certainly owes a debt to the Spiritualist movement, but it was not the only field that gained ground in the nineteenth century. Ceremonial magicians, working in the tradition of the Renaissance, continued to chip away at the boundaries of science. At this time, the tarot came into its own as both a tool for divination and an aid for meditating on the philosophical concepts embodied in the Qabala. Eliphas Levi (1810–1875) was the first ceremonial magician to connect the twenty-two trumps of the major arcana to the Qabalistic Tree of Life, thus cementing a bond between both disciplines.

Papus (Gerard Encausse, 1865–1916) wrote the *Tarot of the Bohemians* and posited that the cards contained an entire system of metaphysical knowledge that synthesized the teachings of many religions, including the Bible.

Papus' ideas were refined by the founders of the Hermetic Order of the Golden Dawn and subsequent members of this famous occult fraternity. The most famous initiate was probably Aleister Crowley (1875–1947), another Trinity College student, whose *Book of Thoth* can be claimed as one of the most intelligent treatises on the tarot ever written.

Arthur Waite (1857–1941) an American-born Englishman, also made his mark on the cards. After studying with the original Golden Dawn, he founded his own off-shoot, The Holy Order of the Golden Dawn, which showed a more Christian and mystical bias. Together with artist Pamela Coleman-Smith, they fabricated the Rider-Waite deck, which is still the most popular deck today.

Paul Foster Case (1884–1954), authored another profound book on the symbolism of the tarot, *The Tarot, A Key to the Wisdom of the Ages.* At one time, Case headed the American Hermetic Order of the Golden Dawn, and alleged to have received teachings from Masters on the inner planes of that Order.

Other diviners and mystics of the time included the Theosophists. Russian-born medium Helena Petrovna Hahn Blavatsky (1831–1891) cofounded the Society. Like Case, she attested that her psychic abilities were bestowed on her by various Masters. According to Drury, "it is likely that many of the psychic powers she claimed were . . . clever deceptions."7 Unfortunately, for her own credibility and that of her Order, she enjoyed playing games with the public and was eventually unmasked by the SPR.

Reverend Charles Webster Leadbeater (1847–1934) was a curate in the Anglican Church, who became a Theosophist and later founded the Liberal Catholic Church. He possessed a genuine psychic ability as an aura reader and clairvoyant, and wrote about these faculties in *Man Visible and Invisible, Clairvoyance,* and *The Hidden Side of Things.*

Astrology kept growing in stature during this time. Evangeline Adams (1865–1932) did much to legitimatize the practice. A descendent of John Quincy Adams and popular astrologer, at the height of her fame, she had advised 300,000 querents by letter.

Alan Leo (1860–1917) is often called the "father of modern astrology." He produced the monthly magazine, *Modern Astrology,* and founded the Astrological Lodge of the Theosophical Society. Driven by a desire to reach the masses, Leo wrote prodigiously in the field.

Palmistry found a champion in Count Louis Hamon, better known as Cheiro (1866–1936). Famous for his knowledge of chirognomy and chiromancy, this war correspondent, publisher, and newspaper editor wrote a classic work called *The Language of the Hand,* which is still studied today. Cheiro was a talented astrologer and numerologist who predicted world events by using these tools. Mark Twain, a noted nonbeliever in such things, nonetheless was so impressed by Cheiro that he wrote *Pudd'n Head Wilson,* which features the art of palmistry. Of Cheiro, he said, "He has exposed my character to me with humiliating accuracy through reading my palm."[8]

LEGACY OF THE SPIRITUALIST MOVEMENT

Largely due to the Spiritualist movement, interest in paranormal phenomena of all sorts gained strength throughout the latter half of the nineteenth century and veritably snowballed into the twentieth. In the next chapter, you will read about the direction the field has taken over the last one hundred years. Before you go on, you may wish to read the following on séances and do a little experimenting on your own.

LITTLE GUIDE TO SÉANCES

A séance is a meeting of believers who, under the auspices of a trained medium, try to communicate with entities from other planes of existence, especially spirits of the dead. It can be a tricky business, and no matter how many good intentions a group possesses, and how hard they try, they may fail to make contact. This is why Spiritualists of the nineteenth century followed rigorous rules and regulations when conducting séances. Through experience, they learned that to do otherwise might open the door for uninvited, possibly even violent entities to enter the bodies of the medium and other sitters. If you wish to conduct your own séance, here is the "kosher" way of doing it.

Who Gets Invited to the "Party"

Anyone who thinks a séance is a spooky, silly party is definitely not invited. Otherworldly communication is "deadly" serious business, and you may consider yourself privileged when the spirits deign to talk to you. Anybody who is hostile, of a highly nervous disposition, or in ill health should not take part. Negative energies drive away spirits, and those who are sick or nervous can be adversely affected. Strangers are discouraged because the participants do not know enough about their temperaments and intentions.

Anywhere between three and twelve sitters seems to work well, with eight being the best manageable number. Ideally, the group should be evenly divided between males and females and include participants of all ages, although this is not absolutely necessary. No one should consume alcohol or any other stimulant before a sitting, and it is best if the sitters refrain from eating a heavy meal six hours before a session.

In the heyday of Spiritualism, members of the group were asked to bathe and dress in white before attending the séance. While wearing white seems somewhat superfluous in our dress-down era, the bath seems appropriate because several people will be sitting in close proximity to each other for over an hour.

A developed medium should be present to act as a lightning rod to attract the entities' vibrations. The medium focuses and transmits these vibrations to the members of the circle. No more than two developed mediums should ever be present because they tend to absorb the energies emitted by the entities.

Perform at least six séances with the same participants. After that, it is possible to retire some and introduce others, one by one, every three-to-four sittings.

Setting the Stage

If you were to invite the President or the Queen to your home, you wouldn't want them to see it in a shambles. Similarly, with the VIPs from other worlds, you will want to make the environment where they will manifest as pleasing to them and to you as possible.

First, tidy up and thoroughly clean the séance room. It is said that the spirits' sensitivities are adversely affected by metals, minerals, and glass objects. So take away all the Waterford crystal, the silver, and gold candelabras that adorn your room! Seriously, it is a good idea to have participants remove all jewelry and leather belts and shoes and store them in another room, so not to impede the energy flow.

If flowers or fruit are in the room, make sure they are fresh. Remove sickly plants. Regulate the temperature so that it is neither hot or cold, but comfortable. When spirits arrive, they often make their presence known by causing an otherwise inexplicable cold draft, but as the séance "heats up" from the release of energy, so does the room.

Entities find strong light too overbearing for manifestation of their ephemeral forces, so it is best to hold the séance in very low light, but not total darkness. Sudden, loud noises drive may drive away would-be communicators, so I suggest you send your kids out for a pizza.

An uncovered wooden table is perfect for a séance because both the wood and the circular construction act as conductors. Provide straight-backed, but comfortable, chairs. If they are not already padded, splurge, and buy some inexpensive chair pads. Avoid rocking chairs; they make squeaky noises.

Preliminaries

Try to hold the meetings at the same time in the same place for no more than an hour so not to deplete the group's or the medium's nervous systems. Do not admit latecomers, as the disturbance can destroy the tenuous links that may have been established with the Other Side. Have soothing, instrumental music playing in the background to help establish the right mood. Personally, I like Celtic harp music or Chopin's *Nocturnes* for the piano, but what you play is up to you. I do not recommend Gregorian chants because they seem lugubrious for the occasion, and music with words can distract.

Participants should settle in comfortably around the table without slouching, and place both feet on the floor in order to take maximum advantage of their bodies as conductors of energy. It is not necessary to hold hands to establish a circuit. If everyone places palms down on the table, the effect is the same.

The sitters should relax and breathe in and out slowly and regularly, and empty their minds of angry or unhappy thoughts. Any time you find your thoughts straying, return to listening to the sound of your breathing.

After a few minutes, the host or hostess should open the proceedings with a short prayer. If you wish to invoke the Archangels[9] for protection, feel free to do so (I include an archangelic invocation to use as a model in chapter 7). If one of the participants possesses a good voice, she or he may offer a song. It does not have to be a sacred song, like a hymn. In fact, it is best to keep things light with a gentle, happy tune that will keep the sitters from concentrating too hard and establish a friendly atmosphere to attract spirits.

After completing the preliminaries, the group should relax and converse quietly. Do not try to concentrate too hard on what you are doing. This may seem like a contradiction to the seriousness of the task, but it has been found in these matters that if you try too hard, you become tense and may be unable to let the energy flow.

What to Expect

At this point, the medium will probably sink into a trancelike state, and contact with other entities may be forthcoming through the instrument of the medium's body. As I mentioned, one of the first signs that a spirit has arrived may be a cool breeze or the rattling of a window when no wind is blowing. Raps may sound faintly and faraway. The table may tremble and even lift off the ground.

The medium's control may appear. This is an entity that acts a liaison between the medium and the spirit world, and who protects the medium from negative, violent entities that may try to possess his or her body. Perhaps the spirit will choose to make direct contact and use the medium's body and vocal chords to speak. In this event, the medium may sound and behave very differently from normal.

Afterward, the medium will probably have no recollection of what has been said and done, so it is a good idea to provide everybody with paper and pen to jot down notes. If at any time during the proceedings sitters feel compelled to write down anything, even if at the time it does not seem to make sense, they should do so. Similarly, if they suddenly feel like speaking or gesticulating, they should not suppress the urge. The spirits may be choosing to communicate telepathically with someone besides the medium. They do this because some entities' thought processes work many thousands of times faster than any one person's, so it makes sense to talk with more than one human at the same time. If you do feel compelled to write something down, do not think about interpreting it until after the séance has concluded. The entity may use some of your personal symbols, which you will need to explain to the entire group.

After all spirits have left and the medium has emerged from the trance, send a prayer of thanksgiving to Hermes, lord of spirit communication, for facilitating contact between the worlds. Thank the Archangels for their protection. Thank the spirits, entities, and unseen guests who took part in the séance, and send them back to their realms in peace and love.

Everyone should share the experience after the meeting, so if you are hosting the event, make sure coffee, tea, and munchies are on hand. Each participant may have picked up on information that went undetected by the others. If it is discovered that inaccurate facts has been passed, do not rush to blame the medium or the entities. Communication between the worlds is often difficult and contradictory. Refrain from letting value judgments seep into your interpretations of the facts, but be sure to say what you saw, heard, and felt. One member of the group should be appointed to keep a log of the sessions so that progress can be measured and remembered.

Notes

1. From the testimony of Mrs. Fox in A. C. Doyle, *The History of Spiritualism,* Vol. I (London: Cassell and Company, 1926), pp. 61–65.

2. *Journal for the Society of Psychical Research.* Vol. VI (1894), pp. 355–357.

3. Dr. William Brown, *Science and Personality* (New Haven: Yale University Press, 1929), p. 157.

4. From the inaugural address of the SPR in *Proceedings of the SPR,* Vol. I (1883), pp. 3–4.

5. Baron von Reichenbach discovered an emanation that radiates from crystals, the human body, magnets, and heavenly bodies which he called the *od* or *odic force.* Experiments in the detection and ramifications of this phenomenon were conducted by Reichenbach and others.

6. New York, Herbert B. Turner, 1907. This popular book has gone through many reprints.

7. Nevill Drury, *Dictionary of Mysticism and the Occult* (San Francisco: Harper and Row, 1985), pp. 30–31.

8. Cheiro, *Cheiro's Language of the Hand* (New York: ARC Books, 1968), p. 1.

9. The Archangels Raphael, Gabriel, Michael, and Auriel are the Guardians of the Four Watchtowers, or the Quarters of the Universe. They preside over air, water, fire, and earth. For a more detailed discussion of the Archangels and their functions, and how to invoke them for protection, see my book *Web of Light: Rites for Witches in the New Age* (Atglen, PA: Schiffer Publishing, 1991).

CHAPTER THREE

THE PARANORMAL IN THE TWENTIETH CENTURY

The Science of Parapsychology Takes Root

I believe the growing knowledge of psychic ability has given a glimpse into a new, creative dimension of human nature, giving renewed hope and determination to mankind.

—Peter Hurkos, psychic detective[1]

By 1910, Spiritualism's hold on the people's imagination had ebbed, but enough wealthy adherents were still around to bestow research grants for psychic research on Harvard, Stanford, and Clark universities. When the president of the SPR, William McDougall (1871–1938), took the Chair of Psychology and Philosophy at Harvard in 1920, he adapted a term from German to give the name "parapsychology" to the nascent science. His protégé, J. B. Rhine, delineated its boundaries, which stayed in place until undergoing expansion with research in recent years.

In the nonscientific community, Pulitzer prize-winning author Upton Sinclair (1878–1968), together with his wife Mary, made a significant contribution to the study of telepathy. Sitting alone in a room, Sinclair acted as sender. He transmitted mind-to-mind messages to his wife, who was sequestered in another room, in the form of pictures which she then drew. Over the course of their experiment, they logged 155 partial or total successes. The telepathically transmitted pictures later came to be known as "target drawings." Sometimes the couple relayed as many as five or six drawings during a sitting. Mary remarked that often the impression of the second picture registered in her mind before she had finished drawing the first one. The author wrote about their journey into the paranormal in his 1932 book, *Mental Radio*.

J. B. RHINE (1895–1980)

Joseph Banks (J. B.) Rhine entered the field as a skeptic. He and his wife, Louisa E. Rhine, were busy obtaining degrees in botany at the University of Chicago when they attended a lecture on Spiritualism given by Arthur Conan Doyle. Rhine was interested enough to read physicist and SPR member Sir Oliver Lodge's book on *The Survival of Man,* where the author describes his conversion to Spiritualism after contacting his deceased son through a medium. The Rhines became fascinated by the question of survival after death.

The couple traveled to Boston to meet Professor McDougall and arranged a sitting with Mina Crandon, aka Margery (1888–1941), whom at the time was probably the most famous medium in America. Crandon was famous for manifesting ectoplasm, phantom thumbprints, limbs, and hands. She was studied by the ASPR, who could not reach an agreement about the genuine nature of her mediumship. Eventually the "ectoplasmic manifestation" was discovered to be fabric treated with a phosphorescent substance, and the "thumbprint" was found to have been taken from a wax impression of Crandon's dentist's thumb.

Immediately the Rhines detected Crandon's ruses. They even saw her pick up the floating trumpet, which lay within reach of her bound hands and project the voice of her control, Walter. Rhine penned a strongly worded letter to the ASPR unmasking Crandon's deception. To those who steadfastly believed in the medium's powers, the criticism amounted to blasphemy. Doyle even took out an ad in a Boston newspaper that read, "J. B. Rhine is a monumental ass."

The rift in the ASPR over Margery's case instigated in part by Rhine's letter eventually led to a split in the organization and the formation of the Boston Society for Psychical Research (BSPR) by Walter F. Prince. This was the first, but certainly not the last time that Rhine provoked controversy. Although he never lost interest in the topic of survival, he knew that if he followed that path, his research would be ridiculed. Even after he became a renowned researcher, and in spite of pleas from his students, Rhine vetoed any examination of this area.

When McDougall left Harvard to head the Psychology Department at Duke University in 1927, he asked Rhine to join him. At Duke, Rhine refined tests that had already been invented and created new ways to confirm the existence of and measure telepathic and clairvoyant faculties. We are indebted to Rhine for the term *extra-sensory perception* (ESP). Because of the rigorous scientific methods he imposed and his all-encompassing work in the field, he has earned the title of "Father of Parapsychology." Largely due to Rhine's efforts, and in spite of what diehard skeptics may say, the question is no longer, "Does ESP exist?" but, "What are its capabilities and limitations?" The road to the legitimatization of the field was cut, but it would be more than thirty years before parapsychology was approved as a science by the American Association for the Advancement of Science.

The Experiments

Following the lead of his SPR and ASPR predecessors, Rhine continued to conduct card guessing experiments. Since this was before the computer age, in order to reduce the headaches of numbers crunching, he switched from the deck of fifty-two to using a set of cards developed by Karl Zener. This deck consists of five cards each of five kinds, totaling twenty-five. The simple designs—a star, a cross, a circle, a square, and three wavy lines—eliminate guesses based on subjects' innate superstitions about playing cards. Chance guesses, called MCE for "mean chance expectation," are five out of twenty-five. A higher score indicates that clairvoyance, telepathy, or a combination of both are at work.

Rhine also had subjects guess "down through" the pack; that is, guess the ordering of the cards face-down on the table from top to bottom. Sometimes the subject was asked to indicate the order even before the cards were shuffled as a test of precognition. Careful attention was paid to make sure the subject did not touch the cards, and subjects and experimenters were separated into different rooms. This way, neither party could be accused of exercising an intentional or unintentional influence. As time went on, an automatic shuffling machine was developed to further distance the researcher from the experiment.

Fortunately, Rhine attracted several subjects early in his career who excelled at card guessing. The group included Adam Linzmayer, George Zirkle, and perhaps the most remarkable subject of all, Hubert Pearce. A divinity student at Duke, it was Pearce who suggested guessing down through the deck, a feat which he was able to perform with a high degree of accuracy, even from another room in a remote building.

Rhine experimented with psychokinesis (PK), too, by throwing dice and having the subjects try to influence which faces landed face-up. As with the cards, machines were devised to eliminate the experimenter's influence. The machine cast the dice down a runway, where they came to rest on a flat surface.

Target drawings along the lines of Upton and Mary Sinclair's experiments were attempted. Rhine also sought to discover whether drugs affected performance. He chose sodium amytal, which seemed to produce a negative effect, since even his best subjects did not score much above MCE while under the drug's influence. Caffeine appeared more promising because it seemed to help some subjects concentrate.

Rhine even delved into animal ESP, and investigated German Shepherds' abilities to sense land mines. He was attracted to animal research, in part, because the subjects were easy to control—they did not try to cheat or exaggerate as some humans might.

Knowledge about psychic phenomena was identified, named, verified, and broadened during the Rhine era, either by him and his associates or by other researchers, at home and abroad. For example, it was discovered that both telepathy and clairvoyance may come into play during card guessing, which led to the realization that they present two aspects of the same ESP phenomenon. Together these faculties were termed general extra-sensory perception (GESP).

While experimenting with target drawing, telepathy was tested by having subjects all over the world "tune into" and draw a picture of the images on which the experimenter concentrated. It was revealed that subjects sometimes drew the right picture two to three nights before and after the target date. The result showed both precognitive and retrocognitive abilities. The same phenomena were ascertained to operate in card guessing. For example, one gifted subject consistently missed the target, but beat chance odds by a billion to one by guessing the following card.

Psychological factors that influence subjects' performance were uncovered. When subjects were forced to speed up the time they took to guess, they concentrated better and therefore performed better. Subjects' attitudes like enthusiasm, boredom, preoccupation with personal problems, and self-consciousness all affected how they did, although intelligence was ruled out as a factor. One English subject's performance, when subjected to machine shuffling, was negatively affected until she overcame her aversion to the machine.

Subjects tended to guess the first few cards in a twenty-five card run correctly, drop in accuracy through the middle, then rally toward the end of the run, rather like a horse spotting the barn door. This phenomenon became known as the "decline effect."

The fact that a subject's mood affects precognition and telepathy was further related to psychokinesis (PK), by exercising the will to influence the outcome of an event, like throwing dice to make certain faces land up. This theory was proposed to Rhine by William Gatling, who believed that PK and the power of prayer might share common qualities.

Volunteer "lucky" gamblers and divinity students, who held strong beliefs about the power of prayer, were put into two teams and pitted against each other in a dice throwing match. Although neither the gamblers nor the divinity students clearly won; after 1,242 runs of throwing six dice from a cup at a time, both teams had beaten the odds against chance by a billion to one.

On the basis of this and other experiments, Rhine concluded in his book *The Reach of the Mind,* that "ESP and PK are so closely related and so unified logically and experimentally that we can now think of both mind-matter interaction as one single fundamental two-way process."[2]

Criticism of Rhine

All these advances might lead you to conclude that Rhine and his colleagues had legitimized and solidified the field of parapsychology forever. Unfortunately, this is not what happened. Rhine had to contend with fierce opposition over the entire length of his career. No matter what he did to eliminate conscious and unconscious influences from his experiments, skeptics lashed out at him for "stacking the deck," so to speak. This is why he "discarded" hand shuffling and kept subjects from touching the backs of the cards or even seeing them. When the experimenter was secluded behind a screen to keep the subject from detecting any unconscious body and facial movements, critics charged that the experimenter with "emitting unconscious whisperings." Rhine responded by separating the experimenter and subject into different rooms.

When, after rigorous controls were instituted, many subjects' scores declined, skeptics took it as confirmation of their suspicions about inept research. They never considered that boredom with mindlessly repetitive experiments with little to hold the subject's interest and focus, conducted in sterile laboratory environments, might have contributed to the lower scores.

When Rhine achieved spectacular results, despite all odds, critics denigrated them. They posited that he may have interpreted the findings incorrectly, or ran tests only until he accumulated the data he wanted, or selected only the evidence to support his theories, or made recording errors.

In order to counter the attacks, Rhine took his results for examination by Sir Ronald Fisher, an eminent statistician who declared them to be sound. He also reminded the accusers that several of his subjects had performed well from the very beginning of the experiments, thus disproving the allegation that he suspended experiments after obtaining certain ratios. No evidence was ever found that Rhine deliberately slanted results to prove his theories. On the contrary, most recording errors (of which there were only about 175 out of 175,000 records) were found to favor chance, not ESP.

It seemed that nothing then, or now, will satisfy those who would discredit psychic phenomena. The Parapsychological Association was finally accepted as an affiliate by the American Association for the Advancement of Science (AAAS) in 1969. Nevertheless, at an AAAS meeting ten years later, physicist John A. Wheeler railed against parapsychology in his papers "Drive the Pseudos out of the Workshop of Science," and "Where There's Smoke, There's Smoke." Wheeler calumniated the elderly, ailing Rhine with having fabricated results and blasted the whole field with, "Every science that is a science has hundreds of hard results, but search fails to turn up a single one in 'parapsychology.'" He likened psi scientists to "confidence men" who "can be sent to jail."[3]

Rhine was recovering from a stroke, but rose up once more to strike down the libeler, and Wheeler was forced to retract the slurs. Rhine died a few months later in 1980.

Some of the irrational reactions to Rhine and his work result from prejudices against anything remotely supernormal that have become so ingrained in some people's psyches that it is unlikely that they will ever accept the existence of psi, let alone open their minds to the possibility that psi awareness can be useful to humanity in the coming centuries. Why the cynics persist in making belligerent denials in the face of the mountain of evidence in favor of psi is difficult to understand. Perhaps vestiges of the many fraudulent occurrences during the Spiritualist era, the gullibility of some researchers at that time, and early experiments that did not follow the rigorous scientific standards of today still "haunt" the naysayers. Then again, they may fear that if they acknowledge the existence of psi they will have to rethink some of the current laws of physics.[4]

In order to prepare myself to write this book, I infiltrated a local chapter of an international skeptics' organization. After spending some time with these people, I concluded that if some of the members were made to admit that a force lurking outside their carefully constructed and compartmentalized world was actually running loose in the universe, their whole worldview would turn topsy-turvy and their reason for being might cease to exist.

Unfortunately, some researchers since Rhine have fallen prey to the dictates of this vociferous faction of the scientific community, and continue to try to refute the accusations. They do not understand that they will never satisfy the more outrageous critics and that they are playing into skeptics' hands by slowing the research process by continually performing tedious experiments on trying to prove the existence of phenomena that have already passed muster.

This may be one reason why a significant number of survey respondents take a dim view of the science of parapsychology as it exists today. When asked, "What do you think of research societies like the ASPR and scientists and parapsychologists who investigate psi and ESP?" only forty-nine (less than half) rate these groups as good to excellent. Many respondents grudgingly acknowledge the value of parapsychology. They feel that since our society demands instruments of validation, research fulfills this need by helping to legitimatize the field and disseminate information. Yet, they still believe that parapsychology only grazes the tip of the iceberg.

While sixty-five respondents find the research useful, others express ambivalent or negative attitudes. Some respondents believe that the research produced useful material in the past but that the studies are now too mechanistic and limited in scope. Sue Burton-Hildago complains, "I have lectured at the J. B. Rhine Institute at Duke (now called the Foundation for Research on the Nature of Man) and find that these researchers seem to be more interested in phenomena than in soul growth."

"They will never commit on definite conclusions," says Patricia Hayes, who has worked with Rhine's associates. "They are too worried about their peers." Nancy Myer adds, "They have been around for a long time and they're not making much progress. They need to move away from [trying to disprove] what it [ESP] isn't . . . This is only a good start."

Lynda Hilburn-Holland, a tarot reader and psychotherapist, comments that she finds some of the research interesting, "but how sad that they have to try to prove that such a normal ability exists."

Some cite the fact that psychical research is sparingly staffed because of lack of funding. Others emphasize that some experiments try to impose physical rules of measurement on a basically nonphysical phenomenon that cannot be quantified because it has been developed by some practitioners into an art.

Kurt Leland, who channels Charles, reiterates this point of view. "The more interesting psychic abilities result in experiences too personal ever to be adequately tested by the scientific method," he explains. "For example, an out-of-body experience can prove to anyone who has had one that the soul exists separate from the body. But that kind of subjective experience could never be corroborated in a laboratory."

Research Since Rhine

Although the respondents' criticisms may be well-founded, not all the research since Rhine has been limited and unimaginative. One boon to research, computer technology, has taken over the numbers crunching and data entry burdens, thereby enabling much more raw data to be generated and processed accurately. Computers have also freed researchers to move away from forced-choice targets to random targets concocted by machines called Random Event Generators (REGs). Subjects are being "treated" to computer games and other free response targets that keep them excited and involved in the experiments.

Today, SPR-type organizations flourish all over the world and parapsychology is taught in hundreds of institutions of higher learning. Since many researchers no longer preoccupy themselves with proving the existence of ESP, they have moved into more provocative areas. For example, the relationship of personality traits and other psychological factors to psi abilities is being explored.

Back in the mid-1980s at Princeton, Gertrude R. Schmeidler tested both believers and nonbelievers in ESP, whom she called "sheep" and "goats" respectively. As one might suppose, the "sheep" scored higher than average on ESP tests, but the "goats" scored much lower on tests than dictated by chance. This surprising result led to the conclusion that those who do not believe in ESP subconsciously block their faculty by a process called "psi missing." Other experiments have shown that the most successful subjects are those who seem to be able to relax, make their minds become passive, at least for a while, and turn their attention inward away from external distractions.

Although ESP remains largely a latent, spontaneous faculty in most people, the results of these and other experiments demonstrate that it is possible to develop the ability and measure one's progress. In altered states research (ASR), a popular branch of parapsychology, researchers work with biofeedback, drugs, and sensory deprivation, as well as with tried and true standbys, like hypnosis and meditation, to identify and increase subjects' ESP.

Louisa E. Rhine (1891–1983), J. B. Rhine's wife, studied 100,000 subjects and found that 65% expressed spontaneous psi in their dreams; that is, they may have communicated telepathically with relatives and friends, and even experienced precognitive episodes, presumably without intention, while sleeping. In 1962, doctors Montague Ullman (b. 1916) and Gardner Murphy (1895–1979) founded the Maimonides Dream Laboratory in New York. Among other discoveries, they found that senders can suggest dream topics telepathically, and that this kind of telepathy seems to operate best when both sender and receiver are males.[5] When a sender is isolated in a sensory overload chamber where images are projected on a screen by polarized light and appropriate surround sound is played, the receiver dreams of the projected images more frequently and in sharper focus.

According to Alfred Douglas in *ESP: A Century of Psychical Research:*

> These and similar experiments have given rise to a theory that perhaps deep emotional involvement in an experience in some way excites the older part of the brain into creating images so strong that they can more easily be transmitted to another brain without the need for sensory contact. If this is so, it would explain why so many spontaneous psi experiences revolve around traumatic events in the lives of the participants.[6]

Hypnosis has also been proven to aid ESP and stimulate creativity. Using a device called a Witch's Cradle, the subject sits bound and blindfolded on a large swing, and is swayed gently. The swinging causes a slight disorientation of the mind which enhances psychic and creative abilities.

Before 1930, when the term "parapsychology" had yet to be coined, some hypnotized subjects were recorded as being able to perceive at a distance real scenes in progress and relate what was going on, where, and when in a manner similar to that described by medieval magician Roger Bacon with his "magick ball." More recently, this phenomenon has been referred to as "remote viewing." The United States government has spent money on research into remote viewing as it relates to military intelligence. Several talented and serious practitioners of this faculty, including groups like PsiSquad, have helped police solve crimes, and remote viewing workshops are popping up all over the country.

PSYCHICS OF THE TWENTIETH CENTURY

Here are the stories of some outstanding psychics who made their mark on the twentieth century by pushing the frontiers of the field. (When available, I have included birth and death dates.) Short biographies of notable contemporary psychics and channelers who are comparatively newer to the field are told in appendix E.

Elwood Babbitt (b. 1922)

A New England trance medium in the tradition of Edgar Cayce, Elwood Babbitt gives life readings, aura readings, past-life readings, and occasionally offers predictions. This farmer with little formal education honed his psychic skills as a young man on the battlefields of World War II. He witnessed soldiers fall mortally wounded, then was surprised to see an exact double of the casualty rise up before his eyes and disappear.

Before giving readings, Babbitt sits in a straight-backed chair and falls into a deep, sleep-like trance. Slowly his face and voice take on the personality of one of his three controls who help him channel spirits. Babbitt's perception of the human aura is so keen that he often sees it to the exclusion of the physical body.

Mir Bashir (b. 1907)

Author of *The Art of Hand Analysis,* this Indian palmist who lived in Britain studied over 50,000 hands and developed theories of disease and aberrant behaviors that could be predicted through hand analysis. His theories, supported by an Atlantean accumulation of data, have been validated by physicians and criminologists.

Rosemary Brown

Englishwoman Rosemary Brown composed musical compositions that she channeled through automatic writing from such icons as Bach, Beethoven, Berlioz, Chopin, Rachmaninov, and Stravinsky. At the age of seven, she claimed that Liszt appeared to her in a vision and told her that when she grew up he would bring her some music. He did.

The compositions are remarkable in that they express many different styles and structures, a feat that would be difficult to achieve for a woman like Brown, who possessed only moderate piano skills. It is possible that, as in the case of Pearl Curran, some sort of self-hypnosis may have enabled Brown to access deeper levels of her own creativity than that allowed by the conscious mind.

Eileen Caddy

Cofounder, with her husband Peter, of the Findhorn Foundation (founded in 1962) in northeast Scotland. The clairvoyant Caddy heard the voice of God, introduced to her as "Elixir," tell her where and how to develop the derelict, infertile, gorse-overgrown land into a prolific, veritable garden of Eden which supports a large community. Some followers believe that they communicate with devas (nature spirits) that advise them on how to grow their crops.

Jeanne Dixon (1918–1997)

This devoutly religious American twentieth-century psychic was acclaimed for her predictions of worldwide import. Although many of her predictions never came true, she is remembered for the spectacular prophecies that did occur, for example, she foresaw the Kennedy assassinations and that of Martin Luther King, Churchill's second Ministry, and invasions and wars of modern times. Dixon believed her ability was a gift from God. She never drank or smoked, arose at 3:00 A. M. each day to pray and meditate, and was a vegetarian. She wrote an autobiography, *My Life and Prophecies,* and Ruth Montgomery wrote a book about her titled *A Gift of Prophecy.*

John William Dunne (1875–1949)

An Irish mathematician and airplane designer, Dunne also experimented with prediction through dreams. In his books *The Serial Universe* and *An Experiment with Time*, he put forth the theory that time was experienced differently by the unconscious mind. He hypothesized that by tapping into the universal mind, dreamers could travel psychically into the past and future. Dunne was not just a theorist; his writings are based his own experience having made many astounding predictions that came true.

Arthur Ford (1897–1971)

Both a psychic medium and Spiritualist, Ford was also a member of the ASPR. He was acclaimed when Episcopal Bishop James Pike declared that Ford had put him in contact with his deceased son. The medium also claimed to have contacted the spirit of Houdini and received the key to breaking the code that Houdini had left behind as proof of survival after death. Charges of fraud were leveled against Ford, although they were never proved. During the struggle to redeem his name, he fell ill and eventually retired.

Eileen Garrett (1893–1970)

Arguably the most thoroughly studied trance medium of modern times, Garrett was born within sight of the Hill of Tara in Ireland, where as a child she communicated with the "Little People." Death was no stranger to her, as she lost her parents early in life, and later a husband and some of her children.

She was a world traveler and hostess for many of the intellectuals of the era. In this role, Garrett became the prototype for the main character in Patrick Dennis's novel (and later played by Rosiland Russell in the film) *Auntie Mame.*

Garrett lectured around the world on psychic phenomena, and in 1951 founded the Parapsychology Foundation in New York. Although she was not always right in her predictions, she enjoyed a high degree of accuracy and never took money for her work.

Peter Hurkos (1911–1988)

Peter Hurkos was a Dutch psychic detective who developed his unique faculties after falling off a ladder while painting a house. He was in a coma for three days, after which he began to "see" things differently.

During World War II, Hurkos was active in the Dutch Resistance. After the war, the French put him through a battery of tests to assess his authenticity, after which he worked for the police for five years. He also helped solve crimes in Holland, the U.K., and U.S., specializing in missing persons and murders. Among his most famous cases is the work he did on the Boston Strangler murders, where he insisted that the man charged with the killings was not the murderer.

Gladys Osborne Leonard (1882–1968)

This estimable British trance medium's control, Feda, an Indian girl, was ascertained by researchers to not be merely a projection or secondary personality of Leonard, but a distinct entity with its own characteristics. Leonard was adept at "book tests," where she could indicate the contents of a certain page of a specific book that she had never before seen as containing a message for a sitter. She also exercised precognitive faculties to "read" newspaper articles in advance of publication, including the page number and placement of the article on the page.

Ruth Montgomery

Originally a writer on the Washington political scene, Montgomery grew curious about psychic phenomena after attending a séance in Florida. She interviewed many psychics, but was not convinced of their legitimacy until she met Arthur Ford. His guide, Fletcher, gave her some extraordinary information and encouraged her to try automatic writing.

After months of practice, a perfect lily was produced by Montgomery's hand, and became the sign of her guiding entity. For a while, Lily appeared to Montgomery each morning, but was later replaced by other beings that identified themselves only as "The Guides." The overriding message was that Montgomery would not pursue a career as a trance medium who gave private client sessions, but would use her ability to impart truths to help all of humankind.

She wrote several books—some channeled, some not—about mediums, psychic phenomena, aliens, past lives, the Ouija board, and predictions for the future of the Earth. Among her best known works are *A Gift for Prophecy* (the story of psychic Jeanne Dixon), *A World Beyond* (channeled to her by Arthur Ford), and *Here and Hereafter* (about her own past lives and those of others). She was labeled "the First Lady of psychic writing."

Dr. George Gilbert Murray (1866–1957)

Onetime president of the SPR who was also a telepath, Murray's interest in psychical phenomena was born when he, his wife, and their children discovered a flair for telepathy while playing guessing games. Perhaps because he was a professor of Greek literature and philosophy, Murray likened telepathy to the Greek idea of "sympathy." His experiments in the realm of the paranormal took the form of a kind of remote viewing of historical scenes.

Rosaleen Norton (1917–1979)

This Australian occultist and artist believed she could contact ancient deities while in a trance and paint their pictures. Some of her paintings were graphic enough to have obscenity charges leveled against her. She represents a precursor of today's spirit portrait artists.

Jane Roberts (1929–1984)

Roberts' parents divorced when she was very young and her mother was bedridden with painful arthritis. As a girl, she spent much time with her grandfather, and when her mother could no longer care for her, she was sent to a Roman Catholic orphanage.

For a while, Roberts yearned to become a nun, but she received a fellowship to Skidmore, where she studied poetry and art.

One October evening in 1963, while puttering with the Ouija board, the energy essence Seth introduced himself to her and her husband, and she became his channel. Roberts channeled to her husband several books by Seth on philosophy, reincarnation, and the nature of spirit.

Later, she channeled books by other spirits, including one by Cézanne, called *The World View of Paul Cézanne.* The book earned the praise of the art community, no mean feat, since art critics are generally known to be a skeptical lot about such matters. Other channeled material included messages from Carl Jung on the meaning of numbers in dreams.

Many questions have arisen around the Roberts phenomenon. Researchers wonder whether Seth was truly channeled or if this was a projection of her own unconscious mind because she never fell asleep during her trances and often could recall the "messages." This aspect of the Roberts/Seth experience is often referred to as a "bleed through."

Willi (1903–1971) and Rudi (1906–1957) Schneider

These Austrian brothers discovered their talents while fiddling with a planchette during a family séance. Willi could make the instrument move without touching it, and soon a control named Olga came through. Between them, the boys could levitate and produce a substance that was invisible on film negatives, but capable of absorbing infrared rays and setting off photographic flashbulbs.

Rudi was the most accomplished of the two, but both were thoroughly investigated by the SPR and found to be genuine. Willi eventually lost his ability and became a mechanic. Neither brother was able to predict the future.

Ted Serios (b. 1918)

Ted Serios represents a modern-day example of something like a nineteenth-century spirit photographer, but without the deception—perhaps. Through concentration, he was able to produce architectural photographic images—often of buildings he had never before seen—and transfer them to film. He was investigated by Denver psychologist Dr. Julie Eisenbud and two other researchers from Virginia. While fraud was never detected, Serios often behaved in an unorthodox way, insisting on taking with him a small object into the experiment room. He was temperamental, did not always follow the rules laid down by the researchers, and often could not produce results on demand for the researchers. Therefore, his ability, though sometimes remarkable, falls under the category of a demonstration rather than an experiment.

Ingo Swann (b. 1933)

At the age of two, Swann remembered leaving his body for the first time and staring down at himself on the operating table in the hospital while his tonsils were being removed. Afterward, he was able to recall minute details of the operation that he had no other way of knowing. Swann became famous as an aura reader. He could perceive auras around people, animals, and objects, and painted them. He also participated in remote viewing experiments. He believed that psychic abilities are not mystical or paranormal, but part of the normal, creative processes of the human brain.

In the next part of this book you will meet the psychics from the survey, and through them, learn more about the state of the art today, who practices, and why, what they do, and how it all works. Before you go on, you may wish to begin to begin developing your own abilities by practicing psychometrics.

PSYCHOMETRICS

Psychometry[7] plunges deeply into the still largely uncharted territory of the mind and reveals to us the possibilities of faculties that most of us do not consciously use. The origin of the term combines two Greek words, *psyche* and *metron,* which mean "soul measurement." Psychometry is the art and science of touching or holding a material object and extracting information about the character, surroundings, history, or influences of the possessor and/or the object itself.

Sometimes psychometrists apply this skill to help archeologists, anthropologists, and historians discover information about artifacts and their associations with ancient civilizations. They may also be called upon to psychometrize physical evidence from crime scenes to aid the police. In a private reading, the client hands over personal effects like eyeglasses, jewelry, rings, or something written on paper like a letter, a signature, or a question. The psychometrist then brings forth information about the person's past and present, attitudes and emotions, relationships, strengths, challenges, and future possibilities.

This method is introduced to you here partly because it seems so mysterious to the layperson that skeptics dismiss it as "just so much bunk." If you take the time to investigate, you find that psychometry is a measurable ability, most people possess it, and they can develop it to a greater extent.

Psychometry disciplines the intuitive portion of your mind and helps train you to rely on this skill whenever you perform any kind of psychic work. At the same time, you become adept at distinguishing between actual psychic impressions and your mind's fabrications.

By learning to trust your intuition in psychometric work, you may come to the realization that everything in the living universe interconnects on some level with everything else. These connections manifest in the same way that in music; vibratory harmonic frequencies come together to create chords. According to Stewart and Janet Farrar in their discussion of psychometry in *The Witches Way*, all objects and beings vibrate at slower to faster and lower to higher frequencies. The psychometrist's own vibrations, or aura frequencies, come in contact with those of the object being read, and they intermingle, creating a "chord" that the psychometrist perceives and interprets. The frequencies that the psychometrist distinguishes may be those of the object, its possessor, or both. The Farrars give the following illustration:

> A diamond ring for example is alive in the frequencies of its gem and its gold, which are both far slower than that of the woman who wears it. But there are harmonic frequencies between the two, just as striking top C on a piano with the pedal down will cause the bottom C string to hum. . . . If the ring is on her finger for years, all the events on her non-physical levels will cause a harmonic response in the corresponding levels of the ring, and the ring will "remember" them. A sensitive psychometrist, handling the ring, will pick up these "memories" by the same harmonic resonance.[8]

It is not as difficult as you might think to perceive and interpret these resonances, but, as with any other skill, it takes practice to perfect your technique. In the end, whether you find that you excel more at reading tarot cards, casting runes, or aura reading, your initial exercises with "psychometrics" will be time well spent. In this section, I will give you step-by-step instructions to help you discover and perfect this faculty that lies latent within you. The survey respondents will also offer their advice.

Suiting Up for "Psychometrics"

First, you need to acquire an object to psychometrize. What you choose depends on whether you are reading the object or the person. When selecting an object, remember that you must separate "object" and "people" impressions. Do this simply by telling yourself that you will read either the object or the person. For example, if you are reading an individual, do not to choose this person's eighteenth-century French pillbox, as it will carry strong historical resonances that may "leak through" into the personal reading.

Twenty-four survey respondents, whether psychometrists or not, indicate that they absolutely require some sort of physical link to the person they are reading, and the majority of the others prefer such a link. The top choice is a photo, but some, like Liaros, need only that the inquirer clearly visualize the person in question. Others find that the human voice supplies a strong tie. Popular alternatives with respondents include a spoken or written name or question, a handwriting sample—especially a signature, or a strand of hair. Personal objects like keys, jewelry, pens, or watches all seem to work well for the psychometrist. Once, when I requested a year's forecast, the psychometrist asked for my desk calendar. Even though it was at the beginning of the year and I had only penciled in a few appointments, the calendar supplied her with enough focus to prognosticate a year's worth of events for me with stunning accuracy.

Age, location, date of birth or death, either written down or spoken, also serve as a vibratory point of contact. Several readers like to see a birth chart, even though they may not be astrologers. Jerry comments that he has received accurate information from inaccurate charts. Many tarot readers seem to use psychometric skills because several comment that they like the inquirer to handle the deck. In this way, the deck is instilled with the inquirer's vibrations.

Shepherd reminds us that the most important item to request when performing a psychometric reading is permission. "Although I can remote view or 'spy,'" she informs, "the accuracy of such information when the subject has not given permission tends to be less." This advice is especially important to bear in mind when you are just beginning to practice, because in your enthusiasm, you may get carried away and read objects that belong to people who do not want a reading.

Time to Exercise!

Once you receive the object, exercise your faculty by relaxing. To relax does not mean to slouch down in your easy chair or cross your legs. Good posture opens a clear channel to energy; poor posture closes it down. Put aside your personal cares, still your mind, and try not to think of anything in particular. If you would like hints on how to remain relaxed, yet alert, turn to chapter 7.

Pick up the object with your left hand. I recommend the left hand because it connects to the right, nonanalytical, creative side of your brain, which is the resource you want to tap for psychometry. If you wish, hold it to your third eye to reinforce the psychic connection.

As I mentioned, the energies you perceive vibrate at different rates. The problem is that you will receive the different energy vibrations all at once, so you need to learn to filter these impressions. There are several ways of accomplishing this. For instance, you can "program" yourself to select only the pertinent data. If someone hands you a pair of eyeglasses and tells you that they belong to his lover and he wants to know how long their relationship will last, you don't need to tell him that the glasses show she likes to read science fiction and play the cello. You are looking for specific data. Use only descriptive terms, like adjectives and adverbs. Do not try to make sense of, organize, or evaluate your impressions. You don't want to open the door for your analytical or emotional minds to take over, because they may be wrong.

At this point, you may be thinking that you wish you had received such a basketful of impressions, but when you pick up the object, nothing happens. For both those who get too much or too little input, I have some recommendations. While you make your way through the following checklist, seek to move beyond the actual shape, size, color, and physical characteristics of the object. Have a notepad nearby to write down your impressions quickly. For each question you ask yourself, use one entire sheet. You may go back and fill in more data later as it occurs to you.

Psychometrics Checklist

1. Ask yourself questions that involve the five senses. Moving beyond the physical object, what visual impression does the object conjure for you? How does it smell, taste, sound, and feel? Can you link it with a color? Is it light or heavy for its size, soft or hard for the actual texture? How does the object make you feel? (Just give an impression with this, not a value judgment about the client's situation.)

2. Can you categorize the object according to the four elements of air, fire, water, and earth, and the more ineffable element of Spirit? For example, do you get an airy-fairy feeling of unconnectedness, or perhaps an idea of swift, decisive action when you hold the object? Both reactions involve the element of air. Does the object feel fiery and angry, or bursting with positive fire energy?

3. Do any personal or universal symbols leap to mind having to do with numbers, flowers, trees, animals, god and goddess forms, or any personal associations? Again, do not try to interpret these symbols.

4. Do you visualize any pictorial representations? Once, while holding a woman's diary, I saw a baby blanket with pink and blue flowers on it. When I told her, she blushed and admitted that the blanket was one she had as a child and that it held a very specific significance for her. No, she insisted after I inquired, the symbol had nothing to do with having children nor with her childhood, but that the meaning was very clear to her. (See how if I'd skipped the reference to the blanket and talked about children how I would have bombed?) If you perceive a picture, draw it. If not, get yourself started by drawing a line—any sort of line. It can be short, long, vertical, horizontal, straight, squiggly, undulating, jagged, or loop around. Draw it without thinking. Then take your finger and trace it with your finger over and over again, very slowly. Now write down your impressions. Tracing works well with written words, like signatures.

5. Finally, write a short paragraph describing your impressions. Go over everything you have written down and add anything that seems important. You will find that many impressions seem to reinforce each other, but a few do not. Discard what you think was not right.

Here is an illustration from a reading I performed for a client I'll call Verna. While holding Verna's keys, I picked up the following: dark blue, stagnant, soft, drowsy, heavy, listless, cold, depressed, a clock winding down, papers with writing on them fluttering in the breeze, Thoth (god of communication) standing protectively in the background, a wilting lemon verbena plant, and a woman sitting under an apple tree laden with fruit, sadly contemplating the rushing water of a nearby stream.

I told Verna about these images and asked if they made any sense to her. Sometimes clients need a gentle push to put the story together. In such situations, I may make one or two suggestions in order to clarify concepts, but I try to keep myself out of it as much as possible. In this reading, with very little prodding from me, Verna came up with the following story:

She had been feeling frustrated and unhappy (blue) because she could not finish a writing project. Her creative juices were stagnating, she felt listless and cold, as if her fires had burned out. Her ability to communicate was wilting like a lemon verbena plant (symbol of communication). Yet Thoth, the scribe and great communicator of the Egyptian pantheon, stood solidly behind her, and the pages fluttering in the breeze were covered with writing, which showed that she could salvage the situation. Verna was capable of keeping this "dry spell" from taking root. Life did not have to pass her by like the rushing stream. If she changed her attitude, Thoth would guide her. All she needed to do was reach up and pick the apples (symbol of knowledge, wisdom, creativity) over her head that she was ignoring. If she did, she would move with the flow of life once more. Verna changed her outlook, finished her book, and three months later, bagged herself a well-known agent. Besides finding out the nature of her inquiry, I only offered suggestions about the symbolism of the lemon verbena plant, Thoth, and the apple. The bulk of the reading consisted of me relating my impressions to Verna.

A word of advice: even if you feel negative impressions, part of your function as a reader is to help people begin to see their way out of their troubles. Do not lie to the client by saying that everything is cheery and bright if it isn't. On the other hand, you don't want the person, on the basis of your reading, to go home feeling hopeless. Be realistic, but positive.

Next Envelope, Please!

An excellent way to practice psychometry is with photographs, pictures from magazines, and small, flat objects sealed in opaque envelopes. For this exercise, you need to gather a few indulgent friends. Have one person choose the items. Ask someone else, without glancing at them, to seal them in envelopes. Ask a third person, who has not seen any of the pictures or the sealing process, to shuffle the envelopes and give them to you. In this way, you reduce telepathic interference and concentrate on the pictures themselves. Proceed with the exercise as you did when reading specific objects.

Once our coven tried this exercise in a group, and the psychometrist who was teaching us used color-coded the envelopes. I found I had some difficulty with "reading" the contents because, being visually oriented, the colors on the outside of the envelopes affected my perceptions. From the experience, I learned to keep all codes off the envelopes. When you finally want to know how you did, just open them up and look inside.

Remember to have fun with these exercises. So what if at first, you get most of it wrong? Celebrate what you perceived correctly, and keep practicing!

Notes

1. Margaret Nicholas, *The World's Greatest Psychics and Mystics* (London: Octopus Books, 1986), p. 126.

2. J. B. Rhine, *The Reach of the Mind* (New York: William Sloane Associates, 1947), in Alfred Douglas, *Extra-Sensory Power: A Century of Psychical Research* (Woodstock, NY: The Overlook Press, 1977), p. 281.

3. *Psychic Powers,* the Editors (Alexandria, VA: Time-Life Books, 1987), p. 61.

4. An example of how psychic faculties run contrary to physical laws is that unlike with physical phenomena, precognition does not seem to diminish with distance over time and space. Survey respondents confirm this fact almost unanimously.

5. The second-best combination was male-to-female, and female-to-female came in last.

6. Alfred Douglas, *Extra-Sensory Powers: A Century of Psychical Research* (Woodstock, NY: The Overlook Press, 1977), p. 302.

7. The term "psychometry" was coined by Dr. J. R. Buchanan.

8. Janet and Stewart Farrar, *The Witches Way* (London: Robert Hale, 1984), pp. 209–210.

PART II

THE ART OF
DIVINATION TODAY

CHAPTER FOUR

PSYCHICS AND CHANNELERS TODAY

Who Are They and What Do They Do?

Mediums and mediumship are among the least understood people and practices in this imperfect world, although there is nothing frightening or mysterious about most practicing mediums today.

—Peter Underwood, psychic researcher[1]

I am sitting on the edge of the glossy, white, unyielding bench waiting to be called into one of the closed cubicles for my reading. I have never been to see a Spiritualist medium, and I have no idea of what to expect. Twenty minutes ago, I pushed through the heavy wooden door of London's Spiritualist Association of Great Britain. Nestled among embassies in the upscale Belgravia neighborhood, this organization has reigned as the major promoter of Spiritualism in the world ever since it was founded in the nineteenth century by Arthur Conan Doyle, of Sherlock Holmes fame.

A gust of wind drives a swirl of leaves and rain in with me. Now the water from my umbrella pools around my feet as I try to extricate myself from my damp, wrinkled raincoat without making too much noise in the creaky upper hall of this mysterious building that seems to house side-by-side the living and spirits of the dead. All the while, I clutch the receipt that I will have to produce to show I paid for the reading. The three cream-colored doors to the readers' cubicles gleam in the light of the overhead bulb, shielding from prying eyes and ears what is happening on the other side.

Without warning, the middle door swings open, and from behind the client—who silently vanishes down the staircase with a secret smile on her face—emerges Hilda Holyman. The trance medium beckons me with a cheerful greeting. She stands barely five feet, two inches tall, counting her high heels and blond French roll. She is a slightly-built woman, spry at around sixty years old, in a tailored suit and with an accent I can't quite place—perhaps from the West Country or the Channel Isles.

I rise, return her smile, and give her my receipt as I pass through the open door. During the session, which validates data about my personal situation and helps me distinguish more clearly the path ahead, a corner of my mind keeps wandering to the psychic. Where is she from? What is her background and education? How did she get involved in paranormal pursuits? A million questions flit through my mind like hummingbirds around a tantalizing bouquet of trumpet flowers.

The questions I formed in my mind that day led to many of the inquiries I wrote for the psychics survey. When we need to see a doctor, we want to know something about her. Is she reliable and experienced? What kinds of services does she provide? Why did she choose the field? Where was she educated, and what are her attitudes toward surgical procedures, vitamin therapy, and acupuncture?

It is natural that in the psychic realm you should also want to know something about the reader you are visiting so you can find the best match for your needs. Psychics are often surrounded by an air of mystery because many people believe that the readings they perform somehow separate their lives from the realm of normal human experience. Some potential clients may think that all psychics are either supernormal beings with a direct link to God, or soothsayers and charlatans. Many don't stop to think that psychics are normal people with homes and families, and that they can be humanly fallible without being fakes.

Sepharial, in *Second Sight,* his classic work on mediumship, asserts that the individual who practices divination becomes aware of a different kind of existence, but that this does not necessarily mean that the person is more intelligent or spiritually oriented than anyone else. He writes, "It is nor more a gift or a property of the wise or good man than extraordinary muscular power is an adjunct of higher intelligence."[2]

He goes on to say that he believes the ability can be inherited, and that this inheritance can be detected through a person's natal chart. Sepharial claims to have found correlations between psychics and people whose charts show many planets in mutable signs, and the planet Neptune dominant.[3]

Describing psychics from another point of view are two classic researchers in the field, Carrington and Whitehead. In *Keys to the Occult,* they describe a psychic as "one who senses material things astrally and astral things materially, psychic experiences calling for reciprocal action between the senses of the material body and the corresponding spiritual senses of the soul or astral body . . . the psychic exercises sense in attraction, perception, and inspiration."[4] Such an intellectual definition, while accurate, does little to give the flavor of a psychic's personality, thoughts, and experiences.

The goal of sharing the following information from the statistical page of the survey and partially from the "Personal Involvement" portion of the survey is to help you get to know who these people are. You can refer to appendix A for the actual statistics on the questions. Not every respondent answered every question, and sometimes they responded with several answers to a single query, so the numbers don't always add up to 100 (see appendix A for statistical data).

VITAL STATISTICS

Psychics and channelers who participated in the survey hail from all over the United States, as well as a few from England, New Zealand, Canada, and Latin America. They use their own names in a ratio of 3:1, and many of those with professional titles often choose something very close to their given names. A few go by both their professional and birth names.

Those who answered the questionnaire were born between 1917 and 1977, yielding an age range spanning sixty years. The majority of respondents are in their forties and fifties, but this is to be expected, as it is the time of life when people are most active in their careers.

Astrology buffs will be interested to know that contrary to popular opinion, the supposed most psychic Water signs are the least represented in this sample. That is to say, those born under the signs of Pisces, Scorpio, and Cancer are among the fewest respondents. More Aquarians than anyone else (in a 2:1 ratio to the Water signs) answered the questionnaire, followed closely by Leo. So either Aquarians and Leos are more psychic than anyone else, or they don't mind filling out surveys that the Water signs find tedious!

The respondents prove to be a well-educated group. They compare favorably with the national norm where, by 1995, 81.7% of Americans over twenty-five had completed high school, and 23% completed four years of college or more.[5] In comparison, 97% of survey respondents have high school diplomas, and 51% have earned degrees from institutions of higher learning, including seven Doctorates and two Doctors of Divinity.

BOOKS, CONFERENCES, CLASSES

Books I've read in the field? I could list hundreds!
　　　　　　　　　　　　　　　　　—Shirlee Teabo, tarot reader

My library resembles a small bookstore.
　　　　　　　　　　　　　　　　　—Sue Burton-Hidalgo, soul reader

Along with their high level of education, respondents share a thirst for knowledge. Many seem to consider their profession a continuing course of study in the great classroom of life, and spend a lot of time and effort improving their core skills and branching out into related areas.

Almost 70% of the respondents answer that they regularly read books, and/or attend conferences, classes, and workshops in their field. Some of the well-known psychics underscore that they offer workshops and deliver talks at conferences, write books, and produce videos. For example, Shirlee Teabo speaks at expositions, conducts a weekly radio show, writes a newspaper column, spent three years as a TV talk show host, and still finds time to give consultations and read almost a book a day!

Authors whose works psychics have read recently or recommend as having influenced their outlook cover the entire New Age spectrum, and several recall "classic" writers as prime influences. Frequently mentioned names include: Evangeline Adams, Alice Bailey, Carlos Castañeda, Edgar Cayce, Helene Corinne, Scott Cunningham, Dion Fortune, Enid Hoffman, and James Redfield. Popular subjects range from parapsychology to feng shui, herbalism, spirituality, animal communication, psychic self-defense, angelic communication, Santería, Wicca, UFOs, tarot, leadership, metaphysics, Shamanism, and miracles.

A few complain about not reading in the field because they don't discover any new material; they only find recycling of old ideas. These respondents tend to be older.

"No, I don't read in the field," says Rueckert because, "I am a reluctant channel. I channel because it is my service."

A couple mention that while they do read in the field, they also learn from the spirit world. One respondent studies with an elder who teaches her the magickal arts. Another expands personal horizons by performing tarot spells; still another does ongoing BOTA work.[6] One channeler even journeys around the world to places like Greece and Brazil to deepen knowledge, self-heal, and recharge her batteries.

Fewer respondents (about one-third) attend conferences and workshops than read in the field. One person mentions time and money as deterrents "plus the Midwest is not famous for conferences in this area." A few admit that they consider many of the events and participants "flaky," and that they are "too down-to-earth for that sort of thing." Those who attend do not limit themselves to their niches. Their broad range of interests spans dowsing, parapsychology, holistic healing, tarot, herbs, the "magickal household," UFOs, tantra, scientific exploration, and astrology.

They learn from each other, too. Almost 80% claim to have friends in the field with whom they exchange ideas; 37% note that they developed their abilities through personal contacts. Other methods of accessing information are: intuition, formal classes, divine revelation, family traditions, inner work, personal dream interpretation, hard work and practice, empirical training, reasoning, laboratory testing, and research.

Five point specifically to their inborn ability, and another maintains that he is simply uncovering what was already there. Several practitioners have studied with personal teachers.

RELIGIOUS AFFILIATION

I believe God is there to help and guide me. I also believe that I am doing this for a reason—a calling, if you will—and that I possess the talent to be able to work in this field. I feel very blessed.

—Nancy, tarot reader and psychometrist

I have experienced cosmic consciousness or what is now called "the experience of Light," unrelated to my work as far as I know. Religious beliefs are a piece of personal philosophical configuration that should not affect or interfere with any aspect of work or research.

—Bevy Jaegers, psi researcher and remote viewing instructor

[My] studies . . . develop the intuition . . . Part of the human experience is to help each other. I see my work as a service to others.
> —Jyoti Wind, astrologer, shaman, Hakomi psycotherapist

If "Oneness" and "Higher Power" are religious beliefs, yes, these concepts enhance my abilities. They certainly give them a larger context.
> —Martha Lawrence, astrologer, mystery writer

I practice all and many religions—I want truth.
> —Martin Butz, astrologer

I would never describe the interdimensional truth of all there is as a religion. It is merely the truth, the structure of all that exists.
> —Marisa Anderson, psychic and psychic detective

The above statements represent comments made by the respondents about their religious affiliations and how their religion influences their readings. Many psychics' ideas appear to butt against the norm of traditional religious beliefs. Only fourteen respondents claim to be Catholics, fourteen Protestants, five nondenominational Christians, and four Jews. Some, who are members of traditional religious groups, view their beliefs in broad terms, and infuse into their religious gestalt elements from many belief systems.

Many respondents affirm that they practice nontraditional religions like Wicca, Shamanism, Druidism, Unity, Spiritualism, and some profess to embrace all religions or none.

Half of the respondents feel that their religious affiliations play an important role in enhancing their abilities, and several take pains to distinguish between religious and spiritual beliefs. It is obvious from their answers that these individuals have thought long and hard about the nature of spirituality, the essence of divinity, their own place in the world, and their responsibilities as spiritual advisors.

PROFESSIONALS OR AMATEURS?

I not only earn my living (as a reader), but support twelve people, three churches, and an office!

—Sylvia Browne, trance medium

I counsel and serve, whatever I'm doing. I don't do it full-time so that I won't have to compromise or undermine any integrity or have to court clients.

—Lina, palmist, dream interpreter

Slightly more respondents state that they are able to make a living at their art as opposed to those who can't or don't need to.[7] Some earn half their income through psychic readings, and a few comment that they have never tried to make a living with their ability, but that they are certain they could if they tried. One dowser (Major Paul J. Sevigny, USAF, retired) donates all the fees he receives to the Boy Scouts, 4-H Clubs, and schools, and estimates donations so far to total $112,000.

Judging from the variety of occupations cited, versatility characterizes most readers. Writers (fifteen, including journalists) top the list, with eleven retirees and ten students following close behind. The list of occupations shows varied pursuits, including: United States Air Force, stewardess, nurse, park ranger, teacher, antiques dealer, stocks and bonds representative, accountant, electrical engineer, weather observer, radio/TV host, administrative assistant, office manager, jewelry designer, state employee, public relations, art seller, medical transcriber, metaphysical shop owner, homemaker, intercultural trainer, psychotherapist, hypnotist, tourist resort owner, communications/computer consultant, editor, publisher, researcher, seamstress, police report clerk, librarian, health practitioner, business consultant, and three readers on disability. Obviously you can't tell a psychic by his or her day job!

USING OTHER ABILITIES

People have said to me that they receive more help in one session than in years of counseling or with a therapist.

—Patricia Mischell, psychic reader and author

[Sometimes I am a] counselor, teacher, friend, or Devil's advocate. Divination is only useful when put in a framework the client can accept and understand.

—Maya Heath, creator of the *Egyptian Oracle*

As chapter 6 will discuss, many clients appear to have other reasons for going for a reading than learning the future, and most readers say that they regularly use abilities other than the psychic to assist their clients. Perhaps the wide variety of occupations and interests has enabled psychics to gain the necessary experience to understand and assist others. An overwhelming ninety respondents assert that they resort to abilities other than psychic ones during readings. Fifty-six occasionally perform counseling (one with a Ph.D. in Psychology, and another with extensive experience as a crisis and alcohol counselor, two who also volunteer in Victims' Services, and a trained Gestalt counselor). Thirty-five act as psychologists when necessary, and forty-one note that they sometimes use teaching skills.

Other talents that come into play include: coach, cheerleader, motivator, facilitator, physician-healer, real estate agent, comedian, spiritual advisor, friend and confidante, mother, sister, herbalist, Druid, catalyst, Devil's advocate, dispenser of information and common sense, and good listener.

Anka explains that these skills are not necessarily his own, but belong to the energy that he channels. "The entity in the channelings utilizes psychic abilities, mediumship, teaching, psychology—anything that will serve."

Dale sees her role as "a psychologist, pastor, teacher, shaman in the true sense of the word—a community-based healer . . . Physical, spiritual, mental aspects all interrelate and a problem in one realm may display symptoms in another. So you may treat a problem by calming the mind, restoring correct energy flow through the body, recommending appropriate herbs, and shielding the client from negative influences."

Only a few frown on using other abilities to enhance readings. One psychometrist notes that she is not allowed a choice because she is always in a trance during a reading. Another reader claims that all answers come from a higher power. Yet another says that although she offers suggestions on correcting health problems, she does not give predictions about those issues because it violates the law.

Most respondents, however, seem to perceive their roles in broad terms, believing that they should use every tool available to help others. As Vivienne Adam summarizes, "I call myself a psychic chiropractor. People come to me when they're out of alignment and I serve as a realigner."

First Experiences with the Paranormal

I told my mother the nanny wouldn't be coming back and pointed to my chest . . . she died suddenly of lung cancer at age twenty-nine.

—Marisa Anderson, psychic

At three, I could always predict phone calls and read my mother's thoughts as though hearing her voice.

—Selene, card and pendulum reader

I told my mom not to go down a particular street because there was going to be an accident . . . She went anyway, had an accident, and grounded me for a day.

—Ginger, psychic,
recalling a psychic experience at age seven

Remember the analogy of the doctor and how you'd like to know how long she's been in business? As a potential client, you may want to know how and when your psychic discovered his or her gift. While the survey respondents have been in the field for anywhere from one year to sixty, the majority have logged many years of experience. What's more, they mostly have been interested in psychic subjects or have known about these faculties since they were children.

Four respondents began reading before they were twelve, and an equal number maintain that they have been practicing all their lives. Most seem to have become involved in their twenties and thirties, which may indicate that a certain amount of life experience is often necessary before a reader can feel confident about successfully transmitting knowledge to help others. Sevigny, who is a dowser, states that he has performed and recorded more than 3,500 readings.

Although it seems that psychics discover their abilities at almost any age, and that the realization can surface for a variety of reasons, many seem to recognize that "something is there, something different" between the ages of two and five, with another cluster occurring around ten to twelve, sixteen to eighteen, the early twenties, again at around forty, and rarely thereafter.

Respondents offer intriguing initial experiences. Several describe childhood dreams that came true, and a handful tell of growing up in haunted houses where they perceived otherworldly entities that coexisted with their own families.

For others, a specific incident seems to have galvanized their psychic selves into action. Remote viewer Joseph McMoneagle describes having a classic near-death experience (NDE), and being taken to the hospital where he felt himself "falling through a tunnel, experiencing a review of life events, meeting with and envelopment by White Light."

Sometimes the death of a loved one triggers the psychic ability:

> The death of family members (my mother and my brother) within two months opened the door for spirit communication. (Graybear)

> My friend died and sat next to me in my car (in spirit) and cried. (Pat Rodegast)

> I knew my two great grandmothers were going to die by visually seeing their faces melt. (Browne)

For others, a series of less startling incidents build a cumulative effect:

> In a Scientology class I found I could leave my body and wander around. (Cleopatra)

> As a child I began sensing situations—like I knew who liked me and who pretended to like me. (Joy)

> [I got interested through] an English teacher of mine who was involved with Duke during the time when the university was conducting Parapsychology research. He was gifted with the ability to read auras. (PoTO)

> I had hunches, psychic dreams, precognitive experiences and past-life memories. Then I bought a deck of tarot cards and my abilities began to develop. (Lewis)

Several readers, particularly those who note that they came from psychic families, indicate that they first were introduced to the field by a relative, often a grandparent, who taught them how to read palms or cards. Others found out by "playing around" with decks of cards or Ouija boards. One woman tells how she first used the Ouija board with friends for fun, "but soon realized that others couldn't read as I could."

In the course of receiving a reading from a reliable psychic or medium, others were told that they, too, were psychic and were encouraged to nurture their abilities. "[At twenty-nine] a psychic told me that I was going to travel to teach psychic things and that I would write a book about intuition . . . I thought he was crazy!" (Carol Ann Liaros, author of *Practical ESP*).

WHAT THEY DO

Divination—exploring the unknown or the future by scrying practices, dreams, drugs, omens, or reading of the stars.

—Nandor Fodor, psychic researcher[8]

A variety of clairvoyants, mediums, channelers, and those involved in related fields answered the survey as well as nonprofessionals who read for family and friends. Many indicate that they practice more than one of the mantic arts. The skills listed are impressive: tarot or other cards, channeling, clairvoyance, psychic/intuitive readings, psychometry, psychometry of place, numerology, palmistry, past-life readings, aura readings, spiritual counseling, ghost and spirit contact, deep trance readings, soul/life readings, healing, graphoanalysis, I Ching, Qabala, feng shui, dream work, Reiki healing, Shamanism, animal and nature healings, clairaudience, music channeling, computer channeling, Hexcraft, crystal gazing, incantations, telepathy, Akashic records readings, hair strand analysis, and tasseography!

It's no wonder that most respondents are of the opinion that a psychic should practice more than one art. They tend to support using whatever talents work best in the situation, some seeing truth in all psychic capabilities. Several comment that different tools render different results, and that some tools are easier for some clients to apprehend than others, so the psychic should consider which method to use in light of the client's needs.

> Most of us have had access to a grand banquet of psychic skills from former lives. Versatility is useful spiritually, more mentally exciting, and quite appealing to clients. (Shepherd)

> As we grow we find tools for each spiritual level of attainment. (Heath).

> [I believe it is useful to rely on] one highly developed skill practiced along with several sub-specialties. (Selene)

> Try everything, weed out most, and develop the best of what remains. (Solomon)

> One key cannot open all locks. (Fitzgerald)

> Would you drive a car wearing earplugs just because most of the skills required to drive a car require hand-eye coordination? (Butz)

About one-quarter of the respondents do not agree, citing that resorting to several modes of divination scatters energies:

A jack of all trades in a master of none. (Joy)

Each [skill] requires too much understanding to spend time on other areas. I've been engaged in research to understand remote viewing for nineteen years and barely scratched the surface. (McMoneagle)

A couple of respondents object to the use of the word "tool" to describe these techniques. "It is not the tool, but the reader's ability," says Anhalt. Others comment that these skills are indeed tools, "like screwdrivers, purely focal points for allowing the mind to grasp information." (Jaegers)

PREDICTING THE FUTURE

Next year Science will find, or stumble upon what can be called "the center of soul control" in the human brain. This is an area that connects or integrates the various factors of intellect, emotion, and consequence; i.e., disease, resistance, etc.

—Johanna Gargiulo-Sherman
creator of the *Sacred Rose* tarot deck

Judging from survey respondents' comments, it seems that predictions made by professionals and nonprofessionals alike run the gamut from nonessential personal information to topics of worldwide import. Many psychics seem to specialize in specific kinds of prediction, either because they "just seem to be good at it" or have made a conscious effort to focus their energies in that direction. Typical areas of expertise are: politics, natural disasters, sports match outcomes, lottery numbers, stocks and bonds, medical conditions, deaths, personal relationships, pregnancies, travel, and job issues.

While many psychics aver that they have predicted newsworthy events like the World Trade Center bombing, the TWA Flight 800 disaster, the 1994 earthquake in Los Angeles, and the fact that Americans would beat the Russians to the Moon, more often than not, predictions seem to center around quotidian matters. Psychics point to these incidents as equally important confirmations of their abilities. Here are some examples:

I told a client not to spend his extra money because he would soon have a problem with an appliance. Two weeks later his refrigerator broke down. (a nonprofessional reader)

A friend of mine was considering buying a new Mercedes . . . I advised him against it because I couldn't see any "light" around the vehicle. My friend bought the car anyway. Two weeks later his car was run into by an uninsured motorist. Then an oak limb fell on it! (the same nonprofessional reader)

From personal experience, my astrologer, Martin Butz, whom I have never met, and who lives in another region of the country, predicted that on a certain day I would have trouble with broken glass. As he worries about my safety, he cautioned me to be especially mindful of locking up the house to thwart any burglary attempt. On the very day he predicted, the windows showed up for the addition we were building on our house. One of the windows arrived smashed, and since it was specially ordered frosted, patterned glass, it took almost a year to replace. Although my astrologer may have let his personal feelings intrude when he expressed concern about theft (he emphasized that he did not actually see robbers), his information was essentially correct both in fact and in the psychological sense that the broken glass caused me a good deal of annoyance, almost as if I had, in fact, been burgled.

Not every respondent's readings are predictive:

My readings focus on personal and spiritual growth. (Scolastico)

I don't believe in predictions . . . Creation is creating itself minute by minute. (Rodegast)

Prediction is not my forte. Charles (the entity I channel) teaches that we create our own reality. He may talk about likely outcomes of one's present state of mind or actions. (Leland)

SO WHO'S BEST FOR ME?

It makes sense to find out what sort of reading the psychic you are considering will give. At certain times in your life you may want to know the probable outcome of a venture, or you may need help making a decision. At other times, you may wish to be made privy to a panorama of your entire potential, in other words, receive a life reading. According to respondents, both kinds of readings are helpful, and one of the reasons to seek a reading is to alert yourself to present situations and make changes if you don't like what you see.

Paul Huson, in writing about the importance of divination to Witchcraft, makes some wise observations that are equally valid for anyone seeking a reading:

> Time is not a continuous ribbon but a complex field extending into many different directions and dimensions. Not paradoxically, although the future is always "out there," the Witch does not feel that her actions are already damned to one simple course by rigid predestination. The nearest approach to an explanation would be to say that each of us, at every moment in time, confronts a series of different choices in action. One of these ways we will take, for whatever reason. That way as well as others is already "out there."[9]

Psychics can function as guideposts for you on your journey into the future. In order for you to make the best choice of a reader, you should consider the kinds of readings the psychic does, how he or she got involved in the field, what other resources the psychic uses, and how the data is transmitted to you. In the next chapter, how psychics are able to receive and communicate this information is explored in depth.

Before you go on to chapter 5, you might like to read the following stories of some famous figures in other fields who happened to have recorded psychic experiences, usually foreshadowings of future events. Some of the names may surprise you.

VISIONS OF THE FAMOUS

Although many cases of famous visions have been recorded throughout history, we don't often realize that several of these have been experienced by people renowned in other fields. For example, Winston Churchill was prone to premonitions. One night during World War II, he hosted a dinner at Number 10 Downing Street. The party was in full swing when, for no apparent reason, the Prime Minister ordered everyone to deposit their food on the hotplate in the dining room and follow him to the basement. No sooner were the guests snug in the shelter than the Germans blitzed London. Half the house, including the dining area, caught fire and burned.

Another statesman, Abraham Lincoln had dealings with the World Beyond. During the Civil War, one of his advisors was a medium through whom spirits spoke to counsel the president on topics like what he should do about slavery and where to send troops. Lincoln also experienced precognitive dreams. Through them, he learned of his rise to power, how long he would stay in office, and that he would be cut down during his presidency. Shortly before his assassination, he dreamed he lay in a coffin in the East Room of the White House. Since his death, other White House residents have glimpsed his shade lingering in the bedrooms and halls.

Another precognitive incident associated with Lincoln's assassination comes from Julia Grant, wife of Ulysses S., then vice president. The couple were slated to attend the theatrical performance with the Lincolns on the fatal night of the president's death, but Julia felt an inexplicable foreboding. She convinced her husband not to go, and probably them saved from being shot.

Another "dreamer" was Thomas Edison, who claimed that he gained many insights for his innovations when he slept. One could say that he literally "dreamed up" some of his inventions.

A startling instance of precognition was recorded by author Mark Twain (Samuel Clemens). Both Samuel and his brother Henry found riverboat life fascinating, and the brother signed on as an apprentice on a steamboat. One night, Samuel, who was living far away in another town, awoke from a nightmare, bathed in sweat. He dreamed of Henry laid out on a table in a special metal coffin surrounded by a group of unfamiliar women. On his breast lay a bouquet of white flowers with one crimson blossom in the middle.

Soon he learned that his brother's boat had suffered a terrible accident in which the engines blew up and Henry was scalded to the point of death. In spite of the ministrations of the women in the town where he was brought to have his wounds treated, he soon died. Unable to produce a wooden casket for the burial, the townspeople put together a metal one. The women, who had become attached to Henry, decided to insert one crimson flower into the traditional white bouquet as a tribute to the young man's physical beauty.

Members of the distinguished James family of American writers and philosophers certainly enjoyed their share of psychic experiences. Henry the Elder once saw a terrifying ghost. The shade impressed him so much that he told his family. Henry the Younger wrote the marvelous psychic ghost thriller, *The Turn of the Screw,* based on the incident. Philosopher brother William studied and wrote about thought transference and clairvoyance, and came to believe that the existence of extra-sensory perception showed a "continuum of cosmic consciousness against which our individuality builds individual fences, and into which our several minds plunge as into a mother-sea or reservoir."[10]

The mother of C. G. Jung kept a diary of what she called "odd coincidences" or premonitions. Perhaps influenced by his mother's ideas, Jung, in his 1916 book *Psychology of the Unconscious,* studies the case of a woman whom he identifies as being able to communicate with unknown entities.

In contemporary times, anthropologist Margaret Mead was so impressed by the apparent supernatural abilities that she witnessed in members of the primitive tribes she studied that she became instrumental in persuading the American Association of the Advancement of Science to admit the Parapsychology Association as a member.

If, instead of or in addition to choosing a reader, you have dallied with the notion of developing your own psychic potential, the foregoing examples show that almost everyone possesses psychic capabilities. This is especially true when the information revolves around important personal events. If scientists, writers, and statesmen can do it, so can you.

Notes

1. Peter Underwood, *Into the Occult* (London: George C. Harrop and Company, 1972), p. 114.

2. Sepharial, *Second Sight* (1911; reprint, Santa Fe, NM: Sun Books, 1992), p. 36.

3. A natal chart is a horoscope that shows the positions of all the heavenly bodies in the sky in relation to the location where the baby is born. The mutable signs are Gemini, Virgo, Sagittarius, and Pisces. These signs are associated with changeability, adaptability, and service. The planet Neptune is associated with psychic phenomena, dreams, mysticism, and the astral plane.

4. Hereward Carrington and Willis F. Whitehead, *Keys to the Occult: Two Guides to Hidden Wisdom* (North Hollywood: Newcastle Publishing Company, 1977), p. 80.

5. U. S. Census Bureau, *Education and Social Stratification Barometers for 1997.*

6. BOTA is the acronym for Builders of the Adytum, a magickal society founded in Los Angeles by tarot master, Paul Foster Case.

7. These findings may be skewed because even though I sent surveys to an equal number of professional and nonprofessional psychics, those who replied tended to be professionals. An interesting topic for further research would be for someone to collect data from a large sample of both professionals and nonprofessionals and compare the responses.

8. Nandor Fodor, *An Encyclopedia of Psychic Sciences* (Secaucus: Citadel Press, 1966), p. 97.

9. Paul Huson, *Mastering Witchcraft: A Practical Guide for Witches, Warlocks, and Covens* (New York: Perigree Books, 1970), p. 63.

10. *Psychic Powers,* the editors (Alexandria, VA: Time-Life Books, 1987), p. 24.

CHAPTER FIVE

HOW DO
THEY DO THAT?

Divination Practices

[T]he diviner put[s] aside his rational, logical, conscious mind and tap[s] into the larger, more spiritual, and—many believe collective—unconscious. It is that area of the mind where, if you will, "everything is known" and therefore, knowable.

—Crawford Q. Kennedy, *The Divination Handbook*[1]

Under my relentless prodding, a skeptic friend of mine who was having trouble with her love life went to see a local psychic. Sue was puzzled by her new lover's erratic behavior. Although he seemed to enjoy her company, periodically he lost interest in everything, including her. In her words, he "wound down like a clock." Then, as if by magic, he'd suddenly jump-start himself, and everything would be all right again.

She said nothing of this to the psychometrist, who held Sue's glasses in her hand. After a few moments the woman told Sue that she was dating a man who used drugs in the secretive, lonely way many addicts abuse alcohol. The psychometrist could see the man locking himself in the bathroom and snorting cocaine. She also saw him driving a truck in the countryside and pulling off to the side of the road, sneaking a hit before meeting with a group of people whom he needed to direct in their work. She felt that drugs gave this reclusive individual the courage to be forceful.

"It's the same in his personal relationships," she said. "He needs the drugs to muster the energy to interact socially. He will never be happy with himself until he gets fed up with his dependence and banishes cocaine from his life."

The psychic assured Sue that the man would take steps toward this end within two years, but by then she would no longer be dating him. In a flash of insight, Sue realized that the psychic was right. She remembered all the times her lover dragged himself into the bathroom only to burst out the door a few minutes later, full of energy. She also knew that the psychic told the truth about the roadside pit stops because the man was a team leader in a corporation headquartered in the countryside outside of town, and that he drove his RV to work along lonely, rural roads. He complained a lot about having to deal with his "dysfunctional crew."

She was astounded at the psychometrist's insights. How could the woman, by holding her glasses, see and understand something about a third person's behavior, which despite Sue's intimacy with the man, she had not been able to figure out herself?

Soon after, the couple broke up. Two years later, Sue ran into her "ex" and he invited her to lunch. He confessed that he had suffered from long-term cocaine addiction that came to a head while they were dating, but that he was so much happier now that he had gone to drug counseling.

INTUITION OR REVELATION?

What sources do psychics, as depicted in the above scene, tap to accurately zero in on details about character, relationships, and future events, and how do they contact these sources? Some believe that psychics and channelers commune with heavenly powers and that the information they transmit is divine revelation. Others claim that the source of "divinity" is found within; while still others conceive of it as intuition, which can be developed like any skill. So, is it really intuition, a supposed inherent faculty that everyone possesses, or are some people gifted by divine powers and receive messages through revelation?

The psychics in the survey disagree on this point, which is at the heart of all issues related to the paranormal. When asked, "How large a role does intuition (versus pure psychic revelation) play in your readings?", thirteen (mostly channelers) answer "none," seven declare that it is "all" intuition, seventeen claim that intuition plays "a large role," and two indicate a "small role." Several respond in percentages, with fifteen indicating that they feel that revelations and intuition are evenly divided. Twenty-five do not distinguish between the two. One reader asserts that her mood and her client's needs and expectations determine which she uses. Another clairvoyant says that "it's about 75% intuition and 25% common sense, good advice, educated guesses, and real knowing."

Evidently the topic of intuition versus revelation is a hot issue in the psychic community. This is seen in the responses to the survey. Respondents tend to divide into one camp or another and express diametrically opposed views with an enthusiasm bordering on vehemence like the following:

> All intuitive feelings are the right brain beginning to pick up, so all are psychic! Your understanding of psychic is vague! (Hughes, presumably referring to intuition, which is a right-brain function.)

> I consider intuition and the psychic much the same thing. Perhaps the psychic is developing the intuition. (O'Very)

> Without intuition one could not be psychic. (Ferguson)

> All people have intuition but what I have are psychic revelations—visions— that come to pass. (Mischell)

Sue Burton-Hidalgo sums up the topic with this eloquent statement:

> This is a great question: I am delighted someone recognizes the difference. I'd say my sessions are sometimes more intuition, and sometimes more divine revelation, but most often it's about 70% intuition/30% revelation. After reading professionally for so many people for so many years I actually have to "say no" to my intuition in order to attune to revelation.

Hayes offers another thoughtful insight when she explains that "psychic ability is trained, intuitive sensitivity. Psychic revelations are usually given for a specific purpose," thereby implying that they both can happen to the same person.

Fitzgerald puts it like this: "Intuition gives daily life information while revelation speaks of universal truths. Something can be revealed about daily life, but the purpose is to demonstrate universal truths."

The Effect of the Astral Plane

In the hot topic, "Is it intuition or psychic revelation?" question, I use the term "psychic revelation" instead of "divine revelation" because not all psychics and channelers who believe in an external source for their information feel that the information originates with Divinity. William E. Butler, noted parapsychologist and one time head of the magickal order Servants of the Light, recognized the importance of intuition in developing ESP, but pointed to a kind of astral clairvoyance whereby the psychic tunes into "apparently living beings who have no physical body."[2] He tells how people of all ages and cultures have believed in these beings as a source of knowledge about this world, and have called them by many names—the devas of the Orient, dryads and oreads of ancient Greece, the Lordly Ones of Celtic times, angels, fairy folk, and elemental spirits.

These "spirits," Butler posits, may actually represent consciousnesses that have acquired existences via the concentration of thoughts and emotions of people over the centuries, and inhabit what is known as the astral world. "This great world of the astral," Butler comments, "is well named the World of Illusion. At the same time, the illusions are in the artificially created appearances of that world; in itself it is as real as any other realm of nature."[3]

According to psychical researcher Willis F. Whitehead,[4] telepaths and sensitives share a sympathetic bond with the astral world and find it easier than the rest of us to communicate with "those who live in the celestial infinitude," in other words, non-physical intelligences who dwell in the "astral flame," as he calls this plane of existence. Whitehead likens the astral flame to a sun that radiates thoughts in the form of light. The psychic becomes a kind of solar collector of these light-thoughts from the "Exalted Ones."

Theosophists take a different view, and see the "astral light" not so much as a group of intelligences, but as a gigantic record book where all thoughts, emotions, and events throughout time are imprinted. Since they do not conceive of time as a linear series of events, all future thoughts, emotions, and events (as well as those of the past and present) are recorded in the Akashic records. They believe that psychics possess the "key" to this "diary," and are able to open it up and "read" about events as remote in the past as the life and times of King Tut, as personal and immediate as whom Aunt Tillie is going to marry, and as all-encompassing as the impact of nuclear energy on the twenty-first century world's environment.

Spiritualists believe that this information comes from spirits of the dead residing on the astral plane, who have made a commitment in their lives on the Other Side to help people who are still earthbound to improve their lives.

WHO'S IN CONTROL?

When asked, "Do you have a control or spirit guide that helps you with readings?" respondents answer 2:1 that they do (64% say "yes;" 32% say "no"). Those on the "yes" side name anywhere from one to a dozen spirits with whom they maintain contact. Often they conceive of the entities as protective forces that shield them while they are in altered states. Here are representative replies about spirit guides:

> [Yes, I communicate with guides] a Hispanic man, a Mayan or Aztec warrior who is a protector and guide, a female ancestor, and a higher being from the cosmos. (Lewis)

> A man from Atlantis and a gypsy Arab for protection. I believe it is better for a psychic to have a control. (Joy)

> Though I have many guides, Asonji . . . protects me when I'm in an altered state. (Boyet)

Some readers are aware of a directing force in a more general way. Three say that while they can't see the entities, they know that they are there to guide them.

"I am aware of a collective (versus individual) up there heightening my energies," affirms Shepherd. "There is an energy that connects me to the 'all;' universal energies. I have no name for it; it encases me and opens my chakras to tap into other people's souls." states Ginger.

Respondents speak of being surrounded by entities, but see them as personal guides, not necessarily to be called forth to aid readings. Ina Rae relates, "At first I was not aware of a guide, but she spoke to me constantly, giving me advice, and answers to my questions and problems. She's a blessing to me, but not essential to readings."

Fonte agrees. "Mother Mary gives me guidance and brings me close to God, but not every psychic needs a guide."

Lawrence remarks that she channeled an entity for a while, but found it unsatisfactory after a time. "I grew beyond him."

Respondents, like Hughes, find the idea of a control distasteful. She claims:

> In mediumship, sometimes there is a special entity that comes to "open the door" for others to be able to talk with me—but any psychic/medium who claims to have a "control" or "lots of guides" is not psychic but I believe they really want to talk about "how many" guides know them and "control" them. No one controls me. No entity should be a "control" of your brain! Again, it is the ability of the right brain to "see" and to pick up and to hear!

An anonymous respondent shares the sentiments, "No, I don't want a control! I am a solitary soul. I don't want to share the inner space at all."

Leland, a channeler, elaborates:

> The information comes to me from Charles in the form of energy or images. I do not think of Charles as a personality, but more like the call letters of a radio station or the log-on password of a computer system. When I first began to channel, I was told "there is a sound that will help you gain access to the clearest possible information." That sound, a kind of meditation mantra, was not a word I knew, but it resembled the name "Charles."
>
> Later, when asked who "he" was, Charles gave a different answer every time. This brought me to the realization that I could never verify who or what the source of the information was, but could only vouch for its positive effects on the likes of other people. As a consequence of the experience, I tend not to trust channeled entities with flashy pedigrees—I think that (some channelers do this) to compensate for a low level of self-worth . . . or sometimes a high degree of skepticism."

When it comes to teaching psychic self-development classes, practitioners remain divided. "I do not encourage my students to develop a control," Myers affirms. "I believe that leads to more errors, and less responsibility is taken for what is said . . . Don't use Red Feather [a control] as an excuse when you're wrong. Just apologize . . . No human is ever 100% accurate."

On the other hand, Burton-Hidalgo, who does have a control that filters information to lessen the impact on her because she is too "empathetic and tender-hearted," disagrees. She maintains that:

> [A] control is not necessary, but useful [when I am channeling] for large groups of 100 or more. A control manages the karmic resonances of the crowd so that I do not become sidetracked by deeper emotional or spiritual agendas.

When I teach channeling courses, I introduce beginners to a control. I call it the "gatekeeper." I find this reassures the students that they have someone to share the responsibility/ability to "get information." It also sets up a system to make sure negative or astral energies stay off of them.

THE MESSAGE IN THE MEDIUM

All these comments that show differing points of view about how psychics receive their information may cause you to wonder whether the data transmitted by paranormal means is just a figment of the practitioner's imagination. This would be a premature conclusion to draw because you need to consider that psychics may obtain their knowledge in different ways.

Butler sheds light on how this works. He believes that psychic information travels through the body by way of two different nerve pathways, the involuntary nervous system and the cerebro-spinal system. In the first case, the images, though clearly seen, are not clearly understood. The vision may also not be under the control of the will of the person who is experiencing it:

> Often when it is needed it cannot be brought into action, and at other times, when it is not required, it breaks through into the waking consciousness. The other mode of working, through the voluntary nervous system, has the advantage of being under the control of the psychic, and can be aroused at will. It is also far less dependent upon what, in psychic experimentation, are known as "conditions."[5]

Since the perception of how and where the person receives information differs, perhaps it also feels different to each individual, thereby leading psychics to conclude that the sources are different, as well.

IT'S ALL IN YOUR HEAD!

Skeptics like Louisa B. Rhine, wife of the famed parapsychologist J. B. Rhine, scoff at spirit contacts because "[t]he existence of an extra physical determiner at work in the physical universe would open up new frontiers of physics."[6]

Jaegers echoes Rhine's sentiments when she eschews the idea of a control. "The human mind's potential is unlimited," she stresses. "There is no need for any outside help or assistance."

Perhaps the quantum mechanics' theories described in the introduction about how everything in the universe is related in a way that, as yet, remains hidden from us, marks a starting point for reconciliation between the opposing camps who believe in external sources of information (and those who hold that the source is internal). Psychologist C. G. Jung wrote about the collective unconscious mind, where, on a subconscious level, everything that has ever happened or will happen is known because of an underlying connection. Perhaps this forms a basis for what traditionally has been called the astral light and the Akashic records. The psychic is able to put aside ego, or the "rational, logical, conscious mind" that Kennedy refers to in the quote at the beginning of this chapter, and reaches the part of the mind where "everything is known, and therefore, knowable." Warmoth, who began his career as a professional mind reader, and later became a metal dowser, sums up this idea of the collective unconscious beautifully: "I believe that all is mind and that one mind is my universal mind."

WHY DO THINGS GO WRONG?

According to Butler, psychics tune into this knowledge and receive it back into their subconscious minds as a solid block of information. Then they subconsciously sort it and order it into a sequence that it makes sense to the conscious mind. When this happens, they necessarily select some information to relate and reject the rest. He likens this to questioning witnesses after an accident. Everyone sees the same accident but they all come up with different memories of it. This is why training and development are essential. As Butler writes: "To unfold a faculty is one thing; to stabilize it and have it under control is quite another!"[7]

The survey respondents confirm Butler's theory. When asked if they had ever had any resounding failures and if they could describe one, many are brutally honest. The inability to separate one's personal emotions from facts heads the list why sometimes psychics' "selective memories" choose the wrong information.

"My friend was dying of cancer, and I didn't see it," Rodegast laments. "Fear got in the way . . . (This was) a huge lesson for me."

Heath recalls "projecting about awful things happening to my husband that didn't . . . I probably was tired."

"I interpreted a planetary transit for a friend by saying what he wanted to hear instead of what I needed to say," Lawrence admits. "I learned a lesson in codependency there."

Respondents also cite lack of personal interest in some topics like health, the American economy, business, and politics as a reason for inaccuracy. Without a feeling of rapport with the topic, they find it hard to isolate the right information.

The timing of predictions is named more than any other factor about where psychics can go wrong, and I was given dozens of examples. Respondents tend to feel that since they don't believe time is a linear concept, it is difficult to transpose non-linear information onto a linear world.

Some practitioners, like Ron Scolastico, reject the idea of prediction entirely. Instead, he focuses on personal and spiritual growth.

Anka tells how his "extraterrestrial consciousness" explains it to him:

> Bashar believes there is no such thing as predicting the future per se. He explains that we psychically or intuitively sense the energy in a situation as it exists now. If the energy remains in that flow, we say the "prediction" came true. But sometimes . . . the energy of the sensing will alter the energy of the situation itself. Thus, sometimes the "prediction" will change what is being predicted and will cancel the situation. Bashar has made certain sensings—both personal and global—that have transpired, but only because the situation had too much momentum to change direction.

Other reasons why psychics sometimes get it wrong include trying too hard to come up with an answer when there may not be one, or the answer is difficult to bring through to consciousness. "If I impose my will on a reading, it can go wrong," declares an anonymous respondent. Sometimes signals are misinterpreted. Carol Ann Liaros remembers, "I said someone was going to recover from a serious illness in three months because I saw her singing and dancing in a field of flowers. She died three months later."

Too much data coming in at once out of that "solid block of knowledge" can be confusing. "I predicted that the pope would be assassinated, but he was just shot," says Solomon. Another reader cites mixing up two clients' boyfriends who came together for a reading, although she was right on the facts. This is why she prefers to work with one person at a time, rather than with groups of two or more, who, like couples, might otherwise want to come together for their readings. In this way, she keeps her information straight.

A few respondents mention that while their data has been right, the client misinterpreted what was heard. Others tell stories of being purposely misled by clients who were out to fool the psychic. "Naturally," Joy comments tersely, "the prediction couldn't occur."

On the other hand, Marquette believes that "all responses in a reading eventually help the person for advice. At times, it seems a failure, but in time, the truth surfaces."

Ater sums up the subject aptly, "No one is 100% correct all the time. Just live and learn, and be happy!"

If you are inspired to develop your own psychic faculties, chapter 7 will present you with some training techniques. One of the best ways to sharpen your ability and consistently draw forth accurate information from the reservoir of your subconscious or open yourself to messages from otherworldly sources, is to improve your ability to concentrate. The final section of this chapter, which deals with crystal ball reading, will help give you a push in this direction.

CRYSTALOMANCY

This section introduces you to the venerable method of divination by means of a crystal ball, otherwise known as crystalomancy, or crystal gazing. It has been employed in many cultures in both the Occident and the Orient. Perhaps the most famous crystal gazer in the Western world was Dr. John Dee, the official crystalomancer to Queen Elizabeth I (for more information on Dee, see chapter 1).

Like all the mantic arts, crystal gazing entails far more than predicting the future. It helps discipline your powers of concentration in order to plumb the depths of your subconscious mind and bring forth hidden memories and thoughts, either originating in you, the collective unconscious, or Divinity. Besides learning the future, you can use the crystal ball to groom your imagination to work for you by visualizing positive changes in your life. As Ra Mayne says in his monograph on the subject:

> The crystal acts as an agency towards the development of your mental and psychic powers; instills greater confidence; builds poise, character, and refinement overcomes nervousness, stimulates memory; and brings about a new and peaceful era of understanding and belief. The crystal ball will better enable you to collect your scattered energies into a definite focus where you can handle them efficiently and accomplish much.[8]

Even though this section deals specifically with ball gazing, the techniques described are applicable to scrying in a magick mirror, cauldron, chalice filled with water, still pool, or even a puddle of black ink.

The first step in crystalomancy is to acquire a ball. Purists prefer a clear, pellucid, natural quartz in the shape of a sphere or an oval because they believe that natural rock crystals contain highly magnetic qualities not present in manmade crystals, which facilitate visualizations. The ball should be no less than two inches in diameter—any smaller makes it difficult to perceive visions—around four or five inches in diameter is an optimum size. Some crystalomancers demand a perfectly clear ball with no distracting bubbles, while others search high and low for a ball with a small flaw because it helps rivet the attention. The choice is yours.

It is also up to you whether you place the ball on a stand, on a table, or hold it in the palm of your hand. If you prefer hand-held gazing, place a black velvet cloth between your hand and the ball so it does not become contaminated with your body oils.

Automobile enthusiasts spare nothing to keep their vehicles in tiptop condition. Your crystal ball is your vehicle to "other worlds" and should be treated with the same careful attention. When not in use, wrap your ball in a black velvet cloth, and store it in a drawer or closet away from sunlight, which will eventually score the surface and ruin it for gazing. Clean your crystal by either immersing it in boiling water for twenty minutes, or wiping it with vinegar or brandy (alcohol). Rub dry with a piece of black silk or chamois cloth. Treat your crystal gently so you do not ruin it by scratching it. From time to time, "recharge" your tool by exposing it to moonlight.

Preparing to Read

The environment you choose for reading largely depends on your preferences. Since crystal gazing is a method for developing your mental faculties, you should read in a place that enables you to focus your concentration. Those who have made a life study of crystalomancy suggest the following conditions:

- Read indoors in a quiet room that is dark, but not so dark that you can't see the ball. Some natural daylight should fall over your shoulder onto the ball. Some practitioners recommend candlelight, low electric lights, or moonlight in the background.

- No light should shine so directly on the ball that you can see the reflection of the source. For example, if you use candles, make sure you don't see their image in the ball.

- Read in the same room each time you practice so that the room builds up psychic vibrations (or, if you prefer, train your subconscious to flourish under these conditions).

- Make sure the room is tidy, all sickly plants and flowers are removed, and the room is well ventilated. Spirits are put off by clutter (or, if you prefer, your subconscious mind gets distracted by these things).

- Sit on a chair that is upright, but comfortable, so that you can easily maintain good posture and keep both feet on the floor.

The amount of time you spend gazing, in my opinion, can vary according to your tolerance for sitting still with your eyes open, only blinking minimally, and your ability to keep your mind from wandering. Start with only five minutes so that you do not tire your eyes, and work up slowly to one hour.

Take the ball in the cloth in your hand and hold it for five minutes to infuse it with your warmth (but not your oils!). Close your eyes and relax. Empty your mind of all thoughts by enjoying the peace and quiet. Tell yourself that you will not let any extraneous thoughts intrude on your visioning. If you have trouble making your mind blank, concentrate on your breathing. Listen to and feel the rhythm of your inhaling and exhaling. Any time a thought intrudes, refocus on your breathing. At this point, you may want to practice some of the exercises I recommend in chapter 7.

You are ready to read. Open your eyes and either place the ball back on its stand or hold it with the cloth in your hand. Pass your right hand over the ball, close but not touching it. Repeat with the left hand. This procedure magnetizes the ball, that is, it creates a link between your aura and that of the ball so that you interlock into a harmonious union.

Look steadily into the ball. Do not let your gaze wander, but at the same time, do not force yourself not to blink. Let your eyes blink naturally. Over time, you will train your eyes to blink less often without straining them. Like all skills, it takes practice.

At this point, I would like to clarify that you are not seeing actual pictures in the ball. You see the images in your mind and project this vision into the ball. It helps to realize that the ball merely provides a vehicle for focusing your attention and concentration. Some gazers get good results if they tell themselves that although they are looking at the ball, the vision will appear at some point beyond it. This makes it clear to them that the vision is really in their heads.

On the other hand, in crystalomancy experiments it has been discovered that sometimes visions, even though they may only be mental impressions, affect the focus and the retina of the eye as if the gazer were really seeing an external image. An episode of *X-Files* treated this subject. In the plot, a woman, blind from birth, occasionally perceived images of scenes that were taking place at the moment. Her retina and eye focus changed every time she experienced an episode. It turned out that she was somehow mentally and emotionally linked to her father, whom she had never met, and "saw" what he was seeing in her mind. It would be a good guess that the idea for this episode came from crystalomancy experiments.

If you have a clear idea of what you want to see, it helps to distill your intention by writing down on a piece of paper what you want to envision. For example, affirm that you want to see an image of your future mate, find out how a trip is going to turn out, discover where you made a mistake in the past, etc. If you simply want to see the future in general, say something like, "Show me the shape of things to come in my life within the next week," "Bring me a vision of what my town will be like in twenty years," etc. After writing your intention on the paper, crumple it up and throw it in the wastebasket. Do not look at the paper again, simply rivet your attention on the ball.

Do not be discouraged if at first you see nothing. If you persist with regular practice sessions, you will succeed. One outer circle covener of mine years ago became fascinated with crystal gazing, yet couldn't obtain a vision to save her karma! Doggedly, she kept at it, and by the end of a year was rewarded by seeing her first "clouds." After that, she progressed rapidly.

By clouds, I mean that just before a vision unfolds, a gray or whitish mist may fill the ball; that is, appear to come between it and your eyes. Many gazers never progress further than seeing clouds. This should be considered a success because clouds change form and color just like the clouds in the sky, and the crystalomancer learns to interpret what they symbolize. Some cloud meanings are covered in the "Roman Omens" section of chapter 1, and the symbolism of colors is dealt with in appendix C.

When you progress beyond clouds, you will begin to see gold-colored specks dancing like gold dust in the clouds. Suddenly the ball will clear and fill with a brilliant sky-blue light against which images will appear. These may be objects, like flowers, birds, trees, household items, or they may manifest as vividly colored scenes. The visions you project fall into five categories:

- Occurrences that you have consciously forgotten, but now recall. With these visions you stimulate your subconscious mind to bring to the surface of consciousness the information you require.

- Scenes that actually took place in the past, but of which you could have no direct knowledge. With these visions, you dip down into the collective unconscious to draw forth images.

- Events happening in the present about which you have no knowledge. Some people compare these visions to hunches. This sort of visioning also has been identified in the related psychic field of hauntings as "apparitions of the living." For example, the image of a living person may suddenly appear to a percipient when awaking from a dream to relate some sort of message or warning.

- That which will occur in the future; that is, prediction.

- Visions consciously produced by the seer's imagination.

Envisioning a Better Future

Although prediction is the most popular use for crystal balls, controlled visions from the imagination projected into the ball can aid your efforts at self-development and self-improvement. Here's how to do it.

Begin by focusing your attention on an object in the room other than the ball for one minute. Then close your eyes and try to recall the object in vivid detail. Now open your eyes and attempt to transfer the image in its entirety to the ball.

Move on to an object that is not in the room, like your car, or a tree in the yard, and attempt to project its image into the ball. Follow with faces of relatives, friends, and acquaintances. When you succeed at this, project the scene that "crystallizes," so to speak, an event that happened to you or that you witnessed in the past.

At last, you are ready to visualize something for yourself in the future. For example, if you want to improve your health, project an image of yourself striding down the street on a sunny day, looking happy, healthy, and strong. If you'd like to perform better in school, visualize your teacher handing back a perfect examination paper to you with both of your faces wreathed in smiles. If you yearn to get pregnant, see yourself sitting in a rocking chair or in the most comfortable chair in your home, holding your little bundle of joy swathed in blankets. In whatever way you want to improve your life, envision it in the ball, and you will be training your subconscious mind to help you take the steps necessary to achieve your goal.

As the foregoing demonstrates, two kinds of concentration exist. In one type you let your mind go blank so it can receive impressions of actual past and future events. In the other way, you concentrate your mental faculties on one event, or one idea, and project it into the future. By using both methods, you take full advantage of the honorable art of crystalomancy.

Notes

1. Crawford Q. Kennedy, *The Diviner's Handbook* (New York: New American Library, 1989), p. 10.

2. William E. Butler, *How to Read the Aura, Practice Psychometry, Telepathy and Clairvoyance* (1968, 1971, 1975; reprint, New York: Destiny Books, 1978), p. 31.

3. Ibid., p. 33.

4. Willis F. Whitehead, "Occultism Simplified," in *Keys to the Occult: Two Guides to Hidden Wisdom* (North Hollywood: Newcastle Publishing Company, Inc., 1977), p. 27.

5. Butler, p. 18.

6. Louisa E. Rhine, *Psi, What is It?: The Story of ESP and PK* (New York: Harper and Row, 1976), p. 15.

7. Butler, p. 153.

8. Dr. Ra Mayne, *Six Lessons in Crystal Gazing* (Los Angeles: International Imports, 1992), p. 16.

CHAPTER SIX

ANYONE FOR
A READING?

The Clientele

Why do I feel there has been such a spiritual upsurge in recent times? There is a major enlightening occurring universally. The Hundredth Monkey Principle— When one becomes aware, it is easier for the next. Many are seeking enlightenment in health, education, self-therapy, emotional issues, and spirituality.
—Patricia Hayes; soul, life, angel and Akashic reader

I have a friend in international finance. Fifteen years ago, Elaine tells me, if she had told anyone that she regularly consulted a medium, people would have laughed at for being crazy or suspected she was on drugs. Besides losing the respect of her colleagues and clients, she feared she might even lose her job if she admitted she sought psychic guidance.

Yet somehow, by the end of the twentieth century, prevailing attitudes toward ESP have changed, and many people seem open to the idea of consulting a psychic. Some hold that just as the end of the last millennium spurred people to search for the meaning of life in mystical religious movements that culminated in events like the Crusades, many people today are embarking on spiritual quests.

Some do so out of fear of Armageddon, and may choose safe, institutionalized religions that give them reassuring, ready-made answers. Others favor a more challenging, individualized approach that sects like Spiritualism, Wicca, or Santería offer. Often these religio-philosophical movements make use of practices like divination and channeling to foster self-understanding and spiritual development. Sometimes a seeker may launch a spiritual journey by visiting a psychic.

Add to this the fact that many of the rich and powerful like Nancy Reagan, and celebrities like Shirley MacLaine have come out openly in favor of psychics and psi phenomena, and it is easy to see how psychic readings have gained acceptance with much of the public and are eagerly sought as a valuable tool to insure success in life.

On the other end of the spectrum sit the debunkers who have bought into the limited worldview, where it is believed that all life results from intricate but random combinations of physical interactions. These skeptics claim that the popularity of psychics and channelers results from lack of education and gullibility. They maintain that they witness apparently amazing, endless innovations in the physical world everyday about which they have little understanding, but that they know these events somehow follow the physical laws they have constructed. Yet the layperson, unschooled in scientific theories that allow for the unknowable, come to believe that the powers of science are boundless. It is then a small leap of faith for the public to come to believe in any far-fetched claim. In the debunkers' opinion, this is why the public has jumped on the psychic bandwagon.

The real reasons for the sudden upsurge of interest in psychic phenomena and prediction are complex, and need to be examined in light of both the clientele and those who read for them.

According to survey respondents, people of both genders, all ages, ethnic, backgrounds, income levels, and religions go for consultations. The four groups most frequently listed, somewhat surprisingly, include business people (eight seers claim CEOs as clients), homemakers, lawyers, and doctors (nine mention doctors, but only three name nurses). Even more thought-provoking is the revelation that three respondents are consulted by Roman Catholic priests, two by nuns, and three more by ministers. One respondent has even consulted to the Vatican.

Clients involved in traditionally conservative occupations like banking, finance, the military, international diplomacy, and research science are represented in equal measure to careers that may be considered more experimental and creative, and therefore, more open to psi experiences, like acting, singing, music, art, university studies, teaching, psychology, and social work.

Evidently income does not affect those who will seek out a psychic, because respondents mention as patrons all levels, from middle- and upper-income brackets to factory workers, welfare recipients, and the homeless. Nor does age or sex seem to matter. Several respondents state that their clients are men and women from ages eighteen to eighty-five, although about one-third remark that they advise more women than men.

TYPICAL ISSUES

People see me to gain an understanding of old issues that prevent them from being the best they can be.

—Sarasvati Boyet, channeler

Someone who has never had a reading might be surprised to know that while learning what the future has in store may be one reason why clients visit psychics, it is not the only, or necessarily the most compelling motivation.

My friend Elaine again provides some insights. She lives in a big city. She is a hard-driving person who spends most of her time working, and feels quite anonymous among the looming gray buildings of Wall Street. Deep relationships just don't make up part of her life right now. When she visits her psychic counselor, Elaine feels she is in the presence of someone who knows, understands, and sympathizes with her deepest thoughts and feelings.

"And my reader is cheaper than a shrink!" she crows. "I don't have to talk about anything I don't want to reveal, either. Yet when I do talk, I know I'm being heard by somebody, whether it's the channeler or the entity she contacts. I drive my own session with my questions," she adds, "and leave feeling positive, energized—ready to meet any situation that may arise."

Elaine is not alone. According to several respondents, clients come to them who have reached a crossroads in their lives, and are hoping to find perspective on their situations and information about their options.

SEEKING ANSWERS TO LIFE'S CHALLENGES

Although clients come to me with issues across the board, they also [communicate] a sense of loss, aloneness, a feeling of being lost.
—Dr. Elisa Robyn, astrologer and shaman

The recently "awakened," that is, those who are searching for the right spiritual path, are not the only ones who reach out for a reading. People suffering physical and emotional pain also call on psychics to receive ideas about how to resolve their dilemmas. Sometimes after a reading, fears are assuaged, patterns change, and the client leaves better able to face life with courage and confidence. The client gains hope.

Daily life issues also send people to psychics. In the sample, relationships top the list, with love questions specifically mentioned thirty-nine times. Career concerns also rate highly, as do money topics in general.

Other subjects that surface frequently include: health, children, timing issues, lost pets, lost valuables, the stock market, and treasure hunting. Unusual requests also come up, like meeting spirit guides, finding a soulmate, reconnecting past lives, dealing with infertility, death issues, inner child reclamation, changing residence and emigration, protection from psychic abuse, and even revenge.

THE BOTTOM LINE

Despite daily life issues that loom in the forefront of most people's lives and, therefore, represent prime motivations for obtaining a reading, the overriding reason why clients visit psychics seems to be curiosity about life. People go for a reading who love adventure and want to have a good time. Some clients even consider a psychic reading as a form of entertainment. Mrs. M., a card reader, sums it up brilliantly, "What do you 'get' from a reading? It's wonderfully satisfying to be helped, entertained, and have the best possible time—what could be bad?"

THEY KEEP COMING BACK

More than 80% of the respondents work with repeat customers, and a few claim that almost all their clientele come back. Satisfied customers may want updates; some come around for yearly "tune-ups," or they bring new problems for the psychic to help solve. Others battling ongoing issues seek a fresh perspective. A few, serious about their personal growth and committed to self-healing, return, in Shepherd's words, "looking for a coach in their spiritual development and journey toward self-awareness."

Not all readers believe it is a good idea to foster repeat business. For example, Browne discourages the emotionally insecure who would become dependent on her. Several respondents claim that they absolutely do not accept repeat clients. An intuitive herbalist says that her "goal is to keep people independent as much as possible; that is true freedom." JeanAnn Fitzgerald, who is a clairsentient graphologist and numerologist, remarks that numerological charts don't change and handwriting is slow to modify. As a result, she does not encourage repeat visits, although people do refer new clients to her. One psychic fair worker admits that she probably does get repeat business, but she can't remember the faces unless someone tells her.

PLAYING THE "PROVE IT" GAME

A curious phenomenon practically unique to the psychic world is what may be called the "prove it" game. In other service-oriented professions like medicine, counseling, and the law, practitioners are usually not confronted by paying clients who try to trick them or demand that they substantiate their abilities on the spot. Yet according to a significant number of respondents, some of the clients consciously play "fool the psychic." Only one-fifth claim they have never seen a hostile client, while almost half affirm that they have experienced client animosity at least occasionally.

It seems that these difficult scenes rarely occur during private sessions, but more often pop up in public places like psychic fairs, bars, readings for hire given at parties, and especially on the radio, where the heckler can remain completely anonymous.

Master dowser Sevigny remembers an occasion when a professor from Boston University invited him to speak to a class, and set up a test that was impossible to "pass."

Edens recalls a strange incident when she was reading palms in a group. One man insisted she prove her abilities by reading his dog's paw.

Psychic readers develop unique ways of dealing with such situations. Several respondents say that they charge enough money to discourage game players. Others terminate the reading at the first sign of trouble.

"I tell them to go call a psychic hotline," quips Muench. Butz sends them away because he won't "cast pearls before swine." Lina admonishes skeptics, "Please don't waste my time. You are paying for this information, and it just takes too long to get through the nonsense." Henits informs them that "a reading is a two-way street. If you don't want to participate, feel free to seek another reader." Fox observes that "[These people] are only fooling themselves when they [do this]; so I give them back their money."

On the other hand, some respondents, like Browne, rise to the challenge. "I change them," she declares. "I just tell them something that knocks their socks off."

"I tell them things I divine which they cannot refute," says Solomon, "and win them over by demonstration. The stubborn skeptics can't be convinced, so I charge them double!"

Telepath Myer is not put off by bad attitudes. She reflects, "Sometimes I enjoy pulling something (personal information) they'd rather not talk about to jolt them . . . [I was doing a public demonstration and] PsiCops[1] had a student who said he had an identical twin challenge me to tell him his sibling's state of mind. I told him that she was devastated over the breakup of a relationship and that his twin was fraternal, not identical. The young man was so stunned by my accurate response he confessed in front of the entire audience that he had been sent to set me up."

Liaros notes that skeptics sometimes provoke her to probe deeply into the recesses of their minds and describe to them their inner feelings, shadow selves, and deepest emotions. Others welcome the challenge as an opportunity to educate by explaining what readings are about. They read for a few minutes, and if the client is still dissatisfied, terminate the session and refund the money.

"I confront them, educate them about what goes on in a reading, and how they need to behave to get a good reading," declares the energetic Wolf.

Usually psychics can break through the "wall" the skeptic has constructed, but it can cost them energy. Some decide that it's not worth the price. "I pray to be in truth," comments Rodegast, "and let go of any ego desires I have to impress or convert."

Others take it all in stride. "I let them have their own feelings and I just do what I do," says one reader. "Eventually they relax." Another comments, "I ask them, do you want me to give you a good reading or not? Sometimes they're not stonewalling deliberately, they're just not very open mentally."

Leland, a channeler, offers the insight that he used to get more skeptics than he does "now that I've let go of my own skepticism about my work." In other words, he feels that like attracts like.

WHAT BOTHERS READERS?

[What annoys me is] the fact that when I introduce myself as a psychic to a group of professionals, I'd provoke less controversy and be given more respect if I said I was a prostitute! Sex is something everyone understands. Spirit is something that a huge number of people don't even think exists—much less is it something they understand!

—Jennifer Shepherd, clairvoyant, palm and tarot reader

In spite of skepticism from many people in the scientific and religious communities, often unfavorable reports in the press, and fear from those who don't grasp what they do, one psychic after another dedicates his or her life to reading for others. Why do they do it? One way to gain insight into people's reasons for choosing this profession is to ask what they don't like about the field, then find out what motivates them in spite of the negative factors.

Ignorance tops the respondents' list of pet peeves, whether it be out of lack of education, superstition, or fear of the unknown. This, in turn, provides fodder for the sensationalist press and those who espouse narrow religious, mechanistic worldviews that keep them from opening their minds. The insensibility of practitioners who lack training or willfully commit fraud is often cited as a pet peeve.

"No one in this culture is taught how to deal with [the concept of] psychic abilities or psychics themselves," complains one respondent. "There is a belief that psychics themselves are superstitious or weak-minded," says Heath. Fox puts it down to lack of schooling, "The true role of channeling in history is not taught in the schools," he comments. Lawrence adds, "If one percent of the people who pooh-pooh astrology would study it for even a month, there would be a change in public opinion."

COMMON MISCONCEPTIONS

Widespread lack of understanding leads to misconceptions about the psychic field. Inflexible religious dogma is perceived as contributing to these distortions. "Societal prejudice is learned by religious teachings," comments one psychic reader who prefers to remain anonymous. "We're not so far removed from the burning times," declares Burton-Hildago. "There are still some people out there who think psychic phenomena is Voodoo." "I wish there were not such a conflict between the Church and the New Age movement," numerologist Edens laments. "If I knew how to change it I would."

Hilburn-Holland thinks that infelicitous terminology may contribute to these misinterpretations:

> My favorite pet peeve is calling psychic/intuitive abilities "powers." That is a way to make oneself feel special, set apart. And it opens the door for all sorts of stupid questions from people like "Where does your power come from?" a real constant with the fundamentalist crowd.

Csere believes that people "are fed misinformation by skeptics and debunkers who like to play the media."

Some blame skeptics, who espouse too limited a "scientific" world view. Psychics claim that their field cannot be measured by existing, less than adequate scientific methods. "People expect/demand that I tell them something about themselves to prove that I am psychic. They would not ask for similar confirmation from another professional like a psychologist or a doctor," one crystal ball reader objects.

This attitude can lead some practitioners to consciously or unconsciously commit fraud, which perpetuates the cycle of incredulity. Lawrence says, "I wish people would become more comfortable with 'I'm not sure,' or 'I don't know.' Batters are not expected to hit a thousand—psychics shouldn't be either. I think we'd all have more credibility if we were rigorously honest."

Lewis vents frustrations that many psychics feel:

> I am as offended by negative reactions to the field—"Oh, are you into that stuff?" as I would be about negative comments about my skin color or gender. I believe in what I do, and don't appreciate comparisons to or comments about 900-numbers, psychics, or New Age flakes. I resent the sensationalism attached to this field!

Other respondents point the finger at some practitioners, whom they believe lack training or who behave irresponsibly, either because they don't realize what they're doing or because they want to make fast money.

"It bothers me to see people apply their psychic abilities without loving sensitivity and common sense. Most of the time it is because they have never been trained properly and don't have the spiritual understanding and wisdom to go along with their psychic talent," Hayes laments.

An astrologer remarks:

> Superficiality in the astrological field (bothers me)—people who use it to "hook" someone—sun-sign stuff. I realize that anything can be a "draw" and

that's great, but I get clients (needing) healing from other astrologers who have told them things that were downright cruel or totally inappropriate—and they've feared astrology ever since.

Hilburn-Holland gives a good example of irresponsible behavior:

I have overheard readings at fairs where the client will talk about feeling lost, sad, or hopeless . . . and the reader says "that's because you have an entity attached to you" or "you've been abducted by aliens," or "you have a curse on you." Talk about taking a leap into the absurd!

To Thyself and Thy Clients Be True

Lack of responsibility toward clients upsets many psychics, even though an overwhelming ninety-six respondents emphasize that they believe a psychic has a moral responsibility toward the client. The very few who answered "no" say that they tell their clients that they are not always 100% right, and they believe the clients should also exercise good judgment, common sense, and self-responsibility.

"Usually an individual comes to a psychic after other avenues have failed. To abuse this (possibly) last ray of hope a client might have is evil," chastises PoTO.

"With a few words of advice," Ginger reminds us, "a psychic can alter or manipulate a person's life. To me, this is a tightrope. If there are no moral aspects, then there is no definition between spirit information and ego."

Leland believes that mystification is a problem:

It's easy to impress people with stories about Atlantis, angels, extraterrestrials, past lives, the fourth dimension (or higher), etc. Most of this kind of information has little more than entertainment value in my mind. It can sometimes be spiritually dangerous in that it distracts people from the task of realizing the soul's master plan for their growth. I believe that enlightenment consists in knowing what to do next under any given set of circumstances. I question the value of material or metaphysical systems that don't start and end with practical advice on how to improve happiness and satisfaction in human life right now, no matter how challenging the work may be. I don't think that spiritual growth is as easy or as simple as some people in our field make it—or as abstruse or complicated.

"I don't like readers who dwell on the negative," Mrs. M. complains, "or who insist people are cursed just to extort money. And boy, do I dislike pictures of 'readers' dressed as gypsy women wearing really cheap jewelry!"

According to some respondents, psychics who persist in "looking on the dark side" may do so because they lack training. "Some psychics unconsciously put out powerful negative energy," Wolfsong notes, "because they haven't taken time to look at themselves honestly and clear their own blocks."

"I want to be treated as 'normal,'" Burton-Hidalgo sighs. "I feel that many people in my field are very eccentric. I insist for myself that I act as a bridge to the mainstream community as well as serving the New Age crowd."

SWIMMING AGAINST THE MAINSTREAM

Do the people who float along in the mainstream really understand and appreciate the psychic profession? In replying to the question about reactions they get when they first tell acquaintances about what they do and if there are certain people they can't tell about their faculty, some respondents answer that people are intrigued and react positively. Ogham reader Adam declares that "Most people, even my mother, think it's great."

"I always get good and positive reactions," comments astrologer and author Csere, "since I am discreet about whom I tell. I don't tell Fundies (fundamentalist Christians), for example."

An anonymous respondent credits the media with causing part of the positive change in public opinion. "The media is now presenting psi as something everyone possesses, so [the public doesn't] want to condemn something that has been presented in a favorable light to them."

Others are circumspect about whom they tell. For example, Lina says, "I cannot tell certain people due to them making . . . cruel remarks in front of friends, coworkers, family members, and acquaintances"

Although not everybody is well received, negative reactions don't daunt some.

"I get everything from 'You're doing the work of the Devil' to 'why haven't you found a cure for AIDS?' I'll tell anybody!" asserts McMoneagle.

People with narrow religious views, whom respondents generally group together as Fundamentalists, or "Fundies" for short, seem to cause the most distress for psychic readers.

"I used to be completely up front about it," Shepherd comments. "Later I grew tired of being demonized by others, especially devout Catholics and Christians. Their reactions I always consider ironic, since the vision I had at sixteen (of Christ) should put it in some perspective for them. These days I'm more of a hermit."

"My son is a born-again, so I don't mention it when I meet his people. I live in [a liberal university town] where it is not unusual to raise three kids and be an astrologer as well, but other places might not be so liberal," states another reader, who prefers to remain anonymous.

"I have to be careful because I spend a lot of time around Christians. Many are surprisingly open to psi phenomena, but there are those who believe it all 'comes from the Devil,'" declares Wicca priestess Cleopatra.

Alia adds, "I have a young daughter and I live in a very Christian small town. I do not want her to have problems at school. I write and speak and teach. When people ask, I say I am a holistic healer-teacher. That's okay. My clients all live elsewhere."

Other respondents, like aura reader Gehman, are not bothered by Fundamentalists. "I love talking to Fundies. It provides a great teaching opportunity."

Psi Reading and Counseling

Some psychics, when dealing with the general public, call their profession by more socially acceptable names. For example:

> I get reactions all over the board from fear to admiration, interest, and confusion . . . I usually say I do counseling unless they persist. (Dale)

> Mostly I tell people I've just met that I "do counseling." I do this not only to protect myself from possibly being stereotyped by people who don't believe in channeling, but also because I don't much enjoy being considered a curiosity or interrogated by people who are interested in what I do . . . I'm a very private person. (Leland)

> I'm careful because I'm also a psychotherapist. I always identify myself as a therapist so I will be taken seriously as a professional. (Hilburn-Holland)

E. Harte, who makes spiritual studies from strands of clients' hair and also performs numerology does not ever talk about this facet of her life. "I work for a large financial institution. Enough said!" she writes.

Jaegers tries "not to tell anybody unless there's some good reason, or people tend to confuse myth with reality."

Mischell gives a very practical reason for not revealing her faculty. "I don't usually tell people because they will want a reading. I say I'm off duty."

Qabalist and Satanist Solomon doesn't talk about it much, either. "I don't prostheletize," he says. "I recognize the stigma of my profession as an obstacle to public credibility."

Spiritualist medium Boyet, among others, feels she owes it to her profession to be up front about it. "I honor who I am and if my profession upsets people, it's their loss."

Canadian card reader Manning sums up many attitudes, "If they don't like it, I really don't care," she says. "That's awful, isn't it? But I'm not going to stop what I do because someone doesn't approve."

FAMILY REACTIONS

My parents and several of my children think I'm a card-carrying kook, but my husband is very supportive and a good reader himself.
        —Cleopatra, Wicca priestess and psychic reader

It seems that at least with family, psychics, channelers and other readers are able to let their guard down and open up. In this survey, 57% affirm that their families regard their talents in a positive light. They describe their families' reactions with words like "delighted," "supportive," and "fascinated."

Only 12% identify completely negative judgments, but almost one-fourth admit to receiving mixed or lukewarm receptions from family members. One channeler admits, "One of my brothers thinks I'm possessed." Selene comments that her family thinks "it's a phase they hope I'll outgrow."

Many families (22%) simply seem to accept their psychic relatives. They are curious, respectful, and "accept me for being me, not for the 'strange' things I do," replies one psychic. "My family is happy that I'm happy," says Fisher.

HELP OR HINDRANCE?

[My psi faculties] help me in the same way that two hands are better than one.
—Bertie Marie Catchings, palmist and psychic reader

With all the negative feedback they receive, it's a wonder that more readers don't find something else, more "normal," as Burton-Hidalgo puts it, to do. Yet they persist because they are highly motivated. Reasons are complex, but based on responses to questions like "What motivated you to get into this field?" and "Do you find what you do a help or a hindrance in your personal life and why?" some clear patterns emerge.

The personal benefits derived from psi abilities serve as an inducement for the majority of the survey respondents. Being able to peer into the future can give them an edge. They say it makes them hard to fool because they intuitively know the reasons behind others' behaviors, and their talent enables them to avoid unpleasant situations, act on hunches, and help their families and friends.

"It helps me with everything from what's wrong with the cat to where to go for sales and visualizing parking places," says an anonymous respondent. Selene offers another slant, "If I pay attention, I stay out of trouble."

Some refer to the human intimacy that their abilities creates and how this helps them understand and evaluate other people's worldviews. They say that their faculty has aided their personal quest for spiritual growth.

"The esoteric understanding of the tarot and astrology gives me a solid foundation for a healthy worldview," Henits explains. "It keeps spiritual energy constantly flowing through my system," Hayes adds. "The greater the 'awareness,' the more joyful the psychic experiences." "Enrichment is always welcome," Jaegers suggests. "Why would it be a hindrance?"

THE "DOWN SIDE"

Only three respondents view their talent as an out-and-out hindrance to their personal lives, but twenty consider it a mixed blessing. Anderson comments, "It's a help now, but in the past it was a hindrance because many people couldn't handle what I do."

Shepherd, who is an empath, refers to the fact that "I see everyone's dark side right up front, and other people's more 'negative' emotions flood over me, even strangers'."

Butz admits that he has a hard time turning his ability on and off. For example, he may be in a crowd and begin to absorb people's negativity, like a sponge. This leads to a feeling of disorientation, as if he were walking inside a cloud.

Others mention the difficulty with setting personal boundaries. "It's nice to be able to read others' minds," says Fox, "but sometimes it's intrusive." Browne remarks that "what you see can't help but affect you." Another psychic refers to the faculty as having contributed to the breakup of his marriages.

Some respondents learn to turn off their psi faculties like a faucet. "I try not to use it in my personal life," observes Anhalt, "except to test my vitamins and minerals."

A few take their abilities in stride and claim that they are neither a help nor a hindrance; for them, psi just is. "I don't know if it is a help or a hindrance because I don't know of any other way," PoTO tells us.

Basic Motivations

When things began to happen, how could I have stayed out? Being aware of a number of levels of existence makes living a richer, more complete experience. I feel sorry for anyone who lives only in the physical realm. They miss out on a lot.

—Greybear, tarot reader, astral/shamanic journeys

It saved my life. It gave me a wonderful reason to live and be useful.

—Bob Ater, dowser

When asked what their motivations were for getting into the field, replies ranged from believing it was destiny to having readings where other psychics identified the talents.

"I am walking the path of my destiny," affirms one respondent, "and I love it all. I used to work for IBM and always knew someday I would be doing what I really love to do."

Mischell observes, "I love my work because it is what my soul has called me to do, and I never tire of doing it."

Curiosity piques some respondents' interest. "I wanted to see if my abilities were real or imagined," Dr. Robyn explains.

Alan Vaughan, Ph.D. entered the field first as a researcher. Initially he was curious about how psi works, and then he was challenged to help make it work better.

Evelyn Anhalt reflects that she never ceases to be fascinated "that when I lay down my tarot cards they 'tell' me a significant story about my clients. I enjoy giving fresh insights to them."

Lewis, a practicing psychic and editor of *Psychic News,* claims a long-abiding interest in the Occult. "Since early childhood I've been fascinated by anything paranormal, beginning with the pyramids, the Bermuda Triangle, Atlantis, the Arthurian legends. As I became more aware, I realized the mysteries were a part of a larger reality—one that many people never experience. I thrive on feeling connected to that Universal energy."

Marc Sky echoes Lewis's feelings of fascination, excitement, and love of the field. "I love doing what I like and getting paid for it," he declares.

Joy Green, a New Zealand numerologist and tarot reader, relates that in the process of receiving a reading, her talents were identified and she was encouraged to develop them.

Some respondents who work with spirit guides talk about how their guides made it very clear to them that this is the path they should follow.

"My guides (told me) that this is part of my life's work and part of my karma. It is important for me to help other people and conquer my own shyness," one channeler informs.

Others regard the field as an enriching, metaphysical experience with no parallel to other areas of their lives.

"What I like best is the joy of sharing the metaphysical experience," says Fitzgerald.

"I am motivated by the search for truth and self," Butz reflects. "Being at one with all is to be alive. It's just like flying, it gives you a high."

Edens was drawn to psychic studies because "I needed answers I couldn't get through Science or Religion." Through using their psi energy, readers like Palzere search "for answers to life . . . it makes life more understandable and bearable."

"I have always been fascinated by the challenges of mysteries and solving them," Myer admits. "Of course, the greatest mystery is life itself—I'm still working on that one!"

A True Calling

I believe it is important for psychics to be called upon to reach those who cannot speak for themselves—patients in comas, autistic children/adults can be reached. Many mental patients are not crazy; they have just experienced situations they could not cope with . . . Everyone needs to feel they are important, that they matter. We need to reach out to them, not make fun of their disabilities. Love is the key.

—Anonymous respondent

Although respondents list many reasons for getting involved in the field, the primary motivation that almost everybody mentions is a true, selfless desire to help others.

"It is my religious/social inheritance," claims Qabalist and Satanist Solomon. "I can truly help people . . . in their times of need and stress. I serve a very important function in society as a rapidly disappearing cultural necessity—the tribal witch doctor."

As well as being a channeler, Leland is a composer and a poet. He identifies his other pursuits as "solitary activities with certain narcissistic elements. In my channeling work, I feel that I can give something back to other people, the spiritual community, and the world as a counterbalance."

Catchings illustrates, "My first reading was to try to keep a woman from killing herself. I was successful. People found out and wouldn't leave me alone after that."

Hayes loves "watching people discover their own spiritual abilities and find their purpose in life."

"At one point," Burton-Hidalgo reveals, "I begged God to 'take it away' and give me a family, polka-dot curtains, two kids, etc. What motivates me is that I am very talented, and through my talent I see people change—they heal, they grow. I really like . . . seeing their spirits fill!"

If rather than or in addition to consulting with a psychic, you aspire to develop your own faculties in order to read for yourself and others, the next chapter will give you tips on how to proceed. By way of leading into the topic, the following presents you with information on palm reading.

Learning the basics of this ancient art, also known as chiromancy, will help you in many ways to deliver a superior face-to-face reading. A quick glance at the palm will help you size up clients, or for that matter, anybody you meet in any situation. In my opinion, it is not cheating to gather all the information you can about a client, whether it be through psychic means or through observation of minutiae like posture, facial expression, gestures, dress, or the size, shape, and color of the hands. You should permit yourself to use all the resources available to you so that you can put together the most complete picture possible for the person who is consulting you.

ABOUT PALMISTRY

In the popular imagination, palmistry conjures up scenes of heavily bejeweled, gaudily costumed gypsy women declaring dubious fortunes from the back of carnival wagons, while their men pick the pockets of the unsuspecting crowd. Many people dismiss palmistry as a charlatan's ruse because they do not realize that this legitimate and serious study of the intricacies of the human body and mind has produced some amazing, verifiable discoveries. Even the traditional scientific community has begun to acknowledge palmistry as a way to diagnose disorders such as Down's syndrome, alcoholism, and Alzheimer's disease.

You may wonder how this can be so. The hand and brain are related by impulses that originate in the brain and terminate in the muscles of the hands and fingers. The impulses cause the muscles to move, thereby determining the size, shape, and color of the hands and digits, even mapping out the lines of the palm. The major lines of the hand are etched during the first sixteen weeks of a fetus' existence in the womb, although minor changes can occur throughout one's lifetime. These modifications result from the action of countless brain impulses that send messages to the muscles. Since the palm reflects brain activity, it can also be considered one measure of an individual's character and personality.

Although this scientific basis for palmistry was not understood until recent years, many practitioners from different civilizations over the centuries sensed the importance of the hand to character reading. These ancient sages formulated the principles of palmistry, which have become a reservoir of accumulated knowledge about humankind. Information has been added to this store of knowledge by cultures as diverse as the East Indians, Greeks, Arabs, and Western Europeans. One of the most famous chiromancers, who also wrote about the theories behind palmistry, is Cheiro, whose biography you read in chapter 2.

In this section, you learn how to perform a palm reading. Some general characteristics of the hand are also given. The finer points of palmistry, such as fingers, mounts, lines, and incidental markings are detailed in appendix D.

How to Perform a Reading: Approaches

You should view a palm reading session as a way to assess your client's motivations, talents, and weaknesses, and to see how these energies have been put to use. Palmists are not seers; they do not predict the future. They only reveal situations as they stand now and that show that if the client proceeds along the current route, certain conclusions will be reached. This is because lines are not etched in stone, and if a client hears anything that could be construed negatively, this individual has free reign to change the current path, and thus reshape personal destiny. The minor lines, in particular, will reflect changes in actions, reactions, and points of view.

Before beginning a reading, I suggest you advise your clients of this point, and stress that part of the reason for having a reading is to identify these tendencies in order to modify behavior. It may help to liken a palm reading to Scrooge's visitations in Dickens' popular story, *A Christmas Carol.* Because Scrooge did not like what he saw in store for him, he changed his ways and created a new destiny for himself.

It is also important to leave the client with cause for optimism. This does not mean you need to lie about what you find. But no palm, like any human being, is entirely without assets. How you present your story—what you choose to emphasize or minimize—affects the tone of the reading. For example, rather than tell your subject she has not done much to develop her talents, you can say. "Although your success line has yet to appear, with your high Mount Apollo and flared fingertips, you show an innate ability to achieve unusual results in a creative field. The long little finger and head line bending to Mount Luna indicate you have a dramatic flair. Have you ever thought of going into the performing arts?"

In performing readings, you have chosen to take on the responsibility of helping others to help themselves. In palmistry (as with other modes of divination), this is best achieved by maintaining a positive attitude, even when pointing out weaknesses.

Besides this, the best advice I can offer to you is practice, practice, practice! Begin with your own palm, and move on to those of friends and relatives. Almost everyone is flattered to receive a free palm reading, so read at social gatherings, school, and at work. Examine as many palms as possible, and eventually you will develop a "feel" for this complex art.

The Reading

Begin the reading by observing how the client naturally holds his hands. Are his fingers spread open wide—a sign of willingness to communicate—or are his fists tightly clenched, revealing tension, fear, or uncertainty?

Hold the client's hands in yours for a moment to feel the temperature of the hands, ascertain the vitality of the individual, and establish a psychic link. If ever at this juncture you feel repelled by the hands, refrain from carrying on with the reading. Give any reason—you're tired, you really don't know enough about palmistry to read such a complex palm—any excuse not to continue with the reading. If the client forces you to continue, the results could be disastrous psychically for both of you.

There are two classic approaches to palm reading. In the psychic approach, the reader uses the hands as a psychic link to delve into the client's mind. In this case, the chiromancer practices clairvoyance just as she or he would with a pendulum, crystal ball, or deck of cards.

In the second method, or textbook approach, the diviner studies and memorizes the meanings of the lines, shapes of the hand and fingers, and other indications, then interprets the markings according to textbook definitions. Frankly, I favor a combination of both ways, because they seem to work "hand-in-hand," so to speak, to achieve the most accurate results.

In my experience, a fundamental aspect of palm reading is the evaluation of relative balances in the hand. Check to see whether the fingers are long or short, palms square or round, shorter or longer than the palm. Are the lines straight or curved, long or short? Do a relatively few deeply marked lines occur, or is the palm covered with a fine, weblike structure of lines?

In addition, you must consider the balances between the two hands. The nondominant hand shows inherited characteristics; so this is where you read the client's potential. It is also where you can look for psychic abilities, some of which are shown by lines that occur on the flat part of the palm under the last two fingers, and continue down to the base. Chiromancers read psychic abilities in the nondominant hand because most people do not fully develop their psychic faculties. This is also the only hand to read on young people, as usually their potentials are still latent.

The dominant hand indicates what a person has achieved with innate talents and also identifies areas of weakness or underdevelopment. Sometimes the two hands diverge remarkably, and when this happens, you should make a mental note that the client's life has been very different from what may have originally been expected.

After holding both hands to establish a psychic link, ask your client to raise both hands in the air with the backs toward you. Note the finger span, general hand shape, and length, and if any of the fingers lean forward. Then ask the client to spread hands face-down on the table, and check the same clues from this position.

Next, turn both palms over and compare them. To what degree are they flexible; how far can the fingers be bent back easily? How long are the hands in relation to the rest of the body? Are the palms broad, narrow, round, or flared? What color are they—yellowish, white, blue, sallow, ashen, pink, red?

Concentrate on the dominant hand. Observe skin textures. Ascertain the relative length of the fingers to the palm. Is any joint of the finger disproportionately long or short in relation to the other two? What is the condition of the nails? Long, short, bitten? Examine the shapes of the fingertips. The mounts are the fleshy protrusions at the base of the fingers. Are they high, low, firm, or flabby?

Analyze the lines. Are the major lines clearly marked or do they chain and twist? How long are they? Finally, does the hand reveal any unusual markings like stars, grills, crosses, loops, or circles? Only after this type of analysis can the palmist settle down and begin to put it all together for the client.

Right now you may be thinking that it will take forever to make these kinds of observations. With practice, you can reduce time spent in the preliminary examination to a couple of minutes. One of my favorite past times when I was studying at the university was to watch my teachers' hands when they talked. I especially loved it when they gestured with palms toward the audience so I could distinguish the lines. Believe me, it whiled away the time when someone was up on the podium waxing about the lexicon of Swahili!

While you are still building up your expertise, I suggest you analyze and relate to your client only some of the characteristics of the hand. Start with the generalities. When you feel confident, add observations about the fingers. Expand your repertoire with indications about the mounts. When at last, you are comfortable talking about all these areas, round out your reading by relating information about the lines.

A final word of advice: no single characteristic of the hand in isolation will unlock the door to the client's personality, character, and potential. Always look for confirmational markings. For instance, just because the lines on the hand are reddish, you can't assume the person is aggressive and violent. Be a detective and look for other clues like a short, broad palm; short fingernails; or a battle cross on Mount Mars to corroborate your initial findings.

The next part of this book will give you some more information on how to develop your own psychic skills.

Notes

1. PsiCops is an organization of skeptics dedicated to debunking psychics and psi phenomena.

PART III

SO YOU THINK YOU'RE PSYCHIC!

CHAPTER SEVEN

SO YOU THINK YOU'RE PSYCHIC?

Developing Your Psychic Faculties

I think that I am more capable and self-realized than if I never had become aware of this ability and pursued it. I feel that no matter what happens to me now, I have the ability to understand, accept, and move on. I believe the saying that God never gives us more than we can handle.

—Betty Muench, soul readings

Recently I read a mystery novel[1] in which the main character, Rachel Hennings, had wished she were psychic, but when put through the tests, always scored within or even slightly below chance expectations. Rachel's uncle died and left her his used bookstore that in its time had served as a meeting house for noted authors. One day, while sitting at a table in the gathering place, the new owner opened a copy of *The Great Gatsby*, and as if willed by an unknown hand, penned the signature of author F. Scott Fitzgerald to the flyleaf. She went on to reproduce other famous signatures like Nathaniel West, Aldous Huxley, and William Faulkner. In this way, she discovered her ability to let the spirits of famous deceased writers guide her to produce what is known as "facsimile signature writing," a form of automatic writing.

This easy way of psychic mastery, of course, is fiction. While reading this book, perhaps you have wished that instead of, or in addition to, seeing a psychic you could perform your own readings as effortlessly as Rachel Hennings. Since we all possess psychic skills, discovering and developing your psi faculties isn't as difficult as you may think. All you need to bear in mind is that to achieve any remarkable and sustained results requires a certain amount of dedication and practice.

KNOW YOUR MOTIVATIONS

Self-responsibility and pure intentions are essential—come to think of it, not only in channeling, but in everything in life.

—Pat Rodegast, channeler

What is the most fundamental principle behind people's ability to be psychic? To understand that our strongest beliefs create the reality we experience. We attract that which is on the same vibrational energy level as we are.

—Darryl Anka, channeler

Although foretelling the future for oneself and others is a logical and useful reason to nurture your faculties, it represents only a small part of what you can achieve. As you can see from the above sampling of statements, according to respondent after respondent, psychic self-development is an immensely satisfying and spiritually fulfilling pursuit. What's more, you can enjoy this activity at all stages and ages of your life. No matter the condition of your health, economics, or social status, you will always derive personal benefit.

Modes of divination like palmistry, astrology, and graphology provide frameworks for character analysis. For example, meditation on the tarot can reveal your innermost needs and desires and challenge you to be the best you can possibly be. Students of Ceremonial Magick perform a kind of meditation and ritual called a pathworking in order to strive for unity with Divinity. Through the study of the tarot, channeling, and serious manipulation of psychic aids like the Ouija board, crystal ball, and magick mirror, you are presented with the opportunity to gain information and wisdom, not just for yourself, but to add to the stockpile of human knowledge. Although being psychic doesn't necessarily make you better than anyone else, it may bring you a step further along the road of the quest for human perfectibility.

Another way to achieve self-mastery is to use your talents to aid others. To guide other people on the path of life they have chosen, to present them with new worlds of possibilities is a naturally uplifting experience. Who would not be touched by seeing how your words can ease another person's heartache, loneliness, and pain; and open exciting, heretofore undiscovered byways to explore?

PRACTICE THE THREE "RS"

Never laugh at someone else's problems; those same problems could be yours someday!

—Dr. Catherine Penn, psychic artist

Don't play God. [Develop] feelings of responsibility and honesty for your influence on the lives of others.

—Shirlee Teabo, tarot reader

When you begin to apply these skills for yourself and others, you should be aware that along with all the euphoria come certain commitments. I call these the Three "Rs"—Respect, Responsibility, and Rectitude. You need to be respectful of all people who come to see you, no matter how silly or misguided you may think they are, as Penn notes above. Several respondents emphasize the need to develop a code of ethics. "See beyond reproach in the practice of morals and ethics," Ferguson advises. "Have the desire to do good rather than become rich." Luning adds, "Deeply care about the welfare of humanity, and you'll have many clients who will love you."

Several psychics underscore that once you harness your faculties you become committed to helping others; that is, to create a sort of mini-lay ministry becomes one of your goals and principle responsibilities in life. This concept, in my opinion, resembles what happens to a person after becoming initiated into a magickal order, be it Wicca, Ceremonial Magick, Shamanism, or other traditions. The decision, taken consciously and with forethought, changes your life forever. Neither choosing to become a psychic or joining a magickal order should be taken lightly.

Several respondents note the love of and search for truth as a primary motivation for entering into the field, but they differ in the way the truth should be communicated, as the following comments show.

Leland believes that as long as you are telling the truth clearly, you can't feel responsible for how your client takes it.

> You are responsible for two things only: your actions (that none of them be malicious or intended to hurt or mislead) and your reactions to other people's actions . . . You cannot be responsible for how one uses or misuses what you tell him or her. The fastest way to destroy yourself is to make yourself responsible for what people hear you say. What you are responsible for is stating the truth or wisdom you've been given as clearly as possible.

Anzuz-Auriel, who agrees with Leland, points out how she deals with the legal aspects of responsibility: "I have all personal clients sign a disclaimer saying that they are responsible for their own life choices."

One respondent warns about possible legal ramifications in our litigious society: "Be very careful of health information. We are not doctors, even if we do practice psychic healing. Many times I have clients sign a release form that states that my work is for research purposes with no guaranteed results." A few respondents declare that they refuse to discuss health issues at all because of this problem.

Anhalt expresses her concern for telling the truth. "Don't fake information or give the client what you think he wants. Keep your ego out of it; be humble and thankful for your gift."

"Pursue what you believe to be true, practice what you know is true," McMoneagle reminds us. "Be subject to change in the next five minutes, and reject the words 'can't,' 'no,' 'not possible,' 'impossible,' or any other absolute negative. Practice what you preach, and never do harm to another."

My own advice about whether or not you should tell the truth is based on personal experience as a combination palmistry-tarot reader. Recently I performed back-to-back readings for a fifty-year-old woman and a girl of sixteen. From the woman's cards, I saw that although she had achieved a good position in life socially, emotionally, mentally, and spiritually, she had fallen into complacency and simply did not want to move further ahead. I knew the woman possessed a strong character, so had no compunction about challenging her to extend her limits, even if it meant falling back in the short-run so that she might attain a higher, more fulfilling level. "Quit being slothful," I chided, "forge ahead."

In the young girl's reading, I saw severe health problems, both in the recent past and into the future. Her life line was tenuous with few supporting lines. Her mounts were low, the palm was covered with a web of fine, wavy lines, and she actually possessed a health line, which can indicate poor health. In her tarot reading, health complications also surfaced. I opted to tell her about the past problem and advised her to watch her diet and exercise, and neither smoke or drink in order to achieve and maintain better health. I did not dwell on what I saw in her palm because I did not want this girl, who was at an impressionable age, to become discouraged.

The moral of the story is that I think that while you shouldn't lie to people, you should treat every reading as a separate "entity," so to speak, and reveal as much truth as you feel the client can handle and will be helpful. Since I happen to believe that we possess the free will to change the outcome of a reading through right thought and action, I recommend that a reader suggest what the client needs to look at more closely, yet keep a positive, encouraging tone.

THE MONEY QUESTION

When speaking of a code of ethics, many survey respondents brought up the question of whether or not to charge for services rendered, and if so, how much. I did not ask this question in the survey, so I have no data on how many respondents would have answered "yes, one should charge," or "no, one should not." Enough people made spontaneous comments about the subject, even chiding me for not having included it, that I think their comments are significant.

Most respondents who addressed the issue think that a psychic reader should charge something, although many feel that the profession is riddled with con artists who only want to make a quick buck by playing on the sympathies of the emotionally unbalanced and overcharging for their services. People made vociferous complaints about commercialization in the field. For example, Csere, who is an astrologer, beefs about "computerized, pre-formatted 'readings'" for which some astrologers charge "exorbitant prices."

Dancing Fox, who is a tarot reader, Druid, and counselor believes in donations. "These gifts should be used to help and guide others in need of instruction in their lives," she reasons. "I never set a monetary fee for anything I do. Donations, and I lack for nothing. My desires are simple; becoming a millionaire off of others' misery is not my goal in this life."

Others, like Martha Lawrence, who is both a psychic and a successful mystery novel writer, believe that psychics should be compensated for their time, expertise, and the energy they put into their readings. Mischell points out that the seers in the Bible were all paid for their services. "I have a huge overhead with five full-time employees . . . If I did not charge for my work, I could not provide the kind of services I do for those who come to me from all over the world." Mrs. M further notes that in this society, money is given in exchange for service, and if it is not, the service is devalued.

A problem for some is deciding how much constitutes a fair price to charge. Again, Mrs. M speaks: "If I offered free readings, I would probably feel very self-righteous and definitely out-of-pocket . . . I charge a flat, minimal fee . . . I have given readings in trade, and that has worked well, too."

Selene provides a unique perspective on the fees dilemma:

> When I did this publicly, I charged $5.00 for a reading. I could have gotten $40+, which is the average here, but did not want to jeopardize my ethics . . . . Guilt over charging large sums can subconsciously affect one's ability . . . (so) I prefer the method of donations (i.e.; a $5.00 minimum).

Butz offers this rule-of-thumb to the beginner, "Start small, give free readings, read, network, train, and grow as a person before charging more."

BALANCING ACT

If you're ready and willing to take the plunge and read, but are concerned about how to bring the information you receive from the subconscious across the threshold to the conscious mind, you are not alone. All psychics, whether professional or amateur, deal with this situation every time they read. Although they may tackle the issue in a variety of ways, they mostly agree that it is important to maintain physical, emotional, and mental balance. When asked if mental and/or emotional factors affect their ability to read, respondents answer as follows:

> Yes, after all, this is part of being human. But I try to transcend my personal strengths and weaknesses by tuning into something greater. (Butz)

> If I am in distress or in pain, confused, or distracted, I cannot focus well. (Solomon)

> Being very upset or angry heightens my psychic energy. (Fisher) (Another anonymous respondent makes the same comment, and explains that "being upset" helps tie up the analytical mind and free the intuitive mind.)

I'm sure my mood does limit the "flexibility" or "depth" of the information that comes through, but I don't think it affects the quality or validity of the information. (Anka)

No. I have learned to calm myself, especially since I work with the FBI and police. I see blood and people who have been murdered, and I just can't allow my feelings and emotions to stop me. (Mischell)

They can, but they don't. When it comes time to heal, the "small me" gets out of the way entirely. (Luning)

Carla Rueckert, a Christian channeler who kindly sent me her manual *A Channeling Handbook*[2], offers some profound insights. She states that she does not let mental and emotional factors affect her because she tunes in like a radio and purifies her emotions. She believes that the key to successful channeling is to strike a balance between the intuitive and rational minds and guard against temptations of excess and ego. The way to achieve this goal, in her opinion, is through meditation and prayer. She suggests that as you become more proficient at using your talents you should meditate and pray all the more because the intensive mental and emotional effort that is required to keep focused throughout thousands of repetitions of your work increases. She observes that while it is easy to keep your interest alive when you first get involved, because everything is new and exciting, it is hard to sustain the necessary freshness and high level of concentration over time.

Other respondents suggest that in addition to meditation, you should listen to subliminal tapes, practice affirmations, yoga, and ritual, all by way of blocking out "mental noise." Harte advises to "be still . . . disconnect from physical/material happenings and allow spirit to work through (your) third eye into (your) hands." "Be still," Nancy reiterates. "The help [of spirit guides and angels] is always there when needed to give a good reading. You learn to listen by quieting your mind."

PRACTICE MAKES PERFECT

Besides mental and emotional balancing, an important element for success in seventy-two respondents' opinions is "practice." When asked if they believe a reader needs to train the mind to perfect the skill like a pianist, who warms up by playing scales, several answer that no matter how long they have been in business they do readings every day, even if only practice readings. Some mention that they constantly test themselves, pay attention to their dreams, and make almost daily visits to the astral plane. Other readers talk about preparing by performing breathing exercises, and having body work done, like massage, all of which keeps their channels open.

Only one-quarter of the respondents do not feel the need to warm up. Anka, for example, complains that the question is misleading and that "certain training is necessary to channel more clearly, but I have no need to warm up daily except write in my dream journal."

Carol Skylark, who is an auraportaitist, also declines to practice because, as she says, "I spent many years developing my inner eye to hand coordination . . . now all I have to do is close my eyes to see."

EXTERNAL AIDS

Some respondents underscore the need to "feed the subconscious" (Csere) by using incense, oils, scrying herbs, candles, and symbolic signs to draw forth images. Lina describes, "I take a bath by candlelight with sea salt and special oils. I focus on the flame and listen to a subliminal tape, often holding crystals and/or stones in my hands."

Hundreds of botanicals exist that have been taken by psychics worldwide for centuries. Some are ingested in teas or inhaled as incense, or they are applied externally in oils and baths, or used as talismans in spells to enhance psychic self-development. Typical ingredients in northern climes include mugwort, wormwood, beth root, juniper, fennel, anise, wisteria, musk mallow, sage, thyme, and marigold to enable the seeker to see and communicate with fairies. Apples are an old Celtic-Druidic scrying botanical that the sacred salmon of the River Boyne were said to have ingested from the hazelnuts of wisdom that dropped into the stream. Rose scent is alleged to balance visions as does verbena, which also protects the clairvoyant from malefic spirits. Clary sage lends clarity to the communication.

Seers from semitropical and tropical climates often prefer heady mixtures of vanilla, violet, sandalwood, and jasmine to sharpen their abilities. Other "psychogenic" tropical botanicals include kola nuts, lemongrass, guinea grass, cinnamon, mastic, patchouli, Job's tears, bay laurel, and camellia.

Survey respondents have quite a lot to say about drugs, alcohol, and tobacco, most of it unfavorable. While a few comment that wine and spirits stimulate their psychic centers, even those who occasionally use them abstain when reading professionally. The overwhelming majority reject the "unregulated, chaotic impressions" that these substances produce on the brain. No one in the survey, even anonymously, recommends dangerous botanicals like datura, belladonna, peyote, and psychedelic drugs.

In the so-called "good old days" of Witchcraft—that is, during the persecutions in western Europe and America—many convicted Witches claimed to have anointed their bodies with and ingested Witch's flying ointment in order to communicate with the Devil and spirits. Some of the ingredients they cited included belladonna, datura, water hemlock, opium poppy, henbane, mandrake, yellow flag, monkshood, sweet flag, and speedwell.

My guess is that these substances were generally known in the population as hallucinogens and that many of the confessed Witches claimed to have eaten these concoctions simply to satisfy their torturers. If they really swallowed the ingredients, and if they weren't killed outright, they would have become dizzy, nauseous, and numb. Such a cocktail is extremely dangerous and I do not recommend it. At the end of this section, I will share with you some safe psychic self-development recipes that I have formulated for my coven, and which I have sold for years through my metaphysical supplies business.

DIET AND EXERCISE

Because I have always heard references about how a person's body should be treated like a temple, particularly when performing magickal work, I asked if exercise and diet influence readers' abilities. Forty-one per cent reply "absolutely no," but the 59% who believe it is important seem to go to great lengths to practice what they preach. Age does not seem to be a factor because both twenty-year-olds and the over-sixties crowd rave about the benefits of regular exercise to the psychic system. Wolf, a generation-Xer, works out strenuously to sharpen her intuition. Sevigny, who is in his seventies, still walks up mountains even though he suspects they're getting steeper. Several respondents tout the virtues of exercise as a lymphatic cleanser, which they deem important for successful psychic work. Besides jogging and biking, favorite modes of exercise include walking, yoga, and lifting weights.

The "weight" respondents give to eating habits varies, with once again, about two-fifths claiming that diet makes no difference at all. Among those who do follow a special diet, many are vegetarian, although a couple insist that psychics should eat red meat. Some, sounding like an advertisement for *Prevention Magazine,* sing the praises of low-fat, dairy-free diets, chock full of fruit, vegetables, and whole grains, all washed down with copious amounts of spring water. Ginger, however, enjoys chocolate as an energy replenisher, and Jaegers, who has researched the physical demands of psi work (as well as gathering information from authoritative sources), says that psychic reading depletes potassium and natural sugar levels in the blood, which can be replaced by daily fruit juice drinks. A few respondents mention that they need to eat regular meals or else hunger will distract them, while others prefer to read on an empty stomach, citing the benefit of enhanced intuition. It seems that diet is very much a matter of taste!

Conditions that affect some respondents' abilities adversely include fever, colds, yeast and fungus infections, allergies, tobacco, and menstruation (although a couple of women feel that menstruation sharpens their faculties).

Environmental Factors

Environmental conditions draw more general agreement than diet and exercise. Only sixteen respondents claim that they can, and have performed readings anywhere, including in airplanes and buses, at parties and police stations, indoors, outdoors, at the kitchen table, in groups, or one-on-one. One reader explains, "my angelic spirit is always with me and can converse with me anywhere." However, the majority of respondents (more than 80%) indicate that the environment does make an appreciable difference.

A few respondents prefer bright or naturally lighted spaces, while several mention dim light and candlelight as conducive to reading. Smells enter in, especially pleasant fragrances, like incense and perfume. Respondents also mention bad odors, unsanitary conditions, and pollution as deterrents, and some insist on a well-ventilated facility.

Music enhances some respondents' abilities, especially light classical and soft background music. Many complain about loud rock music and sudden noises or shrieking children and animals as factors that disturb their concentration.

Aesthetics play a key role. Respondents read better in a quiet, calm, orderly place, particularly a private, safe, sacred space, like a purified circle, a kitchen office, or even a favorite metaphysical store that exudes positive energy. One respondent goes so far as to state a preference for pink, color-coordinated rooms. Another suggests that the locale should face south, still others like to be in nature—or at least have a view of it from a window.

Several mention that while the space itself is not particularly important, the attitude of the client is, and that open, loving and preferably psychic clients bring along with them a positively charged psychic environment. Two respondents like to read over the Internet because it provides privacy plus a chance to work one-on-one.

As to the best times to read, some respondents favor early morning, others early evening, or at night. Dawn and dusk are favorite times because it seems that when day and night are shifting into one another, glimpses of other worlds can be more readily perceived. A few respondents earmark Wednesday as a good reading day because it is the day is governed by Mercury-Hermes-Thoth, god of communication. Several prefer reading at or around the Full and New Moons. Some Wiccan respondents refer to the Waning Moon as a traditional time to draw within to analyze events, circumstances, and potentials, and foresee the future. They also recommend sabbats, especially Hallowmas (October 31), because these are traditional times when it is believed that the veil between the Worlds grows thin and spirit communication is facilitated.[3] The days when the Moon is traveling through the water signs Cancer, Scorpio, and Pisces are considered by some to facilitate psychic work. Marcum is the only respondent to indicate a Moon sign that does not seem to work for her, which is when the Moon is traversing Aquarius.

Weather sets an appropriate mood for some respondents. Several believe that rain enhances abilities while others prefer warm, sunny weather. High altitude locations, although not mentioned by any survey respondents, traditionally have been considered repositories of psychic powers.

RECIPES FOR PSYCHIC SELF-DEVELOPMENT

Here are some of my favorite recipes for psychic self-development. Many of the ingredients are easily obtainable from health food supermarkets and aromatherapy shops. If you would rather not fuss with preparing these concoctions yourself, write for a metaphysical supplies catalog to Dunraven House, P.O. Box 403, Boulder, Colorado 80306, e-mail me at hpmorwyn@aol.com, fax your request to (303) 499-7370, or check us out on the Web at www.dunravenhouse.com.

The incenses that follow use colored, commercially prepared wood base, which is a fancy name for sawdust. If you can't obtain wood base anywhere, I recommend you cultivate the acquaintance of a carpenter and ask to sweep his or her floor. Then color the sawdust with dry tempera powder. More precise details on how to prepare your

your own incenses, perfumes, and bath salts are the subject of my book *Witches Brew: Secrets of Scents,* cited earlier.

Burn incense during meditations and when you perform a reading. Anoint your third eye (the space between your eyebrows) with the perfume or anoint your psychic tools like your crystal ball, Ouija board, psychic stones, tarot cards, and reading table. For items that don't take kindly to oil absorption—like tarot cards—dilute the oil in alcohol in the proportion of nine drops of oil per ounce of spirit.

When blending perfumes, use a one-dram (⅛-ounce) vial. After you combine all the ingredients, shake the bottle well, and apply a little to your wrist. Let the perfume dry, then sniff your wrist to see how the formula mingles with your natural body oils. Sniff again a few hours later to measure staying power and changes in the scent. Some formulas will combine better with your body chemistry than others, or you may want to modify the recipes to suit your taste.

Concentration Incense
Focuses the attention and enhances intuition.

¼	cup frankincense
½	teaspoon cinnamon powder
½	teaspoon heather flowers
1	tablespoon crushed fir needles
¼	teaspoon ground cinquefoil
½	cup orange wood base
¼	teaspoon heather oil
¼	teaspoon frankincense oil
3	drops clary sage oil
6	drops Siberian fir oil
¼	teaspoon chypre oil

Midnight Vision Perfume Oil

You received the formula for the incense in chapter 1 (see page 29). Here is the perfume blend. It is one of my favorites for night scrying—fabulous applied to a magick mirror!

- 1 part sandalwood oil
- 2 parts narcissus oil
- 1 part honeysuckle oil
- ½ part carnation oil
- ½ part cinnamon oil
- 1 part tobacco oil

Shaman Vision Incense

Taps into the wisdom of the Native American shamanic tradition.

- ¼ cup copal resin peas
- 1 tablespoon cut and sifted deerstongue leaves
- 1 teaspoon ground meadowsweet
- 1 teaspoon crushed juniper berries
- 1 teaspoon poppy seeds
- ½ teaspoon crushed fennel seeds
- ½ teaspoon powdered thyme
- 1 teaspoon crushed white incense sage
- 2 teaspoons fir needles
- 1 teaspoon mistletoe oil
- ½ teaspoon spruce oil
- ½ teaspoon copaiba oil
- ¼ teaspoon hemlock oil
- ½ cup natural fir wood base

Occult Contact Incense

Facilitates meeting with spirits from other planes of existence.

¼   teaspoon crushed vetivert grass
1   tablespoon myrrh powder
2   tablespoons frankincense peas
1   teaspoon ground cedar
1   teaspoon cut and sifted patchouli leaves
1   crushed bay leaf
½   teaspoon anise seeds
1   teaspoon narcissus oil
½   teaspoon dark musk oil
3   drops spruce oil
¼   teaspoon cypress oil
½   teaspoon heliotrope oil
½   cup black wood base
    A pinch each of cut and sifted mugwort and vervain leaves

Moon Mistress Perfume Oil

Helps put your psyche in resonance with the strongly intuitive lunar currents.

2   parts lotus oil
1   part jasmine oil
½   part magnolia oil
½   part honeysuckle oil
2   drops benzoin oil

Astral Flight Incense

Enhances astral travel abilities.

2   tablespoons frankincense peas
1   teaspoon marigold flowers
1   teaspoon cedar powder
1   teaspoon crushed lavender flowers
½   teaspoon rosemary leaves

1 teaspoon rose oil
1 teaspoon wisteria oil
½ teaspoon India bouquet oil
½ teaspoon eugenol oil
½ cup lavender wood base
Pinch of beth root

Neptune Bath Salts

Attunes you to the vibrations of this dreamy, mystical planet. Mix the ingredients into 1 cup of sea salt and pour into a warm bath. If desired, color the salts green or blue with food coloring.

¼ teaspoon opopanax oil
½ teaspoon oakmoss oil
1 teaspoon dark musk oil
1 teaspoon lotus oil
½ teaspoon ambergris oil
2 drops rue oil

Cerridwen Bath Salts

Pay homage to the Welsh Moon goddess of the cauldron of inspiration and knowledge with this formula. Mix the ingredients into 1 cup of Epsom salts. If desired, color with blue food coloring.

5 teaspoons cornstarch
1 tablespoon baking powder
½ teaspoon heliotrope oil
1 teaspoon light musk oil
½ teaspoon jasmine oil
5 drops vanilla oil
½ teaspoon white lilac oil
Pinch of powdered bay leaf

Mind Reader Sachet

Works on a subliminal level to sharpen your telepathic faculty. Mix together the ingredients of this sachet, enclose in a little sachet bag, consecrate, and place it on your reading table or on your altar when performing meditations. Sleep with it under your pillow at night to help induce psychic visions. Reserve unused portions in a tightly sealed jar.

½	cup orange wood base (try to get oak sawdust and color it yourself with dry tempera paint)
1	tablespoon ground orris root
¼	teaspoon cut lemon peel
¼	cup lavender flowers
1	teaspoon cut and sifted hyssop
¼	cup crushed verbena leaves
½	cup santal pieces
2	teaspoons crushed cinquefoil leaves
2	teaspoons rose oil
½	teaspoon melissa oil

AIDS TO PSYCHIC SELF-DEVELOPMENT

Survey respondents offer several other suggestions as to how you can develop your psychic faculties. Among them are:

Read regularly. Choose the same time every day or several times a week to practice alone or read for others. When beginning, keep your sessions short, no longer than twenty to thirty minutes. The reason to stick to a psychic self-development routine is that every action we perform tends to repeat itself under similar conditions. If you practice regularly, the psi action will eventually become automatic.

Learn from a teacher. A teacher does not have to be a famous seer, just someone who knows the ropes better than you and can help you along until you achieve balance.

Attend workshops and developing circles. In these groups the psi energy of many is pooled, and the student tends to make more rapid progress than when beginning solo.

Experiment with different "media." How many artists have started out with oils and found that their real talents lay with watercolors? The same is true with psychic media. You may initiate your efforts with tarot cards, but get attracted to remote viewing. Or perhaps you feel you can give a better reading if you practice astrology, palmistry, and the Ouija board at the same time. Maybe you prefer to get deeply involved with crystal ball reading to the exclusion of all else. Go with your gut feeling. Do what feels right for you.

Go slowly. Accept what "visions" you receive; don't force results.

THE PSYCHIC "DIET" PLAN

If you're still not sure how to begin, follow this fail-safe "psychic diet plan." If you stick with the psychic diet, it is guaranteed to speed you on your way to psychic self-development. The mantra of the plan consists of five little words: "Relax! Concentrate! Protect! Invoke! Flow!"

Relax

By relaxing, I mean still your active, analytical, left brain and let your passive, intuitive, right brain take the helm. I recommend several kinds of relaxation, including muscle tension release, breath work, affirmation, and meditation. With muscle tension release, you drain tightness from your body so that this vehicle for communication remains free of blockages.

Muscle Tension Release

Sit in a comfortable, upright chair with both feet on the ground and your arms at your sides or on the armrests. Wear clothing that does not constrict you in any way.

Start at the top of your head, wrinkle up your forehead and squeeze your eyes tightly shut. Hold the tension for a moment, then let go. Do this three or four times until this part of your body feels free from tightness. Move on to your nose and cheeks, and wrinkle them up, then relax them. Follow with your jaws, shoulders, arms, hands, stomach, lower abdomen, buttocks, thighs, lower legs, and feet until every part of your body feels free from tension.

Breath Work

Next, concentrate on your breathing. Note how your chest and diaphragm slowly move in and out. Observe the minute changes that take place in your body as you inhale and the air fills your nose, throat, and lungs with the breath of life, and feel how the air is expelled when you exhale. If you get stuck following the other steps of the "diet plan," return to this exercise to help regain your focus.

Affirmation

To put yourself into the right frame of mind to accept and communicate the information that will flow through you, affirm aloud and silently everyday that you are psychic and able to perform accurate readings. Three times a day, nine times in a row, say something like:

Each day I bring myself into communion with my psychic self.
Each day my inner voice grows stronger.
Each day my psychic abilities solidify and are brought into manifestation.

If these words don't work for you, choose your own affirmations, but keep them positive and focused, and make sure you believe in them. Empty words don't fool your subconscious!

Meditation

Are you ready for a guided meditation to elicit and enhance your faculties? As you did in the tension release exercise, seat yourself in a comfortable, straight-backed chair. Do not lie down unless you are certain you won't fall asleep. Tense and relax your muscles and perform your breathing exercise as directed above. You are completely relaxed, but alert.

Close your eyes. Imagine you are immersing yourself in a clear, blue sea. Deeper and deeper you sink until you come to rest on a soft, white, sandy bottom. Around you flows the limpid blue water, sparkling in the rays of the sun that reach down to warm the sand.

All the stress of the day seeps out of you into the flowing blueness and is carried away. Your personal concerns vanish, flushed clean by the pristine salt water. You are perfectly grounded. Completely and perfectly centered.

You realize that you have shed your earthly form and taken on a new identity, that of a living sponge. How good it is to feel the purifying liquid wash through your cavities as you oscillate on the seabed.

As you watch your transformed self sway gently on the seabed, you glance around at the vast, serene, turquoise ocean kingdom. You are aware that you are not alone in this perfect, protected place. You share it with other life forms. Coral, kelp, mollusks, tiny fish, big fish—they're all floating in the water around you, and you feel you are natural, vibrant part of this immense ecosystem.

A school of dolphins glides by, and their smiling faces and playful gestures prompt you to gently dislodge yourself from the seabed and move along with them. As you cavort among the dolphins, your sponge self becomes aware of certain murmurings. The dolphins are talking; they are speaking to you, sharing with you the wisdom they have accumulated over the eons. Honored by their willingness to communicate, you absorb their confidences through the millions of pores in your body.

After a while, you perceive that the dolphins need to move on and you need to change back into your human self. You thank them for sharing their knowledge. They swim away, you slowly rise to the surface. A warm, sunny stone ledge overlooking the sea awaits you on land. You realize that as you clamber up onto its slick surface your arms and legs, hands and feet have grown back, and in fact, you are once again inside your human body. Except that you carry deep within you the secrets imparted to you by the dolphins. Later, as you read for people, you will tap into this reservoir of knowledge. Open your eyes. The meditation is over.

After you have practiced this meditation several times, you can vary the circumstances by imagining that you are a perfect, white river pearl, or a tree whose roots reach deep into Mother Earth. In the river pearl scenario, you might be visited by the wise river salmon of Celtic legend; in the tree meditation, your communicators may be the elemental spirits known as dryads and gnomes, who guard the Earth's "gems" of knowledge.

Concentrate

Relaxation is the first step toward psychic self-development, but in order to become a proficient reader you need to learn to concentrate. Relaxation and concentration are not mutually exclusive concepts. You can relax, but still turn your one-minded focus toward the single purpose of zeroing in on the subject of your reading. By concentrating, you link into the energy vibration of a specific person and object and draw forth psychic information, which you then communicate.

An effective way to improve your ability to concentrate is to review the day's events in reverse before you go to sleep. Start with getting into bed, and work backward to brushing your teeth, donning in your pajamas, hanging up your clothes, until you're back to the first moment your eyes popped open in the morning. Don't just record the big events or thoughts; try to recall them all, no matter how insignificant.

Your subconscious mind, who if the truth be told is a bit of a shirker, will try to interfere and put you to sleep before you've finished the task. With time and patience, you will overcome your subconscious' sluggishness, and harness it to work for you.

Another way to sharpen your concentration is to go to your favorite restaurant and observe in detail everything about it. Notice the color of the walls, texture of the carpet, arrangement of the tables and chairs, who the servers are, and how they move around. Drink in every detail.

The next day at home, write down all the facts you remember. Then go back to the restaurant and make a note of what you forgot.

You can broaden the scope of the exercise by visiting unfamiliar restaurants, friends' homes, the library—any other building. Or describe people you know—your friends, acquaintances, even complete strangers you encounter in the street. As you progress in your mini-self-training course, you will be rewarded with remembering more and more.

Protect

> *Beware of those who would control you. Balance all aspects of your life.*
> —Graybear

Finally, before you invite spirits and other entities to enter your body and mind and speak through you, you have to protect yourself. Not every entity running around on the astral plane is beneficent. In fact, a lot of downright vicious and ugly energies are on the loose, because for every good, positive thought, feeling, action, deed, and entity, its opposite number is lurking somewhere out there.

If you scoff at such ideas, that is your prerogative. If, for example, you believe that what you are tapping into is the latent power of your own mind, your Higher Consciousness, or your intuition, I will not try to dissuade you. In fact, I agree that much of the time, perhaps this is what you are doing. If this is the case, I ask you to think of performing the two exercises that follow in this section as a way to guard against your own "negative" side to make sure it does not creep into your readings.

Another good reason to perform a protection ritual is to banish mental noise from your environment and intensify your focus. In other words, the protection ritual puts your mind right by preparing you to read.

Must you do this every time you read? Yes and no. If you are executing a series of readings say, at a party for friends or at a psychic fair, you should do it once before you start. If you are called away from the reading to the phone or if you are doing a series of short readings for yourself at intervals throughout the day, you only need to challenge the communicating entity again (I will explain the concept of "challenging" shortly). Every time you let twenty-four hours elapse, or you change the setting of the reading completely (that is, read at a metaphysical store in the morning and for a friend in his home that night), repeat the procedure.

One of the most effective ways I have found to invoke protective forces is with the ritual from Ceremonial Magick called the Lesser Banishing Pentagram Ritual and its companion rite, the Qabalistic Cross Ritual. If you follow a different path and prefer to use a ritual that is more familiar to you, feel free to do so.

Qabalistic Cross

Two parts comprise this ritual. The first part, the Qabalistic Cross Ritual, affirms that you are about to enter another sphere of reality. The Qabalistic Cross, which is based on the Western magickal system of the Qabala and the Tree of Life, balances you, stimulates your chakras, and opens your path to heightened self-awareness. It prepares you to perform the Banishing Pentagram Ritual that follows it.

To begin, stand (don't sit) facing east, the direction of light, hope, and beginnings, with your legs comfortably apart and your arms at your side.

Imagine that a stream of bright, bluish-white light shoots down from the cosmos and forms a globe of light just above your head. Touch your forehead with your thumb and forefinger, and say:

Ateh ("Thou, to Thee")

Lower your right hand to your solar plexus, and as you do, visualize that a ray of bluish-white light extends from the globe straight down through the middle of your body to your feet. Say:

Malkuth ("Kingdom")

Shift your attention to your right shoulder, touch it with your hand, and form another pool of cosmic light there. Say:

ve-Geburah ("and the Power")

Send out a jet of light across your chest to your left shoulder, where it accumulates another globe. Say:

ve-Gedulah ("and the Glory")

Finally, bring both arms up to your shoulders, fold your hands to your chest, as if in prayer, and say:

Le Olahm Amen ("throughout the eons")

The Cross of Power that you formulate will scintillate through the universe, and you will feel that you are a point of light in this vastness extending infinitely outward in four directions.

Banishing Pentagram Ritual

You are now properly prepared to chase away negativity with the Banishing Pentagram Ritual. This ritual calls forth the protective forces of the Four Quarters of the Universe—Raphael for the east, Michael for the south, Gabriel for the west, and Auriel for the north. These Archangels are collective archetypal images through which the potencies of the universe, including the power to protect, are transmitted. They stand for the four elements. Raphael, "God as healer," typifies air. Michael, "like unto God," represents fire; Gabriel, "strong one of God," symbolizes water; Auriel, "the enlightenment of God," is related to Earth. For complete details about the Archangels and this ritual, see my book, *Secrets of a Witch's Coven* (Atglen, PA: Whitford Press, 1988).

In this rite, you will visualize shaping four enormous pentagrams from the bluish-white light in the east, south, west, and north. From each pentagram, a ray of light of the same color will extend out and around you at chest-level until it forms a protective, vibrating circle of light. At each quarter (cardinal direction), you will also invoke an Archangel to anchor the position in front of the pentagram and expel intruders.

Trace each pentagram figure with your right, extended forefinger, beginning at your left hip. Move diagonally up to the top of your head to mark the upper point, then down to your right hip for the second angle. Move to your left shoulder for the

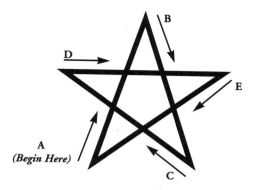

Banishing Pentagram

third angle, across to the right shoulder for the fourth, and complete the fifth angle at your left hip where you began. Remember to close all the angles of the pentagram. All the while, envision that a ray of light has entered your body through your head, courses through you, and exits from your forefinger like a kind of electric ink with which you make the drawings. You are a channel for this protective light.

After completing the Qabalist Cross, still standing in the east, draw the first pentagram. Then stand back, and lunge forward with your right arm, and with the point of your forefinger, penetrate the center of the pentagram. This sends the figure spinning out into the universe. At the same time, say:

Yod Heh Vau Heh ("Self-Existent One")

Keeping your arm at shoulder-level, move to the south, where you formulate the next pentagram. Don't forget to carry along with your finger the stream of bluish-white light that will form the protective circle around you.

In the south, inscribe another pentagram, lunge forward as you did in the East, and send the pentagram whirling out into the universe. Intone:

Adonai ("Lord")

In the same way, carry the point of light to the west, trace the pentagram, activate it with the tip of your finger, and call:

Eheyeh ("the One-Self")

Repeat the formula in the north, and say:

Ateh Gebur Le-Olahm Adonai
("Thou art the power throughout the ages")

Keeping your arm raised and still pointing your finger in front of you, seal the circle of light by returning to the east. Picture that the ring of bluish-white light swirls around you and that the light swells into pentagrams that scintillate at the quarters. Spread both arms out to your sides at shoulder-level and call upon the Archangels:

Before me, Raphael,
Behind me, Gabriel,
To my right, Michael,
To my left, Auriel,
Around me flame the pentagrams,
Above me shines the six-rayed star.

End by repeating the Qabalistic Cross. You are now fully protected from the Dark Forces of the internal and external worlds.

Invoke

You may want to enlist the aid of angelic forces to aid you in your divination. Although it is not necessary to invoke these powers, you will find that if you do, you will achieve excellent results in your readings. Appropriate entities to call upon include certain angels of the sphere of Mercury, since Mercury is the planet of communication and governs foreknowledge. The angels of this sphere are called the seventy-two genii of Mercury. However, you will only invoke three of them.

In a prayer of your own creation, call upon the forces of these intelligences: Sitael, the third genius of Mercury, who governs telepathy, hypnosis, and suggestion, and tells the future from the Akashic records; Achaiah, the seventh genius, who reveals the fate of individuals and of nations; Ariel, the forty-sixth genius, who reigns over prophecy, instructs about the past and present, and interprets dreams.

Say something like:

O Sitael, interpreter of the Akashic records,
Achaiah, communicator of the fates of individuals and nations,
and Ariel, governor of prophecy, come, join me in this Circle of Light.
Guide my divinations so I can aid humanity. So mote it be!

I know these rituals seem complicated, but once you perfect your visualization technique, you will find that you can do them in under two minutes.

Flow

At last, you are ready to read! As an example, let's say you are divining with a Ouija board. I know that most people do this in pairs, but I happen to work with the Ouija board alone, and have done so for years.

First, light appropriate incense (use any of the recipes in this chapter), and anoint the tip of the planchette (the pointer that spells out the messages) with a drop of anise oil.[4] Rest your fingertips lightly on the planchette and wait for it to begin to move. If you want, you can speed up the procedure by calling, "Is anybody out there?"

The planchette may now start moving slowly and jerkily, gather speed, and furiously spin around in a circle until it comes to rest in the center of the board with your fingertips still on it. You are witnessing the result of the energy entering the planchette. After the planchette pauses, question the entity: "Who are you? What is your name?"

The planchette will spell out a name, often something that seems strange and difficult to pronounce. Don't overly concern yourself with the name; just use it to address the energy.

Now challenge the entity with: "In the name of Truth and Light, will you answer all the questions I put forth to you clearly and accurately?"

If you get no response, or a "no" answer, thank the spirit for appearing, send it back to the realm from which it came, and terminate the reading. If, however, the entity says "yes," you may proceed with your inquiries.

When you have finished asking all your questions, thank the energy for its help in the name of Truth and Light, and send it back to the realm from whence it came with Love until you meet again.

Whether you are divining with a Ouija board, runes, crystal ball, tarot, channeling, or any other way, let the reading flow at its own pace. Accept the information you receive, even if it seems incomplete or lacks sense. Do not force an answer, no matter how desperately you desire it. Sometimes you will get nothing, and this, too, is okay. Save your questions for another time. Go with the flow!

As I have mentioned elsewhere in this book, part of going with the flow of the reading is learning to not analyze the information you receive or make judgments.

Here is another illustration. Recently I was chatting with my good friend, Lorraine Moller, who is a world class marathon runner and remote viewer from New Zealand. I had just returned from a trip to Scotland, where I met an interesting fellow. I asked Lorraine to "view" a sample of his handwriting without telling her anything about the individual, including where or when we met.

She scribbled down a line doodle that represented her first impression, then retraced it over and over again with the point of her pencil. Then she wrote down adjectives and phrases that referred to the feelings that the doodle evoked. Among those phrases were "mysterious," "degrees of involvement," "deep," and "expanding." In her synopsis, she informed me that whoever this person was, we were going down together deeper and deeper, and that something mysterious was involved. She did not try to make sense of her impressions by concluding that our relationship was mysterious or that it was becoming more profoundly involved with each other. She just said what she felt, "deeper and deeper."

What she could not have guessed was that I met this person at the beginning of a tour into the underground city of Edinburgh that was built centuries ago. As the tour progressed, we moved further down under the city, and back into history. If she had jumped to the logical conclusion about a relationship, she would have been wrong. Being a well-trained remote viewer, Lorraine stuck to only what she felt, and gave a correct reading of the situation.

Along your journey on the road to psychic self-development you will experience many highs and lows, frustrating periods, and moments of sheer exhilaration. You will expand your horizons, and very possibly become a better human being. My steadfast encouragement and sincere wishes for your welfare go with you.

Notes

1. Jon L. Breen, *The Gathering Place* (1984; reprint, New York: Walker and Company, 1986).

2. Carla L. Rueckert, *A Channeling Handbook*, (Louisville: L/L Research, 1987).

3. The eight Great Sabbats are: Winter Solstice (around December 21), Candlemas (February 2), Vernal Equinox (around March 21), Beltane (May 1), Summer Solstice (around June 21), Lammas (August 1), Fall Equinox (around September 21), Hallowmas (October 31).

4. You may prefer to anoint your planchette only once a year because the oily residue tends to eat through the plastic.

CONCLUSION

Divining the Future of Divination

The future is the past unfolded, or entered by a new door.

—Occult adage

Throughout this book, you have seen the role that divination and other psychic pursuits have played in the history of humankind. You have also met some of those people who perform these arts, and learned about the nature of their skills and how they implement them. Also you have been introduced to ways to cultivate your own latent faculties. Finally, you have been exposed to the question that ESP and other psychic phenomena pose to the traditional scientific community.

As we step over the threshold into the new millennium, you may be curious about whether the entire body of knowledge about divination and related psychic phenomena will be washed from the face of the Earth, drowned by the tide of scientific doctrine that does not allow for systems that as yet, cannot be adequately measured, and consigned to the dustbin of superstition. Will our psychic faculties vanish from our human makeup in the same way our acute sense of smell weakened when we emerged from primitive times and no longer needed it? Or is there a place for these distinguished, ancient arts in the modern world? Can our aptitude for the psychic help us to survive and thrive in the future, or is it best left to molder in history books that describe more atavistic times?

WHAT'S HOT AND WHAT'S NOT

As you might suspect, when asked these questions, the survey respondents had much to say. First, by way of establishing what sorts of needs are addressed by the psychic community today in order to project into the future, I asked what fields of divination are "hot." Tarot and related card reading and channeling take first prize hands-down. Astrology and clairvoyance run neck-and-neck as close seconds.

Age-old methods like runecasting, palmistry, and dowsing also put in good showings. One dowser submits that his field will grow even more important in the future because, with the burgeoning world population "thirsting" for water, dowsers will be entreated to find these sources.

Other areas in the forefront of the field, according to the practitioners, include: herbology, numerology, healing, I Ching, computerized astrological charts, angelic communication, pendulum divination, aura reading, African and Santería shell divination, UFO contacts, astral travel, Shamanism, crystalomancy, psi hotlines, Reiki therapy, Ouija boards, past life divination, hypnotism, spirit-guide painting, conspiracy theories, and Armageddon scenarios.

One of my personal favorites, which I think will "take off" in the future, is remote viewing. As more people discover that there is more to this activity than cloak-and-dagger spying, and learn that we all have the capacity to perfect this innate skill, they will find ways to use it for self-development and humanitarian needs. At least this is my personal prediction.

When addressing the question about the future of divination, several respondents note that all techniques seem to be experiencing a revival because, as one individual proclaims, "we are progressing toward a mental state where everyone will be more aware and develop their intuitive sides." Lawrence, for example, believes that aura reading will become a standard skill in the future. Jaegers senses that we are currently "undergoing a revisiting of the . . . (renewed interest in psychic phenomena) situation of the '60s and '70s, but (these days it is) somewhat more widespread and on a slightly higher level, since the pop culture aspects have been removed."

Myer expresses a less sanguine feeling about the resurgence of interest in psi. "It would appear that we are once again in an undisciplined phase where almost anything goes . . . the pendulum is due to swing back to a reasonable middle once more."

A few respondents react negatively toward some of the methods practiced by their colleagues. "Channeling [is hot these days], though I wouldn't consult one myself—it's a load of bunkum! A good Spiritualist takes some beating," Green objects. An anonymous astrologer echoes Green's sentiments, "I've yet to hear anything significant from the mouth of a channel." Hughes complains about the term used to describe the field: "I don't like the word 'divination!' It smacks of fortune-telling, and there are laws against 'fortune-telling.' The genuine psychic, mediumship, and astrology are the fields that are busy and genuine."

Probably the area that comes in for the worst criticism from other psychics are telephone "1-900 hotline psychics." They top the pet peeve list under the question, "Does anything bother you about the field?" In all fairness, I must comment that I received completed surveys from several channelers, palmists, fortunetellers, and hotline psychics, and their history, development, abilities, opinions, and sense of moral responsibility toward clients do not seem to differ in any significant way from the other respondents'—at least in the surveys that were returned to me. In fact, some of their remarks, which I have included in this text, rank among some of the most intelligent, respectable, honest, and high-minded.

WHAT'S IN STORE?

Respondents divide almost evenly into two opposing camps when asked if they "think that new areas of divination, channeling, etc. will develop in the future." Those who don't envision brand-new specialties emerging feel more or less that "there's nothing new under the sun," and that only the names change, or that the lines of pursuit will remain the same, and only the techniques will be refined. Two individuals cite channeling as an example of an activity that has taken place since ancient times under different names. Shepherd goes as far as to say that "divination may actually disappear as we realize that we create our own reality and use our own psychic gifts."

Shepherd's idea that the population at large will take a greater hand in their own psychic development, and hence, psychic reading, is endorsed by several respondents. "I can't describe it," Rueckert admits, "but we are evolving. I see a future of growing awareness of spiritual identity—more and more people waking up."

An anonymous respondent proposes, "People will learn to access their own answers by tuning into other energy frequencies by natural and unnatural (paranormal) methods."

One of these new methods, according to Sherman, is the computer. She foresees "self-readings via computer hookup."

Anderson predicts that other computer-enhanced fields will emerge. "(I see) computer/hologram (methods) where the instrument is attached to the psychic and the hologram displays what the psychic 'reads'."

FAITH IN PEOPLE

Why do respondents see more people becoming telepathic and using their own psi abilities? Wind offers this explanation: "Many people are becoming open to their Higher Selves because the webbing of the crown chakra (the energy center believed to link humans to Divinity) is thinning." Ginger concurs, "Spirit contacts will advance because they want us to know what's on the Other Side . . . the veil is getting thinner. Lewis muses, "It will be interesting to develop psi input from 'space' as well as from 'spirit.'"

Csere puts faith in future generations' abilities to modify venerable traditions and create new ones. "There [will be] pioneers and progenitors of a new breed of people," he assures us. Edens agrees, "A new generation will be born to understand more."

Others believe that new areas of healing and techniques of psychic medical diagnosis will blossom.

Selene, on the other hand, is of the opinion that ancient oracles with which we lost contact during the Age of Enlightenment will resurface and adjust to the needs of present time.

Expressing hope for the merger of technology and psi, several respondents look forward to seeing their field legitimatized. "All areas of divination will be better understood as technology advances in its ability to measure energies," PoTO comments.

Mischell looks toward the future with anticipation. "I feel everyone who wants their own personal psychic will be connected to that special person via the Internet. We will get our answers quicker through the technology that is coming. Another 200 years—the word I use is 'Wow!' How wonderful for all mankind as we take what I do and you do as normal!"

DISTINCT OR EXTINCT?

When asked about whether the field will exist in another fifty to two hundred years, a whopping eighty-seven shout yes, and several underline forever! Some propose that as long as human beings and spirits exist on the Earth there will be readers to act as intermediaries. Those few who are unsure, or do not think so, surmise that the world will change and the characteristics of divination will modify accordingly. "It won't be a field so much as a way of life," Lys predicts. "People will be fluent in mind-to-mind communication," Fitzgerald says. "There will be no need for graphology, but numerology will always be a valid tool." Harte forecasts, "In 200 years we'll have better modes of communication. Hopefully we'll evolve."

THE PSYCHIC'S ROLE IN THE SCIENTIFIC AGE

What do the respondents think about the contrast between their viewpoint and that of traditional science, and what do they think is their place in the modern age and projected into the future? Almost every respondent offers a strong opinion.

Psychics conceive of their function as vital to contemporary life. Overwhelmingly, they believe that their primary duty is to help others. They indicate how they can locate missing children and aid the police in their investigations, give input to medical cases, and heal and counsel. Spiritualists note that they can assuage clients' fears of death. Others offer that they can introduce people to their guides or Higher Selves, and steer them toward the path of self-knowledge and self-improvement.

Heath remarks, "The more technical our age becomes, the more people will have need for direct access to spiritual sources of help and information." Liaros mentions the psychic's ability to assist people in their decision-making process, whether the decisions be in government, business, education, or any other facet of their lives. Dancing Fox tells how psychics redirect people who are confused and upset by removing the burden of "doom and gloom" that many individuals feel in this fast-paced, modern society. For these reasons, and to to help bring the field more into line with the twenty-first century, Myer is working at establishing a training institute.

SCIENCE AND PSYCHICS

As to the debate between scientists and psychics, many respondents, including Dale, perceive psychics as a bridge, a "link between science and spirituality. [We] help evolve rationalism to spiritual principles." Lawrence clarifies, "[Our function is] to bring the human race's intuitive powers in line with its rational powers." Others credit the psychic field with providing solutions that science cannot yet supply.

Psychics discern that the relationship between their field and science is improving, albeit slowly. "Science is having to make room for an expanded view of reality," Graybear elucidates. "It should not be denying anything as impossible just because it does not fit preconceptions. Science should investigate the unexplained, not explain the uninvestigated!"

Others realize that scientists and psychics need to learn about each other and together develop a psychic technology. They reckon that psychics can convince scientists to broaden their horizons. Burton-Hidalgo remarks, "Recently I participated in a distant viewing [remote viewing] project at Duke's department of radiology . . . [and found that] the mainstream field of psychotherapy is literally gobbling up skills that psychic healers and teachers have been using for decades."

"We're already friends with the quantum physicists," Shepherd notes, "and we can duplicate everything modern technology does. [I am speaking of] the cosmic Internet, where we are all connected. I'd say we're here to remind scientists of their souls so we can all move forward."

The concept of psychics as teachers and guides to scientists as well as clients is corroborated by many respondents. Schroeppel, who speaks from eighty years of life experience, concluded that psychics are here to "teach scientists the real abilities and teach proper use of the mind and spirit."

"[Our function is the] same it has been since the beginning of time," Lewis reiterates, "to be a source of information, an interpreter, and a guide."

Owl Woman finds that the function of the psychic is to be a "spokesperson for the planet and foster good will among tribes of the human race."

Leland elaborates:

> [Psychics] are the voice of the soul or of personal revelations that our age has tended to deafen itself to by putting religion or scientific figures of authority between us and our inner knowings in order to better control us. Psychics and channelers can be the voice of spiritual freedom from dogma, whether

scientific or religious. Truth is not the same as proof. Faith is not the same as wisdom. Psychics and channelers have the potential to be spokespersons for both truth and wisdom.

Wolfsong's summary of the issue is short, but no less eloquent, "Today it is a practical science; tomorrow it will be mystical science."

To the psychics, our future looks bright, and no matter what unfolds, they intend to be there to guide us.

As we move into the new millennium, we bring with us the inheritance of our past, which includes the wisdom instilled in us by both our inquiring, scientific selves and the profound, psychic part of our beings. Speaking as an "old-time" Wicca priestess and ceremonial magician, I believe that these two sides of our natures, when reconciled and working together in unity, can bring a harmonious balance to each of us. This sense of harmony, well-being, and light then can be projected to the entire world. May both these aspects of our minds unite to serve as an inspiration for future generations. May the future generations, whose past is rooted in our present, carry forth the message of hope, peace, and love to our galaxy and beyond.

THE PSYCHICS
SURVEY

Here are the statistical results of the surveys. I sent out 500 surveys and received 127 replies, which statistically speaking, is a phenomenal result. Because many surveys were returned late, I only recorded the statistics from the first 100. After reviewing the late replies, I saw that these replies wouldn't have change the results significantly. However, if someone from the late twenty-seven made an interesting written reply, I sometimes included the response. Sometimes the numbers don't add up to 100. This is because not everyone answered every question, or they might have answered the question, only in another area of the survey.

SURVEY RESULTS
PART I: STATISTICAL INFORMATION

1. **Name:**

Those who use their own names when giving readings: 76.

2. **Professional names:**

Those who use professional names, 23 (use both legal and professional names, 4; uses name of corporation, 1).

3. **Address:**

4. **Phone (optional):**

5. **Birth date:**

Respondents were born between 1917 and 1977.

Several respondents did not list a birth date, but those who did fell under the signs of the zodiac as follows: Aquarius, 13; Leo, 11; Libra, 9; Virgo, 8; Taurus, 8; Gemini, 8; Capricorn, 7; Cancer, 6; Scorpio, 6; Pisces, 6; Aries, 5; Sagittarius, 5.

6. **Type(s) of readings you perform:**

Most frequent responses: cards (all types), 32; astrology, 22; channeling, 21; clairvoyant, 17; psychic/intuitive, 12; psychometry, 11; past lives, 11; numerology, 10.

Fewer than ten responses: palmistry, 7; aura, 6; runes, 5; deep trance, 5; dowsing, 3; spiritual counseling, 3; ghost/spirit contact, 3; graphology, 2; healing, 2.

Other single references included: pendulum, natal and compatibility charts by computer, voice channeling, strands of hair, psychometry of place, music channeling, karma readings, Satanic readings, Reiki healing, I Ching, Qabala, dreamwork, pathworkings, soul logus, shamanic work, animal and nature healings, exorcism, hex incantations, Akashic angel readings, tea leaves, automatic writing.

7. **Is this your main source of income?**

yes, 47; no, 43; 50% of income, 10.

8. **If not, what is your main occupation?**

Most frequently listed occupations other than being a reader: writer, 12; retired, 11; student, 8; teacher, 6; nurse, 4; on disability, 3.

Other occupations mentioned include: health practitioner, secretary, hypnotherapist, office worker, radio/TV host, police report clerk, librarian, commerce and industry, real estate agent, park ranger, jewelry designer, office manager, New Age shop owner, editor/publisher, workshop leader, USAF (retired), antiques dealer, researcher, state employee, stocks and bonds, secretary at accounting firm, public relations, radio/TV speaker, electronics, technical field, stewardess, communications/computer consultant, occult mail order, tourist resort owner, fruit tree nursery, administrative support, psychotherapist, mother and homemaker, shaman, minister, medical transcriber, art dealer, merchant, weather observer, herb distributor, advertising, seamstress, business consultant.

9.   **What level of education have you completed? (middle school / high school / 2-year college / technical college / bachelor's / masters degree / doctorate / other degree)**

Middle school, 2; high school, 21; 2-year or technical college, 21; technical college, 9; bachelor's degree, 29; masters degree, 13; doctorate, 6; doctor of divinity, 2; other types of degrees, 18.

10.   **How did you learn your art? (intuition / books / family / personal contacts / formal classes / divine revelation / other)**

Intuition, 69; books, 51; family, 26; personal contacts, 37; formal classes, 24; divine revelation, 38; born into it, 7.

Other responses included: spiritual growth, laboratory testing, study, mother was psychic, dreams, personal teacher and a lifetime of self-study, traveled around the world to work with various shamans, mystic experiences, practice, personal gift, spent nineteen years as a researcher in the field, empirically by watching others, used reasoning, heard voices, internal guidance, "my wife taught me," "experience taught me."

11.   **Do you practice professionally or for family and friends? If a professional, how long have you been in practice?**

For family and friends only, 28; professionally, 72.

Age 1 to 12, 4; 13 to 19, 16; 20 to 29, 24; 30 to 39, 36; 40 to 49, 11; 50 to 59, 3; over 60, 2; "all my life," 4.

12.   **What is your religious affiliation?**

Most frequently named religions: none, 17; Protestant (named denominations, including evangelical), 16; Roman Catholic, 15; Wicca, 15; all religions, 9; Christian non-denominational, including Unity, 8; Spiritualist, 7; Jewish, 5; Mormon, 3; Shamanic, 3; Russian Orthodox, 1; Judeo-Christian, 1.

Other religions that were named when plurality of faiths was mentioned include: Church of the Earth Nation, Christian Science and Science of the Mind, Druidism, Qabala, Metaphysics, Native American, Animism.

13.   **Were you born into this religion?**

Not enough respondents replied to this question to get a representative sample.

PART II:
YOUR PERSONAL INVOLVEMENT IN THE FIELD

1. **Do you consider your ability a) a gift; b) a talent that can be developed; c) an ability that everyone possesses; d) something else?**

   a, 56 (several of these said the ability can also be developed with practice); b, 61; c, 52; d, 4; several said "all of the above."

2. **How did you first learn you were psychic? How old were you? Can you describe the incident?**

   Specific ages given (number of respondents citing this age): 2 (4), 3 (13), 4 (7),5 (7),6 (1), 7 (3), 8 (1), 9 (5), 10 (4), 11 (1), 12 (7), 13 (1), 14 (2), 16 (3), 17 (2), 18 (1), 21 (1), 22 (3), 23 (1), 24 (1), 25 (1), 26 (1), 27 (1), 29 (3), 30 (2), 34 (1), 35 (1), 40 (4), 45 (1), 63 (1).

3. **Do you believe you need to practice training your mind to perfect your skill like a pianist who warms up by playing scales? (yes / no) If so, what do you do to "warm up" and "keep in shape?"**

   Yes, 72; no, 27.

   Meditation, 36; prayer, 15; practice (readings or self-testing), 12; self-healing, 7; spiritual studies, 6; ritual, 5; open up, 5; commune with nature, 4; dreamwork, 3,

4. **a) Is your ability consistent? (yes / no) If not, how can you tell when you're having an "off" day?**

   Yes, 76; no, 24.

   Illness, 18; fatigue, 10.

   b) What do you do when you're not up to snuff, but you have to do a reading anyway?

   Do it anyway, 33; Postpone, 30.

5. **Do diet, exercise (or lack of it), or any other physical factors affect your ability? (yes / no) If so, how?**

   Yes, 59; no, 39; don't know, 2.

   Diet, 25; exercise, 17.

6. **Do mental or emotional factors affect your ability? (yes / no) If so, how?**

   Yes, 66; no, 34

PART IV: GENERAL QUESTIONS ABOUT THE FIELD

1. a) Do you think your field is respected by most people? (yes / no)

Yes, 28; no, 50; yes and no, 14; don't know, 2.

b) Why or why not?

Those who answered "no" most frequently gave the following reasons: public ignorance, 22; religion gets in the way, 15; we're judged by the few weirdos, frauds, and actors in the field, 15; 900-line psychics, 10; media sensationalism, 8; misinformation fed to the public by skeptics, 4; public fear of the unknown, 3.

Those who answered "yes" most frequently referred to: the dawning of the New Age, 5; better education in the field now, 4.

2. a) Do you think men or women make better psychics and channelers? (men / women / neither)

Men, 2; women, 16; neither, 82.

b) Why?

See text.

c) How about children? Explain your answer, please.

Since this question was not couched in yes/no terms, many people did not answer the question directly. However, 64 respondents said "yes," 1 said "no," 2 said that born-again Christians had the faculty repressed in them at an early age, and 3 mention that they grow out of it because they are taught to by society. This issue is not raised in the text.

3. a) The media and traditional science seem to like to expose fake psychics. Do you think there is a lot of fraud in the business? (yes / no)

Yes, 64; no, 16; there is some fraud, 5; yes and no, 4.

b) Why or why not?

Most frequent responses: People are easy to fool, and it's a job where it's easy to get away with fraud, 17; greed, 15; like any profession, there are both good and bad practitioners, 7.

c) At one time or another, even some very famous legitimate psychics have committed fraud. What do you think motivates some people to do so?

Greed or need for money, 35; fame, recognition, ego, 22; pressure to live up to image, 13; fear of losing ability, 11; power, 6.

4. a) Do you think there should be a regulatory agency that oversees psychics to cut down on fraud? (yes / no)

Yes, 29; no, 54; yes and no, 10.

b) Why or why not?

See text.

c) If so, what should such an organization be like and how, ideally, would it go about its business?

See text.

5. **a) What do you think of research societies like the American Society for Psychical Research (ASPR) and scientists and parapsychologists who investigate psi and ESP?**

Although this question does not require a yes/no answer, the most frequently cited responses were: excellent, 19; very important, 2; good, 22.

   b) Do you believe that their findings are useful? (yes / no)

Yes, 65; probably, 3; yes, but they are limited, 3; sometimes, 3; yes and no, 5; no, 9; I don't have enough information, 8.

6. **In your opinion, what fields of divination are "hot" today?**

Most frequently cited modes of divination: tarot or other card reading, 27; channeling, 27; astrology, 15; clairvoyance, 11.

7. **a) Do you think that new areas of divination, channeling, etc. will develop in the future? (yes / no)**

Yes, 60; no, 12; maybe, 1.

   b) Can you describe what they might be like?

See text.

8. **Do you believe that a psychic has a moral responsibility toward his/her clients? Please explain.**

Yes, 96 (20 answered "absolutely yes"); no, 4.

9. **What do you think the place of psychics and channelers is in the modern, "scientific" age?**

Most frequently mentioned areas: to help others/to heal others, 8; to bring balance back into science, 7; help the police, 5; science and psychics will grow closer together, 4.

10. **Do you think that your field will still exist in another 50 years? (yes / no) Another 200 years? (yes / no)**

50 years: yes, 87; more so than ever: 3; 50 years: no, 1; unsure, 2; yes and no, 4

200 years: yes, 82 (one respondent said "forever," and another answered, "another 2,000 years.").

"In 200 years we will have better modes of communication"; 2.

"In 200 years everyone will be doing it"; 2.

11. **What advice do you have for fledgling psychics and channelers just entering the field?**

    See text.

12. **What other important questions would you like to have been asked that were left out of this survey? Please feel free to ask and answer them.**

    Several respondents said that the survey was "pretty thorough." The most frequently mentioned question that was left out was about charging money for readings—whether to charge, and what is a fair price to charge. See text for the responses.

APPENDIX B

ESSENTIAL TERMINOLOGY

Akashic records. Subtle material underlying all life that contains a recording of every thought, action, and event that has, or will ever take place on Earth. It has been called the "cosmic record bank." The information contained in these chronicles is supposed to be available to adepts and qualified sensitives. The concept originated in Hinduism and Buddhism and was brought to the Occident by Theosophists.

Altered state of consciousness. State of being that differs from normal waking consciousness in that the individual eliminates external influences and draws within. Often while in this state, subconscious imagery is permitted to surface into memory. Altered states include trance, hypnotic, dreaming sleep, daydreaming, out-of-body, mystical, meditational, or drug-induced states.

Animal magnetism. Concept introduced by Anton Mesmer that consists of a kind of organic magnetism along the lines of physical magnetism, that can be transmitted from one person to another for healing purposes. The technique was refined and expanded in the following century and renamed as "hypnosis."

Apport. Materialization of an object out of thin air. Typical apports include small stones, flowers, and live plants and animals.

Astral plane. In occultism, another plane of existence, contiguous in space, if not necessarily in time, with physical reality. It is considered the realm of dreams and illusions, and is supposed to be where the spiritual essence of a physical being travels in sleep and after death. Occultists attempt to visit this world in spirit during a meditational process called astral projection.

Astral projection. Also known as an "out-of-body experience" or "astral travel," the feeling that a person has separated from the physical body. In this state, the individual may visit locations on the physical plane, and otherworldly planes of existence. In parapsychological studies today, the phenomenon is connected with "remote viewing."

Augur. Originally, the word referred to a priest in ancient Rome, who interpreted the flights of birds for signs of things to come. Nowadays, the term refers to all kinds of divination.

Aura, aura reader. Ghost-like double, or subtle energy radiation or force field that surrounds all objects, inanimate and animate. An aura reader can perceive this emanation by either clairvoyance or clairsentience. The human aura is divided into several layers, most often referred to as the "physical," "mental" or "emotional," and "spiritual aura." By examining the color, shape, and quality of the emanation, the reader analyzes personality, character, depth of spiritual evolvement, and state of health of the subject.

Automatic writing. Writing or typing produced by a medium while in an altered state of consciousness. "Facsimile writing" occurs when the medium reproduces the signature and/or writing style of a deceased person.

Biofeedback. In altered states research, a technique where the subject tries to tune into bodily functions and emotions and control them with no device other than the power of the mind.

Bleed through. Phenomenon that sometimes occurs when a trance medium does not lose consciousness entirely and unconsciously projects messages from the medium's own personality into the information being channeled from a nonphysical entity.

Book test. Test of a psychic's authenticity and of the existence of spirits that involves the medium indicating the contents of a page of a specific book located in a certain place that contains a personal message for the inquirer without the psychic having seen the location or read the book.

Cabinet. Small, enclosed space where a Spiritualist medium may sit to condense psychic energy so that a spirit materialization may take place. The Spiritualist cabinet is based on the Native American conjuring lodge.

Ceremonial Magick. Type of magick developed over the centuries that invokes specific symbols, and practices elaborate rituals. Much of the theory is based on magickal texts from ancient times, and the Middle Ages, Renaissance, and eighteenth century. Ceremonial magicians stimulate the five senses in order to reach beyond and make physical changes in accordance with the will. In the modern age, the practices of Ceremonial Magick were revived and popularized by the work of the Hermetic Order of the Golden Dawn.

Chakra. Energy center, or repository of the life force in a person's aura, where energy is taken in and flows out. Chakras can be perceived and analyzed by aura readers.

Clairaudience. Ability to distinguish sounds by paranormal means; for example, voices and music. The term derives from French and means "clear-hearing."

Clairsentience. Ability to psychically feel emotions and physical sensations, and to sense smells and tastes. The term derives from French and means "clear-sensing." The older term "telesthesia" is a synonym.

Clairvoyance. Ability to perceive discarnate entities, objects, people, and events over time and space. The term is often generalized to describe many psi abilities such as clairaudience, clairsentience, psychometry, remote viewing, and telepathy. The term derives from French and means "clear-seeing."

Collective unconscious. Concept developed by psychologist Carl Jung that holds that shared images called "racial memories" of all conscious and unconscious thoughts and experiences are inherited by each individual. Examples of these kinds of memories include legends, myths, and religious motifs.

Conjuring lodge. Shelter in which Native American shamans communicate with non-physical entities and practice divination. The famous cabinets of the Spiritualist era derive from the conjuring lodge.

Control. Nonphysical entity, often a spirit, or an evolved energy essence, that takes over some mediums' personalities while they are in an altered state of consciousness. Often the control is perceived as a protector and filterer of information.

Cross-correspondences. A complicated way of assessing that a medium's messages are not faked or due to telepathy, but actually originate with spirits. For example, automatic writers from around the world receive bits of seemingly meaningless information which when pieced together, like a puzzle, spell out significant messages.

Decline effect. In psychical research, the phenomenon that occurs when a subject tends to guess the first few cards in a twenty-five-card run correctly, drop in accuracy through the middle, then rally toward the end of the run.

Developed medium. Expert medium.

Development circle. Group of people who meet regularly, usually in a circle, and follow séance procedures under the guidance of a developed medium in order to improve their mediumistic abilities.

Divination. The art of prognostication; foretelling the future, analyzing character, and identifying guilty parties. The diviner is able to tap into a subconscious source and become aware of past, present, and future events, which are often received in symbolic form.

Divination by analogy. Prognostication by interpreting omens, signs, symbols, statements overheard, and the chance arrangement of objects.

Down through guessing. In psychical research, what occurs when test subjects call the ordering of a deck of cards from top to bottom when the cards are placed face-down on the table in a pile.

Druid/Druidism. The Celtic priesthood in pre-Christian times in the British Isles, France, and northwest Spain. One of the Druids' functions was to offer predictions. Druidism refers to the religion of the Druids, modified to fit contemporary times, which is practiced in those regions and in North America today.

Ectoplasm. Whitish, viscous substance said to be produced by spirits so that they can assume physical shapes. Usually the ectoplasmic manifestation extrudes from orifices of mediums' bodies. It is said to emanate an odor similar to ozone. Most ectoplasm has been proved to be counterfeit.

Entity. Energy essence, or nonphysical being, like a spirit or an angel.

ESP. Acronym for "extra-sensory perception"; the ability to perceive information without recourse to the normal five senses of sight, hearing, touch, smell, and taste.

Floating trumpet. Device that looks like a trumpet that appears to float in the air of its own accord during a séance. Spirits are thought to use the trumpet to magnify their voices. Usually floating trumpets of the Spiritualist era were discovered to be fraudulent.

Feng shui. Ancient Chinese art and science that studies the hidden currents that cover the Earth's surface. It is used principally to orient homes, businesses, rooms, and other structures in an attempt to take advantage of positive forces and minimize negative currents.

GESP. Acronym for general extra-sensory perception; the combination of telepathy and clairvoyance. For example, both faculties come into play during card guessing. This discovery led to the realization that they present two aspects of the same ESP phenomenon.

Guide. Guardian spirit that oversees one's daily activities, warns of impending danger, and may provide paranormal information. Some individuals consider their guides to be aspects of their Higher Selves.

Higher Self. The God-force within; the spiritual essence of the self that links the individual to Divinity.

Hypnosis. Deep form of relaxation induced by psychic means, either by another person, known as a "hypnotist," or by oneself. The subject appears to be unconscious, but is highly receptive to suggestion and may also exhibit psychic abilities.

Inner planes. Planes of manifestation that are different from physical reality. In occult cosmology, they are characterized as being denser than the "earth plane," or tangible world. Examples include the spiritual plane that, as Nevill Drury defines in his *Dictionary of Mysticism and the Occult*, "reflects the universal life-force and people's inherent divinity."

Intuition. Ability to know or learn something immediately, such a perception or insight, without having recourse to conscious reasoning.

Karma. Sum of a person's thoughts and deeds in a specific existence (known as an "incarnation") that are said to determine the conditions of one's life, for better or for worse.

Levitation. Form of PK (psychokinesis) in which animate and inanimate objects seem to defy gravity and float into the air without any known physical agency.

Materialization. Appearance of an object or spirit from nowhere, sometimes occurring during a séance. The purpose of a materialization in a séance is to prove that spirit entities are present and communicating with humans, however, they can also take place spontaneously.

MCE/mean chance expectation. In psi experiments, it refers to the score that is most likely if only chance is involved. For example, in card guessing, the MCE is five out of twenty-five cards.

Medium. In Spiritualism, one who acts as an intermediary between the world of the living and the spiritual dimension. The term has been generalized to refer to anyone who demonstrates paranormal abilities, and/or who mediates between this world and any nonphysical entity or energy from another plane of existence. In this last sense, the term is being taken over by the word "channeler."

Mesmerism. Way of curing patients of their ills, invented by Anton Mesmer, that entails manipulating the mind; a precursor of hypnotism.

New Age. Term coined in the 1980s to refer to a philosophy that espouses such doctrines as astrology, mysticism, Shamanism, natural healing, reincarnation, self-help, and other forms of spiritual enlightenment. The New Age refers to the dawning of the Age of Aquarius, a time of peace, hope, love, and psychic awareness.

Omen. Thing or occurrence that is taken as a sign of some future event; an augury; a prognostication; a presage. Omens are divided into two categories: those found commonly in nature, like the flights of birds; and unusual occurrences in nature, like meteors and eclipses. By tradition, omens are often related in dreams.

Oracle. Person who serves as an intermediary between a nonphysical entity and a querent; also a prophecy, or revelation. For more information, see appendix C.

Paranormal. Phenomena that occur beyond the range of what is considered "normal" by current scientific standards for the laws of nature.

Parapsychology. Scientific study of psi and other paranormal activities that cannot be explained by current scientific theories.

Percipient. See Receiver.

Physical medium. A medium in whose presence evidence of the existence of spirit occurs. Such evidential phenomena include telekinesis, ectoplasm, apports, spirit rappings, and voices.

PK. Psychokinesis; the influence of mind over matter without resorting to physical or sensory means. Under this heading fall phenomena like telekinesis, materialization, and spirit rapping. Related phenomena include astral projection and remote viewing.

Planchette. Pointer instrument that accompanies a Ouija board and spells out messages by placing the fingers on it lightly so it can gently glide across the board. Some planchettes have pencils attached to the point so they can reproduce automatic writing and drawing.

Precognition. Foreknowledge of future events without recourse to the normal five senses or any other physical means.

Premonition. Forewarning; intuitive, paranormal awareness of something that is about to happen, often a warning of danger or death.

Prophecy. Vision or prediction of the future of humankind made under the influence of divine guidance. To "prophesy" means to make such a prediction; that is, speak as a prophet.

Psi. In parapsychology, the combined psychic phenomena, ESP and PK.

Psi missing. Psychological phenomenon where the subject subconsciously avoids the intended target, enough times that the misses add up to a score higher than what chance would dictate.

Psychic. As a noun, it refers to a person who is sensitive to paranormal occurrences, or who demonstrates a faculty for paranormal abilities, such as telepathy, clairvoyance, precognition, and the ability to see auras. As an adjective, it refers to paranormal faculties, events, or studies.

Psychical research. Study of psi abilities and paranormal phenomena; parapsychology.

Psychic detective. Individual with enhanced psychic abilities, often a psychometrist or remote viewer, who uses this faculty to aid police departments and others with their investigations.

Psychic medium. A person who acts as a channel for information communicated from spirits and other nonphysical entities to the living, and/or who receives telepathic or clairvoyant messages from a living person at a distance.

Qabala. System of esoteric teachings based on the glyph of the Tree of Life and interpretations of scriptures from Jewish mysticism.

Querent. Inquirer; the individual who comes to have a psychic reading; client.

Rappings. Sharp knocks with no apparent physical cause, purportedly made by spirits of the dead in the presence of a medium. Spirits are said to communicate by these rappings and answer the querent's questions.

Rappomania. Popular reference to the Spiritualist craze of the nineteenth century, so named after the "rappings" supposedly produced by spirits to communicate messages to the living.

Reader/psychic reader. Individual with enhanced psychic abilities who divines the future, perceives the aura, or answer querents' questions by relying on paranormal faculties.

Receiver. Individual who perceives information relayed by paranormal means; percipient. The data the receiver gets may be communicated consciously or unconsciously by a source known as the "sender."

REGs. In psychical research, random events generators; machines that free the researcher to move away from forced-choice targets and give subjects test material that is more likely to sustain their interest.

Reincarnation. Doctrine that the soul is reborn into a different body after death.

Retrocognition. Knowledge of past events obtained by paranormal means.

Séance. Meeting of individuals, often Spiritualists, who usually sit in a circle around a table and attempt to contact spirits of the dead. Often a developed medium leads the sessions.

Second sight. Old Scottish term referring to the ability to sense events at a distance in time and space, often in symbolic imagery. It is considered to be hereditary to a degree.

Seer. One who foretells the future; a diviner; a prophet.

Sender. Also known as the "agent" in ESP experiments, the one whose role is to relay messages or an image to another person, known as the "receiver," by paranormal means, usually using telepathy. Sometimes a sender may transmit information unconsciously.

Sensitive. One who is able to perceive paranormal phenomena, but who does not necessarily need to enter a trance to receive these perceptions. Although the term is synonymous with "medium," most psychical researchers prefer to use this term because it is not associated with Spiritualism.

Sitter. Querent, client, or inquirer; one who sits in a session, called a "sitting" for a psychic reading performed by a medium, often in the attempt to contact disembodied spirits.

Sixth sense. Perception beyond the range of the normal five senses, hence its name.

Spirit. In this text, a supernatural being; a nonphysical entity; the essence of a soul that has died on the physical plane and lives on in another plane

Spirit photography. Practice of taking photographs of purported discarnate entities that mysteriously show up on exposed film of pictures taken of living beings. Wildly popular during the Spiritualist era, the practice was exposed as fraudulent. Also known as "psychic photography."

Spiritualism. Philosophical, socio-religious doctrine developed in the nineteenth century that revolves around the belief that the dead survive in some form as spirits that can be contacted by the living through the agency of a medium.

Spontaneous psi. Paranormal event or experience that occurs naturally without premeditation.

Subconscious mind. Mental activity that occurs without conscious perception.

Target drawings. Images that are telepathically communicated as drawings in psi experiments.

Telepathy. Mind-to-mind transference of thoughts, feelings, and images between a sender and a receiver.

Trance. Altered state of consciousness where the powers of concentration are mobilized to bring meanings and perceptions across the threshold of the subconscious mind. Sometimes while in this state, the individual may be under the control of a nonphysical entity, like a spirit, and communicate messages to the living.

Trance medium. A psychic who enters a trance in order to answer the querent's questions.

Vision/visionary. State of consciousness in which an individual sees something by means other than normal sight. That which is seen may be an object, person, scene, apparition, or prophecy of things to come. A "visionary" is one who is able to perceive beyond present-day physical reality in the above ways.

Wicca/Witchcraft. Neo-Pagan nature religion and way of life based on the worship of the Great Goddess and the Horned God, who represent aspects of the life-force. Many Witches believe in the paranormal and the power of the mind to influence physical reality, and they strive to improve their own abilities in order to help others through divination.

Zener cards. Also known as ESP cards; a deck of cards designed by Karl Zener to be used in psi experiments. The Zener deck consists of twenty-five cards of five simple designs; a star, a circle, a cross, a square, and three wavy lines. The cards eliminate guesses based on a subject's innate superstitions about playing cards.

APPENDIX C

THE MANTIC ARTS

This appendix defines various modes of divination. As you will see, the variety of methods employed and objects and occurrences used are as limitless as the imagination.

Acuto-manzia. Form of divination where the practitioner takes thirteen straight pins and three bent ones, shakes them, and throws them on a table covered with talcum powder, flour, or powdered sugar, and interprets the patterns left by the pins in the powder.

Aeromancy. Divining the future from interpreting cloud formations, the paths of comets, wind currents, or any other aerial phenomena.

Alectromancy. Observing the flight, pecking patterns, and other actions of birds, especially black cocks and hens, to receive knowledge about the future.

Aleuromancy. A kind of ancient Greek version of a fortune cookie, where under the auspices of Apollo, sentences were rolled up in balls of flour and distributed to seekers, who opened the balls and read the words of wisdom contained therein as pertaining to their personal lives.

Alomancy. Divining the future by observing the random patterns made by salt sprinkled on a flat surface.

Alphitomancy. A way to discover the perpetrator of a crime. Suspects were given barley leaves to eat, and the one who suffered indigestion was assumed to be the guilty party. (Obviously this custom dates back to the days before Beano and Tums!)

Anthropomancy. Habit widespread in antiquity of examining the entrails of a sacrificial humans for portents. The grisly custom was practiced by famous diviners like Heliogalabus and Julian the Apostate.

Apantomancy. Suddenly coming upon a wild animal, like a hare, eagle, or buck, and depending on the type of animal met, interpreting the encounter as an omen.

Arithmancy. An early, simple form of numerology practiced in ancient Greece by Platonists and Pythagoreans and in Chaldea whereby the numerologist calculates the values of the letters of a family name and makes a prediction based on the sum. In this way, Achilles' defeat of Hector was foretold. Ideas culled from arithmancy have been incorporated into the Qabala.

Armomancy. During times when human sacrifice was practiced around the world, shoulders of potential victims were examined to see if they would make suitable candidates. Certainly this would be an incentive not to work out one's deltoids too vigorously!

Aspidomancy. Form of divination originating in the Indies where the magician draws a circle, sits in the center, and conjures the Devil to receive answers to questions. This is reminiscent of the practice performed by eighteenth-century ceremonial magicians who, in order to invoke qlippothic entities, drew circles and elaborated them with mystical signs, divinational botanicals, and colors and symbols of the four elements.

Astragalomancy. Throwing like objects of the same size on a table or the ground to divine the future. Examples include dice, bones, runesticks, and stones.

Astrology. system based on the belief that the positions of the stars and other heavenly bodies in the sky at birth influence a person's character and destiny. Two main types of astrology are "horary," which determines the outcome of a particular event or action taken at a certain time, and "mundane," which predicts worldwide phenomena like wars, disease, fates of nations, and natural catastrophes.

Astrometeorology. Science of applying astrology to forecast weather patterns and natural disasters. *The Farmers' Almanac,* available in most supermarkets, gives typical examples of such predictions.

Austromancy. Seeking omens in the sound made by the wind and interpreting cloud signs.

Automatic writing. Technique used by mediums to communicate with the spirit world, which involves a spirit control. The trance medium's hand is guided by the control to spell out messages, or even poetry, music, and in some cases, entire novels. Similar techniques are used for painting, drawing, and speaking.

Axinomancy. Mode of divination that requires an ax. To locate a treasure, heat the ax head until red-hot, and fix the implement in the ground by the handle with the head standing perpendicularly in the air. Next, place a piece of agate on the edge. If it rolls off three times in the same direction, the treasure will be found near that place. If the agate stays on the edge, no treasure will be found in that location.

Belomancy. Chaldean, Greek, and Arabian practice of divining by thrusting feathered arrows into the ground and seeing whether they fall forward, backward, to the left, or to the right.

Bibliomancy. Oracular practice of seeking guidance by opening a book at random and reading the first passage that comes to view. The types of volumes chosen are usually holy books or works of spiritual wisdom. The bibliomancer then meditates on the deeper meaning of the passage and applies it to a current situation. During the Middle Ages, the *Aeneid* was popular in Europe, and Virgil, therefore, gained a posthumous reputation as a magician. John Wesley, founder of Methodism, was fond of opening the Bible and reading aloud whichever passage he first saw to parishioners who came to him to unburden their troubles. If you don't want to use the Bible, I highly recommend *The Book of Tokens* by Paul Foster Case, which is a series of profound tarot meditations and glosses.

Botanomancy. In this botanical mode of divination, vervain and brier branches are carved with questions, then burned.

Capnomancy. Eliciting the meaning from patterns made by smoke rising from a fire after burning jasmine petals and poppy seeds in the flames. In another method by the same name, the smoke rising from sacrificial fires is interpreted.

Cartomancy. Foretelling the future by using any number of decks of cards, including, for example, the myriad of tarot decks that are available on the market, playing cards, or Zener cards. Some readers prefer special fortunetelling decks like The Gypsy Witch and Madame Leonormand. Readers may also choose to combine card reading with numerology, aura interpretation, and astrology (to name a few fields) in order to read the querent's future. Others say that the cards simply represent a vehicle for focusing their psychic attention.

Catoptromancy. Divinatory method originating in Greece where the practitioner holds a mirror under water or in a fountain and interprets the reflection. Also known as "chaomancy."

Ceraunoscopy. Divination by observation of air movements. Instead of waiting around for a breezy day, why not take advantage of twenty-first-century technology and purchase a fan? Write various responses to your question on little squares of paper, and place them upside down on a table or the floor. Then switch on the fan and move it gently over the papers. The first paper to turn up gives you the answer to your question.

Ceromancy. Also known as "cereoscopy," it involves melting wax over a very low heat (so it doesn't burst into flames—a double boiler works well), then slowly pouring the melted wax into a bowl of ice cold water. The operative word here is "slowly," and if you do not get impatient, the wax will first spread into thin layers, and then form distinct shapes to be interpreted. The technique is similar to tea leaf reading, but the shapes are larger and well defined. The ancient Greeks melted beeswax or paraffin in a brass bowl suspended over a slow-burning wood fire, then poured it into another brass bowl that contained the cold water.

Chirogynomy/Chirology. Examining the shape and flexibility of the hand and fingers, nail shapes and sizes, as well as texture and color of the skin in order to determine character. See "palmistry."

Chiromancy. Form of palmistry that involves examining the lines on the hand to determine a person's character, attributes, and likely destiny.

Cledonomancy. Interpreting chance remarks or events in order to determine the outcome of a personal dilemma or a future event.

Cleromancy. Practice of throwing lots with a handful of small, like objects with distinguishing marks onto a flat surface and divining from the patterns that are cast. Examples include dice, small bones, pebbles, beans, peas, and seeds. In ancient Rome, since Mercury was considered the patron of this procedure, the practitioner offered an olive leaf in an urn to this god so that he would lend his power to the reading.

Cleidomancy. Observing the movements of a hanging key to predict the future. By tradition, this should be performed only when the Sun or Moon is in Virgo, and ideally by a virgin or someone born under the sign of Virgo.

Coffee grounds. Like reading tea leaves, the diviner concentrates on interpreting the patterns formed by the grounds at the bottom of a cup of unfiltered coffee after it is drunk and poured with a little water onto a flat, dry, white surface like a saucer. The technique was invented by the Turks and refined in South America. In order to better see the fine images that are formed, it helps to soften your vision by squinting. See "tasseography."

Critomancy. Finding omens in the random patterns made by casting a handful of barley flour or the flour from an offering cake on a flat surface.

Crystalomancy/Crystal Gazing/Crystal Visioning. Seeing visions in a spherical or oval piece of pellucid quartz. Practitioners claim that genuine quartz crystals (as opposed to leaded glass crystal balls) possess highly magnetic qualities that are conducive to clear, precise imaging. Carrington and Whitehead name four possible causes for this phenomenon. conscious or unconscious thought transference from another person; the gazer's conscious or unconscious observations; spirit communication; clairvoyance or prophecy.

planet	day	metal	stone	symbol
Moon	Monday	silver	crystal	crescent
Mars	Tuesday	iron	ruby	sword
Mercury	Wednesday	quicksilver, tin	carnelian	wings of Mercury
Jupiter	Thursday	tin, platinum	topaz	eagle
Venus	Friday	copper	emerald	entwined lovers
Saturn	Saturday	lead	garnet	coiled serpent
Sun	Sunday	gold	diamond, chrysolite	lion's head

Dactylomancy/Dactyloscopy Planetary Correspondences

Dactylomancy/Dactyloscopy. Divination by using a ring in various ways. In one technique, a ring is strung on a thread and like a pendulum, swung over the letters of the alphabet to receive a message. This is a venerable form of divination, alleged to have originated in Egypt or even Atlantis. By tradition, seven different metals representing the seven traditional planets, with individual stones etched with symbols of the ruling planetary deity are used. Each ring represents one of the traditional seven planets, and depending on the nature of the question or the day of the week when the inquiry is undertaken, a specific ring is used. The following chart lists the composition of these rings. If you are intrigued to pursue this method, but don't have the funds to buy the gemstones, substitute colored glass. (See table above for planetary correspondences.)

Daphnomancy. A kind of divination by herbs that uses the leaves of the bay laurel plant *(Daphnis nobilis)*. If the branch thrown on an open flame crackles, good news is on the way. If the leaves smoke or burn silently, then the news is bad or false. If the branch snuffs out the fire, dire tidings are presaged. Bay was highly prized by ancient civilizations, especially the Greeks and Romans, who fashioned victory crowns from the leaves. Many interesting spells involving bay leaves have been passed down to us over the centuries. See this entry in my book *Green Magic* for more lore.

Daturomancy. Indians of the Southwest U.S., Mexico, and South America ingest the pulverized seeds of the *Datura stramonium* (also known as jimson weed) in order to diagnose disease and dream of the future. Datura is a powerful hallucinogen and extremely dangerous. Six ingested seeds can kill an adult. Not recommended.

Demonomancy. Ceremonial magicians of former centuries would evoke qlippothic entities (demons from the Tree of Evil, as opposed to the angelic beings found on the Tree of Life) by casting a circle and invoking them by name in order to persuade them to predict the future. This practice is dangerous because the evil spirits, once unleashed, can wreak havoc on the magician's life. Not recommended.

Dice. A numerological form of divination, also known as "astragalomancy," that does not need anyone other than the querent to make the interpretation. Draw a nine-inch in diameter circle on a piece of paper, hold three dice (small cubes with spots on the six faces, often used in games of chance) in your left hand over the paper, silently ask a question, and throw the dice. Read only the dice that fall within the circle. The total of the number of spots that land face up give the answer according to numerology. You can use dominoes in more or less the same way. Psychic researchers often test subjects to see if they can predict of fall of the dice, or influence the dice to land with certain spots face-up.

Dowsing. See "rhabdomancy."

Dream Interpretation. See "oniromancy."

Eromancy. Persian form of divination whereby the querent filled an urn with water, then went outside, placed the urn where the breezes could play over it, covered his/her head with a napkin, leaned over the urn, and spoke the inquiries. If the water formed bubbles on the surface, it was taken as a positive sign.

Extispicy. See "haruspicy."

Folk divinations. Predicting the future by using old-time methods garnered from agricultural cultures, generally of European heritage. These methods rely on items available on farms and revolve around aspects of rural life such as observation of animal behavior and natural phenomena. For example, how thick the fur grows on barnyard animals is thought to presage the severity of a winter. Slowly dropping egg whites into a glass of springwater is alleged to foretell how many children a person will have. Regrettably these traditions are falling by the wayside as people lose their connection with the Earth.

Gematria. Complex system of divination based on Qabalistic theories for discovering the hidden, mystical meanings of numbers, the alphabet, words, and sentences. The system is based on the Hebrew alphabet and scriptures.

Geomancy. Mode of divination practiced worldwide where the diviner interprets the random patterns made by objects or a handful of earth when they are thrown on the ground or a table, or also dots drawn at random on paper. The types of objects used include river stones, gems, sticks, seeds, shells, earth, etc. The systems used to interpret the patterns vary from simple (e.g.; African bone divination) to complex (e.g.; the I Ching).

Graphology. Science of analyzing handwriting to reveal the writer's character and personality. This is not a mantic art, although many people treat it as if it were.

Gyromancy. "Heady" form of divination whereby the practitioner draws a small circle, inscribes it with the letters of the alphabet, then walks around and around it without stopping. Another person stands by and takes down the letters where the walker stumbles and creates a message from the letters. The object of this nauseatingly giddy procedure is to eliminate any conscious interference of the will. However, when shamanic dancers perform a similar act by hopping and twirling on one foot, the idea is to produce a trance state from where the shaman makes prophetic declarations.

Haruspicy. Etruscan, Greek, and Roman method of foretelling the future by examining entrails of slaughtered animals.

Herbomancy. Divining with herbs, or using botanicals as an aid to other forms of divination. For example, magicians and Witches may encircle the magick mirror with mugwort before scrying. Other divinatory herbs include bay leaves, wormwood, patchouli, beth root, and sandalwood. Calendula and thyme are alleged to help a person see fairies, who in turn, relate messages from the world beyond. Here are some examples of how to practice herbomancy:

Write "yes" on one side of a lotus root slice, and "no" on the other, ask a yes/no question, and flip the root into the air to see which side lands up.

Take equal parts of dried, pulverized mugwort, patchouli, and wormwood, stir together, and spread the mixture on a mirror. Without looking at the mirror, begin to draw random patterns in the dust with your left index finger. When you feel the time is right, stop drawing, and decipher the patterns you formed.

Stuff a six-inch-by-six-inch pillow with mugwort and add fragrant oils of wisteria, cinnamon, and violet. Tuck the little pillow under your regular sleeping pillow, and go to bed. By morning you will have remembered at least one prophetic dream.

The way St. John's wort and sage grow in the garden are supposed to predict the rise and fall of the family's fortunes.

Hippomancy. An ancient Celtic divinatory practice that relies on interpreting the gait of a white horse as it walks behind a sacred cart.

Horoscope. A map of the heavens in the form of a circle divided into twelve signs representing the twelve signs of the zodiac. This map shows the relative positions of the planets and the sun at the precise moment of birth. The positive and negative relationships, known as "aspects," are interpreted by astrologers in a "natal chart" to show a person's natural proclivities. A "progressed chart" is drawn up for a specific date that is as many days after the person's date of birth as the person's age. The chart shows planetary influences on the natal chart for a specific period of time, and is often cast for a calendar year.

Horoscopy. Scanning the sky for stars in order to divine omens.

Hydromancy. Any method of divination by water, where patterns and colors of running water are searched for omens. The hydromancer may also cast stones into a still pool of water and interpret the ripples. An odd number of ripples means a favorable reply, while an even number gives a negative answer.

Try the following form of water divination with your coven. Have the coveners write as many wishes as they choose on little strips of paper, and toss them into the bottom of a clean, empty cauldron. Then fill the pot with pure spring water. Whichever wish rises to the surface first will be the first to be granted; second, the second to occur, etc. Wishes that never rise to the surface will not materialize any time soon.

If you're having trouble choosing a lover, write the names of the lucky candidates on pieces of paper, and roll them up tight like cigarettes. Drop them in a sieve set over a pot of boiling water. Whichever paper unrolls first in the steam names the winner! (See "lecanomancy" for more information.)

I Ching. Chinese method of divination practiced for at least the last millennium. Built around the hexagrams formed by casting yarrow sticks. The meanings are derived according to ancient Taoist and Buddhist books of wisdom. In place of yarrow sticks, coins are also sometimes thrown to make up the hexagrams.

Ichthyomancy. Predictions made by examining fish entrails.

Kephalonomancy. Barbaric practice hailing from ancient Lombardy of examining for omens the boiled head of a goat or ass.

Kleidoscopy. Variation on pendulum divination using a key a piece of string, a ring, and a Bible to reveal the location of hidden treasures. Attach the key to the ring by the string so that when you wear the ring the key is free to swing. Open the Bible to the first page of the Gospel of John, then close the book, marking the place with a finger of your left hand. Extend your right hand wearing the ring horizontally so that the key hangs down from the ring, and concentrate on various possible hiding places. If the key begins to swing, the last place you thought of supposedly conceals the prize. See "cleidomancy."

Lampadomancy. Interpreting the flame rising from an oil lamp or a lighted torch to answer questions and give omens. See "lycnomancy" and "pyromancy."

Lecanomancy. Similar to "hydromancy," only in this method, other small objects such as stones or gems are dropped into a bowlful of water. The sound the object makes as it drops as well as the ripples of water are interpreted. Alternatively, the lecanomancer may cast a drop of oil on the surface of the water and interpret the patterns.

Libanomancy. Seeking omens in the smoke that rises from burning incense. See "pyromancy."

Life reading. Psychic reading that addresses the querent's entire potential. Life readings were made famous by Edgar Cayce.

Lithomancy. Method of determining omens whereby precious stones or pieces of colored glass are scattered on a dark surface to see if they reflect light. The stone that reflects the most light provides the omen. Stone colors carry the same meanings as their planetary correspondences. For example, orange is for communications, purple for power, pink for friendship, etc. They may also reflect the zodiac sign with which they are associated. See my book *Green Magic* for specific stone meanings.

Lychnomancy. Divination by candles. In themselves, lighted candles help create subtle, psychically charged environments conducive to divination, but in this technique lighted candles become the tools of divination. They are examined for color, quality, and movement of the flames.

Choose a candle that represents the planetary color under which your question falls. Select gold or yellow for the Sun, red for Mars, orange for Mercury, purple or sky blue for Jupiter, brown for Saturn, green or rose for Venus, blue or silver for the Moon, purple or green for Neptune, electric blue for Uranus, and black for Pluto.

Place the candle in a holder in a draft-free room, light it, and sit back and meditate on your question for a few minutes. Then voice your query aloud. If the flame burns white or blue, if it surges and gains strength, and if it moves to and fro (toward you), the answer is positive. If the flame sputters, burns low, dark yellow, or red, smokes, or moves from left to right, the answer is probably "no" If the flame rotates in a circular motion, the outcome is uncertain, or you should try your question later. Sparks point to a volatile situation. Expect an upset if the candle flares, then dies down.

Traditionally, lychnomancers use a candelabra in order to arrive at more subtle interpretations. For example, the candle to the left may represent the past, the one in the middle the present, and the candle to the right, the future. One candle burning brighter than the others may mean that the querent is in for a windfall.

Magick mirror. Method of prediction that uses as a focus a round piece of glass painted black on the convex side, placed in a frame for the seer to contemplate. The technique resembles "crystalomancy." Also called a "speculum."

Margaritomancy. Like "cleromancy," only instead of throwing pebbles or peas, the practitioner scatters pearls and studies the haphazard arrangements for signs of the future. As a way to identify a criminal, a pearl is placed near a fire and covered with a vase. The names of the suspects are then read aloud. If the pearl jumps and hits the top of the vase, the name read at that moment is the guilty party's.

Metaynomy. Predicting the future through hypnosis.

Meteoromancy. Finding omens in the paths cut by meteors and shooting stars.

Metopomancy. A form of phrenology where the creases on a person's forehead are examined for clues to character. The forehead is divided horizontally into sections, and the lines on each section are associated with a planet, then interpreted according to that planet's characteristics.

Mind reading. Also known as "mental telepathy," it involves knowing the unexpressed thoughts of another person. It is supposed that the power of the will is invoked in some cases, especially when the reader hypnotizes the subject.

Moleoscopy. Looking at moles on the skin to show personal traits and to predict future events. The mole's location as well as color are taken into consideration. A mole on the toe means success in the arts, on the ankle an ambitious nature, on the knee an extravagant personality, and on the breast an irascible person.

As with so many forms of divination, the color meanings are arrived at by their associations with planets: black for Saturn, bluish-white for the Moon, purplish-brown for Jupiter, light brown for Mercury, honey-colored for Venus, yellow for the Sun, and red for Mars.

While we're on the subject of moles, if you find a mole that pops up suddenly, changes in size, or has irregular borders, see your dermatologist immediately. It may be a melanoma, a dangerous form of skin cancer that can be cured completely if caught right away.

Molybdomancy. Similar to "ceromancy," only in this technique, the diviner pours molten lead or tin slowly into cold water, and makes sense from the ensuing shapes.

Muscle reading. Technique of picking up on the minute, involuntary bodily movements of the querent during a reading in order to identify the person's thought processes, attitudes, and orientations. The psychic may practice this technique consciously or unconsciously, believing that it is divination, and slant the reading to fit the querent's expectations.

Myomancy. Interpreting the movements, coloring, and cries of mice and rats as omens of things to come, usually portents of evil. This practice was popular in ancient civilizations like Egypt, Rome, and Assyria, and is even mentioned in the Bible (Isaiah 16:17).

Necromancy. From Greek words *nekros*, "dead" and *manteia*, "divination." This peculiar tradition, mentioned in the Bible and other ancient works, involves summoning spirits of the dead to give answers about the future. Ceremonial magicians of the eighteenth and nineteenth centuries "resurrected" the procedure by researching ancient texts. The custom goes in and out of style over the centuries and currently in this culture is at a low ebb now, except, perhaps, in some Gothic imaginations.

Necyomancy. Related to necromancy, in this grisly practice, the practitioner examines the nerves of a deceased person to ascertain omens.

Nephelomancy. Predicting the future or answering personal questions by watching cloud formations. The technique shares a common bond with "tasseography."

Numerology. The study of numbers to predict future events and to show strengths and weaknesses of character. In numerology, letters of the alphabet carry numerical equivalents, which in turn, are considered to be fraught with symbolism, so much can be determined by adding together the numerical equivalents of the name and birth date of the querent. Double digit sums can be added together and reduced to a single digit.

Based on the works of Pythagoras and the sixteenth-century magician Cornelius Agrippa, the symbolism of the single digits briefly is: 1 = origin of all things, god; 2 = communion, marriage, coupling; 3 = wisdom, enjoyment; 4 = foundation, permanence; 5 = justice, strife; 6 = beauty, creation; 7 = life, movement, magick; 8 = balance, prosperity; 9 = completion, cosmos.

Oculomancy. Studying people's eyes to understand their character.

Oenomancy. As proof of how important wine was in ancient cultures, this form of divination relies on the appearance of wine once it is poured into a cup.

Ololygmancy. Finding omens in the howling of dogs.

Oneiromancy. From the Greek words, *oneiros,* "dream" and *manteia,* "divination." The Greeks considered this a method of intuitive divination where dreams actually augur the future. Even Aristotle used the word in this way, although he admitted that he believed that sometimes dreams were couched in symbolic terms.

Onomancy. Technique related to numerology in which the letters of a person's name are assigned a number, added together, and reduced to a single digit to give a character analysis or reading. The vowels are ascribed special values. For example, if the vowels add up to an even number, there may be a weakness on the left side of the person's body; if the sum of the vowels totals an uneven number, the weakness is on the right side. No one ever says what happens to the body if a person decides to change his or her name, for example, through marriage. If two people are competing for the same goal, the person whose letters add up to the largest number is predicted to win out. In this system, the etymology of the name is also interpreted.

Onychomancy/Onimancy. Method related to palmistry where the shapes and shadows formed on the surface of the fingernails and the shadows they cast in the sunshine are interpreted.

Ophiomancy. Examining snakes and the trails they cast in order to predict the future.

Oracle. A person who serves as a link between the querent, a supernatural being and a tool for illumination of the individual's present situation, or a shrine where a god speaks directly to humans to answer their questions.

In the first case, the medium becomes possessed by the entity, which then speaks through him/her. The technique is particularly used in Spiritualism, and in the Afro-Brazilian religions of Candomblé, Umbanda, and Macumba.

As a tool for guidance, passages from holy books like the Bible or the Koran are read and meditated on so the querent can gain insight into the current situation. Such books are considered to contain words of wisdom gathered from the collective unconscious of a culture. Methods like the I Ching and even the runes are considered oracles rather than predictors of future events.

Orinthomancy/Oriniscopy. Omens deduced from the flight patterns and songs of birds. In ancient Rome, the method became an integral part of the state religion and merited its own priesthood.

Osteomancy. Interpreting the appearance of a person's bones to show signs of the individual's destiny.

Ouija board. Developing out of the Spiritualist movement, this method of divination involves using a plastic planchette that moves around a board in a game created by William Fuld, or a glass overturned on a table surrounded by cutouts of the letters of the alphabet. Usually two people operate the glass or planchette to point out "yes/no" answers or to spell messages.

Ovomancy/Oomantia/Ooscopy. Using eggs to divine the future. This technique is popular in folk and gypsy divination. One way to practice this method is to boil an egg for a couple of minutes. Take care the yolk is still very liquid. Cut the tip from the small end of the egg and drop the yolk out of the shell drop by drop onto a sheet of white paper. Wait until all the flecks and spots have dried completely, and interpret the images they form.

Palmistry. Alleged to have originated in India and brought to the West either by Gypsies or by Aristotle, who is rumored to have discovered a gold-lettered treatise on the subject. This character reading and medical diagnostic science is based on reading the size and shape of the hand as well as the lines and other distinguishing marks on the palms. Palmistry is also referred to as "chirognomy" and "chiromancy."

Past-life reading. Type of psychic reading that depends on a belief in reincarnation, where the sensitive delves into the Akashic records to draw forth information about the former lives of a querent in order to help the individual deal with recurring karmic issues in this lifetime.

Pegomancy. Observing the bubbles created by spring water or the gurgling of a fountain as a mode of divination.

Pendulum divination. Also known as "radiesthesia," it is a form of "rhabdomancy" where a small weighted object, often made from metal, is attached to a string or chain and allowed to swing free to answer "yes/no" questions. This is one of the most basic modes of divination, and a good technique with which beginners can hone their psychic skills.

Pessomancy. Studying the images formed by pebbles in stream beds to obtain clues to the future.

Phrenology. A way of determining character and mental attributes by studying the bumps on the head. The technique was developed by two Viennese doctors (Gall and Spurzheim) between 1756 and 1828, and was popular in the nineteenth century. The mental attributes fall into two general categories, called the perceptive and the reflective faculties.

Phylorhodomancy. So many unique customs have evolved around botanical divination! For example in phylorhodomancy, the diviner slaps rose leaves (not the petals!) against the hand and, from the sound they make, determines the outcome of an event. The louder the noise the more successful the venture. Let's hope the diviner remembers to dethorn the stems!

Physiognomony. Reading a person's character mainly through facial features, but the whole outer body can be taken into account. The technique was refined by Johan Kaspar Levater (1741–1801). He drew on astrology and planetary correspondences as a framework for his theories. Characteristics include the way a person walks, dresses, gestures, talks, and smiles. The body parts that are examined include the forehead, eyebrows, eyes, nose, mouth, lips, teeth, chin, throat, neck, ears, head, skull, hair, facial hair, height, body proportions, skin, and wrinkles.

In general, a person influenced by the Sun looks cheerful and handsome; Moon people appear cold and pale; the Mars influence produces a pugnacious, crude, masculine countenance; Mercurial faces are slim, fine-featured, and ever young; Venusians are identified by sensuality, attractiveness, and beautiful, feminine features; Saturnine looks are dark, depressed, sallow, and mournful. Sometimes the body parts are likened to animals and behavioral comparisons are drawn.

Psychometry. The art and science of touching or holding a small object and extracting information as to the character, surroundings, history, or influences about the object itself or its owner. Typical objects used include glasses, watches, rings and other jewelry, or a handwritten page.

Pyromancy. Method of predicting the future by interpreting the quality, color, and burning strength of the flames of a wood fire, and by throwing twigs, incense, or dried herbs on the flames to see how they burn. If the fire lights easily it is a good sign, also if it burns quietly in the form of a pyramid. The omen is negative if the fire is difficult to kindle, sputters, or burns dark or smoky. If the flame bends, it signals ill health for someone in the household; if it is suddenly extinguished, the portent is disaster.

Remote viewing. Ability to perceive at a distance real scenes in progress and tell what is going on, where, and who is involved. "Astral projection" is related.

Rhabdomancy/Rhabdoscopy. Also known as "dowsing," the technique for finding water, minerals, oil, buried treasure, pipes, cables, and unexploded bombs involves holding a pendulum or forked stick between the hands and walking slowly over the ground or holding the divining instrument over a large-scale map until it points suddenly to the spot.

Rhapsodomancy. Similar to "bibliomancy," only the book that is opened to a random passage is poetry, and often the entire poem is interpreted rather than the couple of words the diviner first happens to see.

Rune-casting/Runes. Oracular form of divination involving casting on the ground stones that are marked with special symbols. The technique originated in ancient times in Scandinavia, Britain, and the Germanic cultures, and is steeped in myth and tradition.

Sand tray reading. A way of reading one's unconscious thoughts based on Jungian psychology. The seeker takes a tray of sand and is allowed to choose from a myriad of miniature objects ranging from figures of people and animals to trees, flowers, Buddhas, household objects, geometrical shapes, etc. Then the seeker arranges the objects in the tray and mounds the sand to make a little tableau. Sometimes water is used to fashion a tiny stream or pool. When the arrangement is completed, the inner meaning of the tableau is interpreted. The procedure usually takes place in a group under the auspices of a leader trained in Jungian psychology, and everyone helps the seeker make sense of the three-dimensional "tarot card" he or she has created to reveal the person's hopes, fears, wishes, life path, etc. Sherry Hart, of Sherry Hart Art Farm in Boulder, Colorado, is a main proponent of this technique.

Scrying/Skrying. Gazing at the surface of a crystal ball, black mirror, still pool of water, or any smooth, polished surface in order to obtain messages about the future.

Selenomancy. A form of folk divination by which the general shape, color, and phrases of the Moon are studied to give clues to future events, especially those surrounding weather. For example, a ring around the Moon presages wet weather. Much selenomancy has been proved to have a scientific basis.

Shadow reading. In this ancient East Indian mode of divination, the shadow cast by the palms and fingers are measured. Then ancient multilingual tomes are consulted about their meaning.

Shell divination. A type of oracle originating in Africa and brought to the Caribbean and Brazil by slaves. By tradition, the shell game (*jogo de buzios* in Portuguese, *juego de caracoles* in Spanish, also known as *diloggun*) can only be performed by a high priest or by a priestess of the goddess Oxum. The technique usually consists of throwing four, eight, or sixteen shells several times to obtain groupings of shells landing face-down and face-up. Each grouping is associated with a deity, a legend, warnings, and remedies. The shell divination process resembles oracles like the I Ching in that the meanings are complex, deeply symbolic, and require a good deal of training in order to interpret them well. However, the process differs in that the meanings have been handed down orally from generation to generation, and only recently have found their way into writing.

Sideromancy. Studying the shapes produced by burning straws with a hot iron.

Sieve divination. An old Gaelic custom where villagers convened in a barn and hung a sieve from the rafters in order to learn the identity of the perpetrator of a crime. As an elder read aloud the names of each inhabitant, everyone watched the sieve. If it shook or swayed when a name was read, this identified the criminal.

Solistry. Similar to palmistry, this is the study of the shape, size, and markings of the soles of the feet. The art is practiced mainly in the Orient.

Sortilege. Divination by lots. In order to find a clue to the future, people draw straws, cards, or coins, then the card is read, or the short and long straws are interpreted in the hope of finding a good omen. Forms of sortilege include "rhabdomancy," "cleidomancy," "belomancy," and throwing dice.

To eliminate interference from the will, try the following. Write as many responses to your question that you can think of on strips of paper, and fold them up tightly. Go out for coffee with a friend, and without saying why, ask your friend to pick out one piece of paper from those you have folded in the extended palm of your hand. If you're serious about ruling out the will and are really gutsy, ask a stranger to choose one of the papers. Unfold it and read the answer to your question.

Spodomancy. Interpreting images found in the cinders or ashes of a dying fire. In ancient times the ashes were comprised of the remains of sacrificial animals. Modern Witches seek messages in the ashes of the sabbat needfire, which is composed of nine sacred woods. One Summer Solstice we read the cinders and saw a perfectly formed pregnancy rune in the middle of the bottom of the cauldron. One of our members was pregnant, and wouldn't know it for another three weeks. See "tephramancy" for more information.

Stareomancy. Using any of the four basic elements of the Witch's circle for divination. These elements include incense (for air), fire or a lighted candle (for fire), a bowl or chalice of water (for water), and sand or crystal (for earth).

Stolisomancy. Interpreting ways of dressing as clues to character and the future.

Sycomancy. listening to fig tree leaves rustling in the wind, and making predictions based on the sound. Alternatively you can write a question on a fresh leaf, and if the leaf dries slowly, it is a positive omen. If it dries up quickly, then the answer is negative.

Table Tipping/Table-turning. Popular during the heyday of Spiritualism, this mode of divination counts on the participation of spirits of the deceased. The practitioners sit around a card table and rest their hands on it lightly while invoking spirits from the Other Side. The spirit announces itself by suddenly raising or tipping the table. Those in the circle ask questions that the spirit answers in a kind of code by raising the table and making it rap once for "yes" and twice for "no." Numbers can also be assigned to the twenty-six letters of the alphabet, and the messages are laboriously spelled out. Sometimes the members of the circle negotiate with the spirit to abbreviate some words and letters to make the process move along more quickly.

Tarot. Divination by using tarot cards, which include the minor arcana (the four suits of playing cards with the addition of a page) and twenty-two major arcana, whose symbolism is tied into the Qabalistic Tree of Life. See "cartomancy" for more information.

Tasseography. Also known as "tea leaf reading." This ancient Chinese art of interpreting the patterns left by tea leaves in the bottom of a teacup has captured the imaginations of tea drinkers around the world. For a complete discussion of tea leaf reading and an appendix of common tea leaf symbols, see my book *Green Magic*. A word to the wise: in tea leaf reading, as in many of the mantic arts, I advise you not get weighed down by adhering to the precise meanings of the symbols. Listen to your inner voice and let it guide you.

Tephramancy. Another botanical mode of divination where attention is paid to the ashes of burned tree bark, in a way similar to "spodomancy." In this form of divination, words or names are traced in ashes outdoors, and after the first puff of breeze comes along, the letters that remain legible are interpreted.

Thurifumia. Technique whereby the omens are sought in the smoke rising from an incense burner after a petition to the god has been burnt in it.

Tiromancy. Divination using cheese(!). Firm details are not known about this practice. Perhaps people counted the holes in Swiss cheese or the veins in Stilton!

Xylomancy. Seeking omens from the rate at which wood burns on a fire, the shape of the wood that is used to build the fire, and the size, shape, and configuration of wood found in the road. This is obviously an old form of divination that makes sense in rural Colorado, but probably not in New York City.

Zoomancy. Form of folk divination where the interpreter observes the appearance and behavior of animals in order to gain clues to future events.

PALMISTRY MANUAL

As promised in chapter 6, the following is a short manual on the meanings for shape, color, lines, and other qualities of the palm, fingers, and mounts of the hand. As the field of palmistry is vast, this is meant only to be a general guide. For more complete and detailed information, please refer to the books on palmistry listed in the bibliography. Two palm diagrams, one illustrating the major lines of the hand and the other illustrating the mounts and various important markings appear on pages 218 and 219.

GENERAL CHARACTERISTICS OF THE HAND

Fist clenched with thumb tucked in. Defensive, tense.

Fist clenched with thumb stuck out in prize fighter fashion. Belligerent, foolhardy.

Hand relaxed. Open. communicative, outgoing.

Color

Blue. Circulatory problems.

White. Introvert, lacks vitality.

Yellow. Tense, inclined to brood; morose turn of mind.

Pink. Extrovert, communicative, happy, healthy.

Red. Forceful, active, possibly violent or hasty when aroused; may indicate an alcoholic, especially if the lower outer portion of the palm turns red when the fingers are pressed backwards until the skin is taut.

Size

Very small. Mercurial personality, immature, feminine.

Small. Likes to make a big splash; has big ideas.

Large. Analytical, scientific; can perform delicate work like surgery or dentistry.

Very large and clumsy. Strange motivations; bizarre mind.

Texture

Smooth and fine. Impressionable, capable of holding a grudge forever.

Thin. Sensitive; a lover of the arts.

Thin and firm. Still sensitive, but more intellectually inclined.

Moderately fine. Balanced.

Thick. Energetic, active.

Thick and stiff. Inflexible.

Soft and thick. Weak, physically inactive.

Soft and flabby. Unsure of self; hypochondriac.

Muscular and moderately coarse. Knows own mind; independent.

Very coarse. Lacks sympathy for others; unemotional.

Temperature

Warm. Outgoing, healthy; good vitality, warm heart.

Cold. Inward-looking; possibility of ill health; low vitality, cold heart.

Degree of Flexibility

Very flexible. Easily swayed; able to take on various personalities; a linguist or an actor.

Moderately flexible. Easygoing, open to innovations, enthusiastic; loves life; mark of the world traveler.

Stiff. Need for security; likes to maintain contact with homebase.

Very stiff. Intolerant of other people and ideas.

Shape

Narrow. Introverted, philosophical, religious.

Broad. Aggressive, extroverted, physical, driven; a "doer."

Long, narrow, and pointed. The psychic hand; indicates one drawn to the occult, religious studies; hand of the mystic or poet.

Conic, round. Receptive, idealistic; lover of music and beauty; friendly, communicative, receptive, perceptive; may spread self too thin; a traditionally "feminine" hand; the subject perhaps is engaged in the performing arts.

Square. Balanced energies, enterprising, practical, hard-working; the subject likes to get concrete results; loyal and dependable; generally engaged in down-to-earth occupations, like farming.

Spatulate or Flared

Narrow at the base and broad at the top. Inventive, innovative; works well with hands; sees things differently from others; can be irritable and quarrelsome; perhaps an inventor.

Broad at the base and narrow at the top. Excellent physical stamina; unpredictable; restless, perhaps an explorer.

Oblong. Unusual personality, sensitive, creative, but must apply self to realize goals.

Mixed type. Known as "today's hand," as many people in contemporary times possess this type. Careers indicated are journalism, teaching, technical writing, computers, production; tendency to dilettantism.

FINGERS

Nail Shape

Short. Vivacious, blunt; an inquiring mind; could be a journalist.

Long. Serene, contented, forgiving; lover of beauty who values appearances; could be a model.

Narrow. Inactive, sluggish; low energy level.

Wide. Dexterous, sociable, lively.

Short and wide. Dynamic, full of life, unpredictable, prone to irritability.

Long and wide. Creative, artistic, imaginative; could be a writer.

Short and narrow. Gift for impersonation; keen sense of drama; could be an actor/actress.

Long and narrow. Otherworldly, spiritual; could be a mystic or priest/ess.

Square. Analytical, meticulous, rational; lover of details; could be a plastic surgeon or dentist.

Oval. Friendly, sympathetic, adaptable; tendency to be a conformist; could work as a host/ess.

Spatulate. Inquiring mind; talkative, restless; could be a teacher or scientist.

Pointed. Receptive, compelled to express self; could be a psychic, artist, or entertainer.

Nail Color

Many of the meanings of the colors of the nails are equivalent to the meanings of the colors of the hand already given. According to Bevy Jaegers longtime hand analyst and researcher, in her book *Beyond Palmistry: The Art and Science of Modern Hand Analysis* (New York: Berkley Books, 1992, p. 173), nail colors give the following clues to the state of the subject's health:

Blue ring at tip of nail. Lack of oxygen in blood.

Blue ring at base of nail. Poor circulation (less common, lead poisoning).

Deep red nails. High blood pressure.

Pale Nails. Low blood pressure or anemia.

Yellow nails. May indicate fungus infection or or excess beta carotene.

Pale mauve nails. Poor circulation, lack of exercise.

Bright white nails. Usually on index, may indicate fungus from squeezing citrus fruits.

Splitting white nails. Lack of calcium, mineral deficiency.

Other marks on the nails to note follow. To date events, remember that it takes about six months for the fingernails to grow out entirely from the cuticle, and nine months for the thumbnail to grow.

White spots. Tension, fatigue.

Horizontal ridges. Sudden shock to the system.

Vertical ridges. Poor diet or inability to assimilate food properly.

Positioning of Fingers When Raised in the Air or Spread on a Table

This indicates the subject's temporary state of mind.

All fingers close together. Inhibited, cautious, conscientious, thorough.

All fingers spread wide apart. Independent, untouchable, elegant, sympathetic; quick, flexible mind, high vitality; the subject may be encumbered with too many projects.

All fingers arch forward when raised. Anxiety about the future; subject may be at a temporary loss or may feel constricted.

All fingers arch backwards when raised. Vivacious; attuned to life's rhythms; robust spirit.

Knuckles

Smooth. Impulsive; can make split-second decisions; intuitive.

Knotty. Struggles in life; achievement after hard work; analytical mind.

Large. Thorough, dogged worker; sign of the analyst or computer whiz.

Length of the Fingers

Long (longer than seven-eighths of the palm length). Intuitive, elegant, graceful.

Short. Quick thinker; innovative, impatient, restless, blunt, enthusiastic; could be a detective, journalist, or manager.

Average. Balanced personality.

Long tip. Mystic, idealist.

Long middle section. Practical, prescient.

Long base. Sensual, materialistic.

Short tip. Prefers an active lifestyle.

Short middle section. Balanced; the subject may have difficulty communicating thoughts.

Short base. Prefers intellectual lifestyle.

Waisted bottom section. The subject applies self willingly to tasks.

All three sections of equal length. Balanced personality.

The tips of the fingers reveal intellectual and intuitive abilities; the middle section shows the emotional side of the personality and the ability to communicate and integrate mind and matter; the base indicates the vital, material world of the subject and the state of health.

The digits are named for the mounts at their bases. The names of the mounts, in turn, are derived from planets, and express the energies of the planets as they are reflected in humankind.

Index Finger (Jupiter)

Flexible tip. Respectful, attentive, tactful.

Enlarged top knuckle. Possibility of rheumatoid arthritis (only if all the other knuckles are normal).

Leans forward when raised in the air. Self-confidence suffers.

All other fingers slant toward the Jupiter finger when placed on a table. Active, energetic, sanguine.

Wide separation between the Jupiter and Saturn (middle) fingers. Independent thought and action.

Narrow separation between the Jupiter and Saturn fingers. Cautious, reticent.

The Saturn finger leans toward the Jupiter finger. Ambitious, aggressive, successful; a leader.

The Jupiter finger leans toward the thumb. Objective, open-minded; the subject consciously strives to take the lead.

Short. Impressionable, inhibited; lacks self-esteem.

Long. Authoritarian, courageous; a leader.

Very long. Magisterial, overbearing.

Average. Successful in personal relationships; works harmoniously with others.

Straight. Individualist.

Curved. Withdrawn.

Middle Finger (Saturn)

Flexible tip. Virtuous, reliable.

Leans forward when raised in the air. The subject's philosophical attitudes are in doubt.

Wide separation between the Saturn and Apollo (ring) fingers. Frugal; need for security.

The Jupiter finger leans toward Saturn finger. Serious, prudent, conservative; the subject may be thwarted in current efforts.

Short. Unconventional, lonely spirit; eschews power.

Long. Power to focus; enduring, rapacious, serious, dutiful, deeply perceptive.

Average. Balanced, self-controlled.

Ring Finger (Apollo or Sun)

Flexible tip. The designer's flair.

Leans forward when raised in the air. The subject is uncomfortable in the current environment.

Wide separation between the Apollo and Mercury (little) fingers. Restrictions on options at this time.

The Saturn finger leans toward the Apollo finger. The subject's responsibilities are conflicting with the desire for recreation and/or self-expression at this time.

The Mercury finger leans toward the Apollo finger. The subject is destined for success in the arts.

Short. Creativity is somehow being stymied; the subject may be sheltered from surroundings.

Long. Artistic.

Average. Balance between the unconscious and conscious minds; creativity is elegantly and felicitously expressed.

Bulge on lower third of finger. Possibility of kidney infection or high blood pressure.

Little Finger (Mercury)

Flexible tip. Ear for music, talented mimic.

Leans forward when raised in the air. A need to be loved and accepted.

All fingers slant toward Mercury. Introverted; actions are governed by the emotions and instincts.

The Apollo finger leans toward the Mercury finger. Persuasive, optimistic, independent, unconventional.

The lower knuckle bulges toward the Apollo finger. Possible gynecological or prostate problems.

The Mercury finger leans away from the other fingers. The subject is free to make own decisions.

Short. Overcommitted, quick-tempered; the subject may feel inferior to others.

Long. Shrewd, intuitive; the subject possesses the gift of gab and mimicry; this is the finger of the lawyer, actor, salesperson, and scientist.

Average. Expressive; the subject enjoys a positive relationship with the opposite sex.

Horizontal lines on the middle and lower sections. Dietary problems.

Thumb (Venus)

From the palmist's point of view, the thumb is perhaps the most revealing digit of the hand. Its mobility is one of the indicators that distinguishes humans from other animals on the evolutionary scale, and palmists have always considered that the thumb represents the will. Moreover, this digit is associated with Mount Venus, the fleshy area that lies below it, and which designates vitality and drive.

Stiff. Stubborn, dogmatic, restrained; a long-range planner.

Stiff at first, then flexible. Defensive.

Flexible. Generous, romantic, discriminating, extravagant; unwilling to make decisions for others.

Very flexible (can be bent back to the palm). Agile, adaptable.

Bent like a claw. Grasping; mark of a misanthrope.

Short. Spontaneous; success is achieved after trials and tribulations; when combined with a long Apollo finger, it reveals someone willing to take risks; a gambler, a stockbroker.

Long. Persistent, goal-oriented.

Small. Instinctive, high-strung; lacks staying power.

Large. Resolute; a planner and a motivator; someone who conscious develops talents.

Thin. Well-bred; thin tip, low energy reservoir; thin bottom, nonjudgmental.

Flat. Cerebral, unathletic.

Thick. Forceful.

Thick tip. Energetic.

Thick bottom. Stubborn.

Well-developed. Sensitive; may indicate an artist, dancer, musician, or athlete.

Waisted base. Tactful.

Bump on tip. Active in the arts.

Chunky ball. Quick-tempered, impulsive.

Soft. Lethargic; indifferent sense of humor.

Broad. Unflappable, enduring.

Narrow. Impetuous, lively; a world-traveler.

Held close to the hand. Secretive, reserved.

Held away from the hand. Broad-minded.

Long tip. Tenacious, self-centered.

Long base. Irresolute; the subject may tend to see all sides of issues.

All the fingers set straight across the palm. Courage and self-respect.

Low-set fingers. Timidity and repression.

MOUNTS

Mounts are the padded areas directly under the fingers. They derive their names and meanings from the planets. Mount Jupiter resides under the index finger, Saturn beneath the middle finger, Apollo, or the Sun Mount under the ring finger, and Mercury below the little finger. The padded area beneath the thumb is called Mount Venus. Mount Luna or Moon governs the cushions on the outer lower part of the palm. Mars has two mounts: Active Mars is to the side of the thumb, above Venus; passive Mars is located on the outside of the palm between Mounts Mercury and Luna. Modern palmists distinguish Mount Neptune, a small mount between Luna and Venus at the base of the center of the palm, Mount Uranus, in the center of the palm, and Mount Pluto, on the upper third of Mount Luna.

Mounts display quantity and quality of energy. "Good" mounts, in general, are high and firm. They radiate active, positive energy. Medium-sized mounts show that the energy is mentally directed. Flat mounts, particularly when coupled with broken, meandering, chained lines, reveal nervous, disruptive energy often at cross purposes to itself. However, if the major lines are clearly marked, the nervous energy can be positively directed.

Mount Jupiter

Leadership, authority, professionalism; possible careers include guidance counseling, teaching; protection, honors, flow of ideas, abundance, wanderlust, powers of concentration, love of children and animals, religious inclinations.

High. Dynamite personality; can be bossy; high and broad. Tends to be sybaritic.

Medium. Confident, optimistic, realistic, philosophical; indicates sense of showmanship.

Low. Lacks drive or enthusiasm; the subject may carry a perpetual chip on shoulder.

Drift. If the pad drifts toward Mount Saturn, the subject is conservative, strong, and direct.

Incidental Markings

Cross. Happy marriage.

Little vertical lines. Ambition.

Triangle. Diplomacy.

Grid. Supercharged personality; an egotist.

Square. Teacher, entertainer.

Mount Saturn

Mount Saturn represents attitudes toward duty and responsibility. It also indicates the subject's degree of self-control, discipline, and balance of personality.

High. Morbid, gloomy (especially if flabby), highly sensitive; a sharp, observant mind; the subject is acutely aware of the tragedy of life; may have occult leanings; often this is the mark of the satirist or one who is occupied in lonely pursuits.

Medium. Balanced, self-reliant.

Low. Congeniality of mind; a stable personality.

Missing. Feelings are easily hurt.

Drifts toward Mount Apollo. The subject tends to stabilize creativity and direct it into practical avenues of manifestation.

Incidental Markings

Circle. Physical or mental imprisonment.

Square. Protection from disaster.

Cross. Unhappiness, tragedy, frustration.

Triangle. Occult talents.

Many little, vague, horizontal lines. Depressive moods; the subject may tend to blow events out of proportion.

Mount Apollo (Sun)

This mount shows creativity, originality, and fulfillment of one's inner needs and desires.

High. Unique creativity; the subject is considered "lucky" by others.

Medium. Balance is achieved between the conscious and unconscious sides of the personality; the ability to create in a form that can be apprehended readily by others.

Low. Shy, retiring.

Drifts toward Mount Mercury. Adept at the performing arts; the subject is endowed with flashes of insight and a spark of genius.

Incidental Markings

Star. Fame is achieved in this lifetime; well-developed powers of discrimination.

Grill. The subject must work hard to achieve fame.

Whorl. Creative talent.

Small, vertical lines. Abilities developed in various creative fields; more than three lines means that talents are scattered.

Triangle. Hard work in the arts will be rewarded.

Mount Mercury

Traditionally, the god Mercury is the messenger of the subconscious mind. In the hand, this mount represents unusual qualities that are hard to define, like the knack of self-expression and the capacity to think and act quickly and adapt to different situations.

High. A quick mind that readily transmits knowledge; professions include teacher, journalist, healer, and one adept at the occult; if extremely high, the subject possibly is controlled by the sex drive.

Medium. Clever, perceptive; an astute business person.

Low. Lack of interest in medicine or business.

Extremely large. When coupled with a long little finger, it may indicate a deceiver, a thief, or a sleight-of-hand magician.

Incidental Markings

Cross. Double-dealer.

Square. Able to make quick decisions.

Star. Distinction in science, medicine, the arts, or commerce.

Tiny vertical lines. A healer or a doctor.

Cross. A writer.

Mount Luna (Moon)

This mount of the imagination stores all memories, both conscious and unconscious of one's past, ancestors, and race. Luna also discloses the subject's creative powers.

High. Well-developed imagination; ability to express dreams and fantasies to the outer world; strong writing talent.

Medium. Average use of imagination.

Low. Prosaic use of imagination; the subject likes to stay at home in familiar surroundings and enjoys quotidian pursuits.

Incidental Markings

Whorl. Exuberance.

Horizontal lines. Urge to travel.

Triangle. Prophetic abilities.

Sometimes this mount bulges at the outside of the hand. If this occurs on the bottom third of the mount, the subject is fascinated by racial memories and would make a superior archeologist, Jungian psychologist, or anthropologist. If the bulge occurs in the middle third, the subject is proficient at unraveling ancestral memories, and could enjoy a career as a genealogist. If the top third bulges, the subject recalls childhood memories easily and can turn these into stories. Sometimes a well-developed mount signifies a sailor or someone who likes to travel on water. Coupled with a long, slender hand, the subject possesses the drive to interpret creative thoughts in concrete form. This may also indicate a propensity for the interpretive arts. If a well-developed mount occurs on a long, bony hand, it points to a philosopher. However, if the mount is fleshy and the hand broad, the possessor is a daydreamer, unable to achieve goals.

Mount Mars

Not everyone possesses a well-defined Mount Mars. However, if active Mars is high and firm, the subject is a brave individual who can be relied upon in emergencies. If active Mars is flat and other characteristics so confirm, the subject is reticent and introverted, and needs to live in a nurturing, tranquil environment. A high, firm passive Mars signals ambition and drive to initiate projects. A low passive Mars indicates the reverse. If both mounts are high and well-padded, the subject is aggressive, persistent, and will fight to achieve goals.

Mount Venus

This mount indicates passion and zest for life. Along with other characteristics such as skin color and texture, it reflects the subject's vitality and energy level.

High. Passionate, sensual, emotive.

Large and soft. Lover of pleasure, sensualist, egotist.

Thick and hard. A combative nature.

Medium. Balanced emotional and cerebral life.

Low. Passions are manifested through the intellect.

Incidental Markings

Grill. The subject has a need for affection.

Vertical lines. A dancer, model, or artist.

Horizontal lines crossing the mount and cutting through the life line. Obstacles.

Mounts Uranus, Neptune, and Pluto

Mounts Uranus, Neptune, and Pluto are relatively new to the study of palmistry, and more information needs to be gathered before these mounts can take a firm place within the scheme of the hand. Uranus hardly ever rises as an actual mount in the hollow of the hand, but if the hollow is quite deep, the subject may be prone to fits of depression. The influence of Neptune is viewed as indirect. Neptunian energy revolves around enchantment, mystery, captivation, and deception. A tiny bulge in this area may mean the subject is psychic, loves mystery stories, or enjoys collecting antiques. Pluto is linked to the concepts of regeneration, racial memory, violent upheaval, mass movement, and occult forces. If this mount is covered with a widening, sunburst of lines, the subject may be drawn to aviation or be a world traveler.

THE MAJOR LINES

As you begin to analyze the lines on the subject's hand, consider the following points. A few, clearly marked, deep lines indicate a radiant personality and mature character. Many poorly defined lines crisscrossing the hand like a spider web reveal nervous energy and impressionability. If many lines cross the palm, but the major ones are strong, intense creativity is affirmed. Few, sketchy lines indicate poor health and vitality, and may be a harbinger of a short life if the subject does not take care. Chained and broken lines disclose difficulties in some aspects of the subject's life. Pink lines mean healthy attitudes; red lines proclaim an abundance of emotional energy; blue lines signify an energy block.

Life Line

The life line, which runs from between the thumb and forefinger around the base of Mount Venus, shows the type of physical vigor and mental resolution as well as the capacity to cope with obstacles and reversals. Contrary to popular superstition, the length of the line does not indicate how long a person will live.

Short. The subject's ancestors may have been short-lived; the subject may need to live by the wits; if short and strong, the line shows good vitality and exceptional productivity.

Long. Possible longevity in the family background; "good genes."

Light. Craving for tranquillity; a life best led in the country or suburbs; if light and short, may indicate health problems or low energy reserves.

Deep. Steady, persistent.

Narrow arc follows close to thumb. Shows an introvert with limited energy.

Wide arc. Gregarious, warm-hearted, extroverted, enthusiastic, energetic.

Swings toward Mount Luna. An urge to travel may determine the subject's life pattern; imaginative lifestyle; the subject is restless, animated, and independent.

Arc starts narrow, then widens. The subject strives to throw off fetters and develops an original lifestyle.

Branch to Mount Jupiter. The subject succeeds by sheer determination.

Parallel line on inside of life line. Traditional palmistry says that the subject is protected, especially in matters of health, as if by magic; Jaegers contends that the line shows that the subject has made a successful effort to change life patterns for the better, so that by force of will, the subject has become a stronger person.

Branches rising from the life line. Concentrated effort in endeavors brings success.

Horizontal bars cutting the life line. Illness, troubles, energy blocks.

Breaks in life line. Complete separation with the past; life recommences anew.

Fork on the line. Diminished vitality.

Grill on the line. Period of tension or hyperactivity where the subject's energy is frittered away; obstacles.

Life and head (the first horizontal line above the life line) join for more than one-third of the life line's length. Overly cautious; indicates a subject who is heavily influenced by family and who likes to stay close to home.

Life and head lines touch. Balance between caution and impulse.

Life and head lines separate slightly. Independence of thought an action.

Life and head lines separate widely. The subject may behave rashly, impulsively.

Life line begins chained or with a circle. Childhood illnesses.

Head Line

Crossing the palm from Mount Jupiter to Mount Mercury: The head line relates to the quality of the intellect.

Long. Sound intellect, versatility; a thorough researcher.

Short. Masterful powers of concentration, phenomenal memory, one-track mind.

Straight. Practical; firm thinking patterns.

Curves to Mount Luna. Sensitive, creative, flexible; an unconventional thinker; possibly a mystery writer.

Curves to Mount Apollo. A good memory.

Curves close to the life line. Reticence; the subject hesitates to make decisions.

Wavy. The subject is easily distracted; if only slightly wavy, it shows a malleable mind.

Double line. Intensified mental abilities; the mark of the linguist, or someone who combines the virtues of mystical and practical thinking.

Branch to Mount Luna. An enigmatic, ingenious person who is often aware of own complexity; a writer.

Branch to Mount Apollo. An appreciator of beauty.

Starts inside the life line. Defensiveness, vulnerability.

Deeply hewn line or star at the end of the line. A razor-sharp mind.

Little, knife-like cuts on the line. Tendency toward headaches; if the lines are deep and wide, then the subject may suffer from migraines.

Dots on the line. Stress, lack of potassium.

Heart Line

The uppermost major horizontal line of the hand is called the heart line, and it usually extends from Mounts Mercury to Jupiter, more or less parallel to the head line. It is so named because in traditional palmistry it gauges the emotions, in particular, feelings in matters of the heart. These days, many palmists examine this line as a measure of the subject's circulatory state of health and general vitality.

Long. The subject idealizes the object of the affections and is expressive with emotions.

Short. Selfish view of love; impassive personality, especially if the line is lightly etched.

Straight. Moderate emotions with displays of affection; attraction is more mental than physical; if the straightness parallels the head line, the emotions are firmly under control.

Upward curve. Physical attraction is fundamental to this person; a romantic, possibly self-denying nature in love relationships; a loyal lover; an emotional personality.

Set high on palm. Objectivity in love; the subject does not let emotions affect decision-making.

Set low on palm. Subjectivity in love; the subject tends to take things personally.

Ends on Mount Jupiter. A happy, stable marriage; idealistic opinions in love matters; if the line ends high on Mount Jupiter, the subject is liberal with the affections; if it terminates on the top of Mount Jupiter, it is a warning of a jealous nature; if it finishes low, idealistic attitudes prevail.

Terminates between Mounts Jupiter and Saturn. A more realistic approach to love, but nonetheless affectionate; the subject seeks harmony in all relationships.

Ends on Mount Saturn. The subject searches long and hard to find true love, and may experience many partners; when things are not going well, the emotions may be turned inward and allowed to fester.

Finishes in a fork. The subject is excitable, spontaneous, and oblivious to conventions.

Begins in a fork. Loyalty is not the subject's strong suit; desire to have many partners and few commitments.

Tiny cuts or droplets at the end of the line. Possible indication of diabetes.

Chained and wavy. Emotional upheavals.

Fate (Career) Line

Not everybody possesses a fate line, and the absence of one does not imply that the subject's destiny is star-crossed. It merely may mean that the subject's own measures of success are not the same as those generally valued by society. From personal experience, I can say that the fate line can develop or modify over the years. I have been monitoring my own palm since I was twelve, and have witnessed development from no fate line at all to one that only weakly extended up as far as my head line. Later it strengthened and lengthened, and now I possess a reasonably strong, unbroken line that begins on Mount Luna and ends under my Saturn finger with a large diamond on the top and a branch at the base that attaches to my life line. Jaegers says that the branching shows that I have developed more than one career, and a career that really excites me, which would be my writing.

Hipskind, noting the line's position in the center of the hand, says that the fate line integrates the forces of the active and passive, conscious and unconscious minds. She reflects that its presence shows the subject's desire and ability to work hard to achieve goals.

Clearly visible. Success in endeavors because goals are well-defined.

Indistinct, broken, or wavy. Ups-and-downs in career; changes in plans.

Starts on Mount Luna. Fame as a writer, entertainer, or politician.

Starts low. Success achieved through independent personal effort; ambitions formed in childhood.

Starts high (over head line). A late bloomer, but nonetheless, successful.

Dies out at the heart line. Efforts to earn own livelihood dwindle after about age thirty; often found on the palms of people who make their career in the home.

Terminates past the head line. Ultimately victorious; if the line shifts after the head line, two careers, or a change in calling is indicated.

Stops on Mount Apollo. Triumph in the arts.

Branches to the life line. Progress through personal efforts; possibility of two totally different professions.

Bars across the line. Hindrances to career.

Vertical lines rise from the fate line. Marriage or other partnerships will influence the subject's vocation.

Square at the end of the line. A helpful patron is indicated.

Stars or circles. Fame and fortune; if the star occurs at the end of the line, success is achieved at the end of the subject's life.

Double line. Good fortune; a complex but well-integrated personality.

Minor Lines

Apollo (Sun) Line

This is a minor line that runs vertically under the ring finger. It is not necessarily present in the palm, but when it is, it indicates success in creative pursuits and skillful expression and communication of energy welling up from the depths of the subconscious mind. The longer and straighter the line the more meritorious the effort. Two or more lines indicate versatility in fields of music, the humanities, and the arts. If the Apollo line connects with the life line, the subject's ancestors may have been similarly gifted. If the line curves toward Mount Mercury, the subject will realize talents in a practical way.

Health Line

The health line extends from the life line over to Mount Mercury. It is one of the few lines better not to possess, especially when ill-defined, because it can reflect poor health, especially bronchial trouble. A strong line shows an individual who is well aware of subtle, personal bodily changes. Since the line terminates on Mount Mercury, a robust health line may also indicate sharp business acumen.

Marriage Line

This short line, when it exists, begins at the outside of the hand and moves across Mount Mercury above the heart line. Modern palmists often ignore it, but the traditional meanings which follow are nonetheless fascinating. By tradition, many marriage lines mean several love affairs or marriages. A fork at the end of the line indicates separation or divorce, while a fork at the beginning is said to presage a long engagement. A cross at the end of the line is interpreted as the death of a partner. Small, vertical lines crossing the line signify offspring, or at least (in a female) the number of children the person is able to produce.

Special Markings

Cross of St. Andrew. Also known as the mystic cross, it links the head and heart lines, showing one who will develop great intuitive and spiritual powers in this lifetime.

Ring of Solomon. A line on Mount Jupiter that extends in a ring around the index finger and affirms astute powers of intuition and discernment of character as well as immense spiritual potential.

Many Lines. Known as lines of influence; if horizontal and they extend across Mount Venus to the life line, but do not cross it, they presage financial aid from friends or relatives.

Escape Line. A short, curvy vertical line on Mount Neptune indicates escape through the imagination. If it links to the health line, the escape may be through alcohol or drugs.

Thumb Chain. A chain around base of the thumb accentuates a stubborn personality.

Battle Cross. A cross on Mount Mars shows one who will sacrifice everything to a cause; depending on other signs in the hand, perhaps the subject also lives recklessly, or is aggressive.

Girdle of Venus. A line above the heart line that rings around from the Saturn finger to the Apollo finger and affirms intuitive abilities and an emotional, outgoing nature.

Islands. Usually unfavorable sings. On the heart line under the ring finger, it refers to eye trouble. If the island is rounded with a central dot, watch out for glaucoma. On the outer, bottom edge of a female palm in the middle of the wrist, it may indicate enlarged ovaries or cysts.

Loops. Usually they are a positive sign, referring to such abilities as sense of humor, a good memory, and common sense.

Telepathic Dimple. This term coined by Jaegers, refers to a depression in the lower, outer edge of the hand that shows telepathic communication between minds — the classic sign of a mind reader!

Many Triangles. Well-honed skills.

Stars. Good luck.

Grills or Crosses. Difficulties, obstacles; sometimes protection.

Whorls on the Fingertips. An original mind.

Loops on the Fingertips. An idealistic mind.

The ulnar loop is a large horizontal loop on the lower third of Mount Luna, which can diagnose Downs syndrome in babies. Downs syndrome is confirmed by a a combined head and heart lines that stretches all the way across the palm. Evidently this "simian crease," as it is called, and the ulnar loop are made by restrictions in blood flow while the fetus is in the womb. Jaegers has specified this marking as a genetic marker, indicating inherited genetic problems of some sort. However, if the loop appears higher on Mount Luna, and is not accompanied by the simian crease, it merely means that the subject loves nature and may wish to pursue a career in the outdoors.

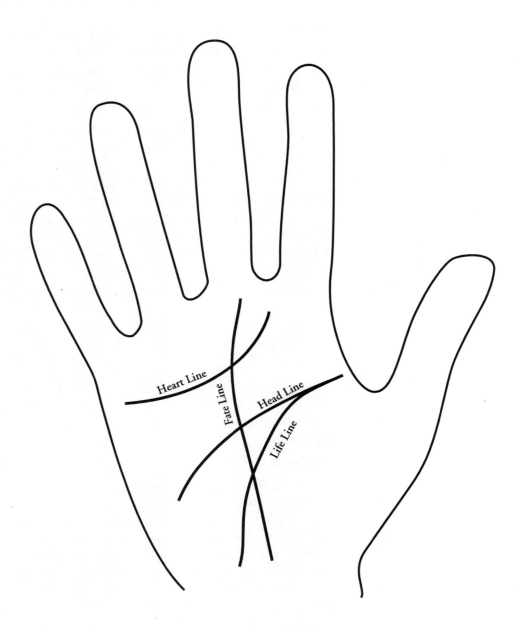

Heart Line

Fate Line

Head Line

Life Line

Major Lines of the Hands

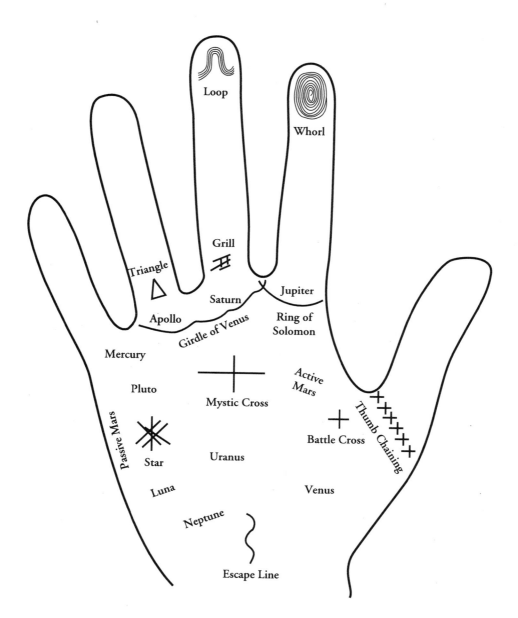

Loop

Whorl

Grill

Triangle

Saturn

Jupiter

Apollo

Ring of
Solomon

Girdle of Venus

Mercury

Active
Mars

Pluto

Mystic Cross

Passive Mars

Thumb Chaining

Battle Cross

Star

Uranus

Luna

Venus

Neptune

Escape Line

The Mounts and Some Markings

PSYCHICS AND CHANNELERS AROUND THE WORLD

The following list contains the names, locations, and areas of specialization of psychics and channelers who answered the survey, and who do not wish to remain anonymous. True to the ideas put forth in this book, which maintains that all people can develop psychic abilities, not every practitioner listed is "famous." Indicated is the name, advanced degree (if any), location, type of reading or focus of ability, and whether the person is an author so that the reader can seek out more information on the entry.

The appendix also includes names of some practitioners who did not answer the survey, but who are well known in their fields. Naturally, in some cases of those who chose not to respond to the survey, full information could not be provided.

The list is not intended to be all-inclusive, as this would take up an entire volume, but it is meant to give an idea of various geographical locations and diverse areas of specialty.

A

Vivienne Adam. Denver, Colorado. Tarot, astrology, ogham.

Alia, D. M. Polson, Michigan. Clairvoyance, numerology, soul cycles, astrology.

Kim Allen. Brooklyn, New York. Tarot.

Marisa Anderson. Scarsdale, New York. Private sessions for personal life, health, business, animal readings.

Evelyn Gurley Anhalt. Denver, Colorado. Tarot, automatic spirit writing

Darryl Anka. Woodland Hills, California. Channeling.

Anzus-Auriel. Certified Gestalt Psychologist. Durango, Colorado. Sacred tarot, Holy Qabala, dream work, spiritual pathways, Gestalt process, numerology.

Robert E. Ater. Monmouth, Illinois. Dowsing. Author.

B

Elwood Donald Babbit. Vershire, Vermont. Full trance channeling.

Bernice Barlow. Wellington, Nevada. Psychometry of place, Shamanism. Author.

Jane Barrett. Schenectady, New York. Card reading.

Joel Michael Beebe. Dearborn Heights, Michigan. Tarot.

Clarisa Bernhardt. Winnipeg, Manitoba, Canada. Aura readings, earthquake (and other) predictions, missing persons.

Jan Billings. Glastonbury, England. Color therapy, aura readings, psychic portraits, tarot, life path readings.

Barbara Bishop. Marysville, Washington. Numerology. Author.

Sarasvati Boyet, M.A. Fort Collins, Colorado. Spiritualist medium, clairvoyance, intuitive healing, counseling.

Carol Bridges. Nashville, Indiana. Channeling, Feng Shui, Wild Grace School of Feng Shui. Author.

Sylvia C. Browne, M.A.. Campbell, California. Past, future events, spirit contacts, deep trance readings.

Sue Burton-Hidalgo. Southgate, Michigan. Soul-level readings, channeling, angelic communication, healing. Author.

Martin Butz. Joliet, Illinois. Astrology.

C

Ken Carey. Channeling.

Bertie Marie Catchings. Dallas, Texas. General Psychic readings, palmistry, psychic detection.

Susan Chicovsky. M.A. Evergreen, Colorado. Spiritual counseling, including physical, past life, emotional, mental (changing patterns). Vision Light, Inc.

Cleopatra. Master of Divinity. Boulder, Colorado. Tarot, channeling.

Thomas Csere. Woodstock, Connecticut. Astrology, intuition, psychic readings. Author.

Lady Sara Cloudwalker-Carter. Glendale, Oregon. Psychic readings, tarot, pendulum, shamanic visioning. Author.

D

Arlene Dahl. Sparkill, New York. Tea leaves, astrology. Author.

Cyndi Dale. St. Paul, Minnesota. Intuition, Christ-based spiritual healing, life issues, counseling. Author.

Deborah. St. Louis, Missouri. Tarot, astrology, numerology.

Joseph DeLouis. Chicago, Illinois. Psychic and spiritual readings, healing, hypnotherapy. Mind Perfection Institute.

Linda Domin. Miami, Florida. Handwriting analysis. Author.

Kathy Lynn Douglass. Willow, Arkansas. "Straight" psychic readings, tarot, crystal oracle, runes, the Alchemist, stone oracle. Author. Clinical Director of the Denali Center.

E

Shirley T. Edens. Peralta, New Mexico. Karmic and life readings, numerology, astrology. Author.

Dar Emme. Westminster, Colorado. Psychic detection, psychometry, general psychic readings, angelic communication, channeling, tarot. Author.

F

Robert A. Ferguson. San Jose, California. Psychic readings, Spiritualist medium. Author.

Ann Fisher, M.A. Albany, New York. Psychometry, astrology, past lives. Author.

Jean Ann Fitzgerald. Reno, Nevada. Graphoanalysis, numerology.

Thomas Fitzgerald. Reno, Nevada. Interpretation of input from individuals' spirit helpers, health readings.

Morris Fonte. New York, New York. Clairvoyance, telepsychic readings.

Dancing Fox. Carson, California. Tarot, Druidic readings, counseling, animal and nature readings, healings.

John C. Fox. Nevada City, California. Technical research, personal readings.

Gavin Frost, Ph.D. New Bern, North Carolina. Runes, tarot.

G

Lee R. Gandee, M.A. Columbia, South Carolina. Hexerei incantations and rituals for healing.

Rev. B. Anne Gehman. Springfield, Virginia. Clairvoyance, clairaudience, psychometry, aura readings, spirit communication.

Ginger. Aurora, Colorado. Clairvoyance, tarot, stones, psychometry, channeling, spirit channeling.

Morning Glory. Denver, Colorado. Tarot, channeling, empathic readings.

Graybear. Cheraw. Colorado. Tarot, ghost/spirit contacts, Reiki healing, astral/Shamanic "journeys."

Paul Guercio. Cambridge, Massachusetts. Business and career readings through computer.

H

E. Harte. Tacoma, Washington. Spiritual studies from strands of hair, numerical life path studies. Author. Editor of the *HARTE Beat.*

Patricia Hayes, Ph.D. McCaysville, Georgia. Soul-life readings, Akasha, angel readings and communication, psychic consultations, psychic portraits.

Maya Heath. Parkville, Missouri. Egyptian Oracle (creator).

Jim Hecker. Wilmington, North Carolina. General psychic readings, cards, psychic detection.

Lynda Hilburn-Holland, M.A., C.C.H. Boulder, Colorado. Psychic readings, tarot, psychotherapy, hypnotherapy, past life regression, future life progressions.

Hilda Holyman. London, England. Spiritualist medium.

Irene Hughes. Chicago, Illinois. General readings, prediction, psychic detection, ghost hunting. Author. Founder of the Golden Path.

J

Bevy Jaegers. Sappington, Missouri. Diagnostic hand prints. No reading for public. Author.

Jerry. San Juan Chamelco, Guatemala. Astrology. Author.

Joy. Auckland, New Zealand. Numerology, card readings.

K

Joyce Keller. Islip, New York. Astrology, psychic readings on the air. Author.

Amelia Kinkade. West Hollywood, California. Animal communication.

Andrea J. Kramer. Los Angeles, California. Clairvoyance, psychic detection.

L

Martha C. Lawrence. Escondido, California. Astrology. Author.

Kurt Leland. Jamaica Plains, Massachusetts. Channeling. Author.

Lee Lewis. Adrian, Michigan. Astrology, general psychic readings. Author. Editor of *The Psychic News*.

Carol Ann Liaros. Buffalo, New York. Psychometry. Author.

Lina. Hudson, Michigan. Palmistry, psychic aura reading, runes, dream interpretation.

Susan Luning. Tigard, Oregon. Soul/subconscious readings and healings.

Anda Lys. Los Angeles, California. Clairvoyance, voice channeling, astrology, telepathy, research.

M

Marie. Auckland, New Zealand. Tarot.

Mrs. M. Chester, Vermont. Tarot.

Matthew Manning. Cambridge, England. Automatic writing, telepathy, precognition, poltergeist and apport investigation, psychic art. Author.

Ruth Manning. Ontario, Canada. Cards, numerology, I Ching. Author.

Armand Marcotte. Mesa, Arizona. General psychic, business, spiritual, and card readings; astrology; psychic detection. Author.

Connie Marcum. Barbers Point, Hawaii. Written readings from photographs and personal items, handwriting analysis, numerology, astrology, biorhythm, psychometric.

Joseph W. McMoneagle. Nellysford, Virginia. Remote viewing. Executive Director of Intuitive Intelligence Application.

Patricia Mischell. Cincinnati, Ohio. Spirit communication; personal, angel, and animal readings; past lives; psychic detection. Author.

Betty Muench. Albuquerque, New Mexico. Soul readings received telepathically from Spirit, psychometry.

Nancy F. Myer. Greensburg, Pennsylvania. Telepathy from personal readings, psychic detection, spiritual healing by direct laying on of hands, psychometry, retrocognition, aura readings. Author.

N

Nancy Elizabeth. Florida. Clairvoyant.

O

Sydney Omarr. Astrology. Author.

Connie Marie O'Very. Adrian, Michigan. Tarot, past lives, psychometry, sun sign astrology, spirit information.

Owl Woman, Scranton, Ohio. Shaman visioning. Author.

P

Jane Palzere. Newington, Connecticut. Psychic reading.

Pat. Albuquerque, New Mexico. Music channeling.

Helena Paterson. Hampshire, England. Celtic astrology. Author.

Catherine Penn, D.M. Lakewood, Colorado. Spirit guide portraits, past lives, aura colors.

Robert J. Petro, M.A. Sedona, Arizona. Trance channeling, psychic detection, exorcism, Shamanic healing. Author.

Robert Michael Place. Saugerties, New York. The Angels Tarot (cocreator) Author.

PoTO. Westwood, California. Intuition.

Jack Pursel. California. Channeling. Author.

R

Ina Rae. Ponderay, Idaho. Pendulum, general psychic readings. Editor/Publisher of *Craft/Crafts Magazine.*

Silver RavenWolf. Mechanicsburg, Pennsylvania. General psychic readings, runes.

Nancy Regalmuto. Bellport, New York. Personal, health, business, animal readings; psychic healings; ghostbusting; finding lost tombs, treasures; clairvoyance.

Elisa Robyn, Ph.D. Wheat Ridge, Colorado. Shamanic readings, spirit guides, astrology. Author.

Pat Rodegast. Naples, Florida. Channeling. Author.

George Roman. Beverly Hills, California. Vedic astrology, Chinese mah jongg cards, relationship predictions.

Carla L. Rueckert. Louisville, Kentucky. Channeling, questions and answers. Author.

Kevin Ryerson. San Francisco, California. Channeling.

S

Iris Saltzman. North Miami Beach, Florida. Psychic astrology, Founder of international Parapsychology School.

Arian Sarris. Emerysville, California. General psychic readings.

Harold S. Schroeppel. Tallahassee, Florida. Direct platform, tarot.

Ron Scolastico, Ph.D. Woodland Hills, California. Deep trance readings, spiritual counseling. Author.

Selene. Chico, California. Spiritual consultations, clairvoyance, intuitive tarot, past lives, spirit guides. Author.

Selene. Arlington Heights, Illinois. Playing cards.

Major (Ret.) Paul J. Sevigny. Danville, Vermont. Dowsing.

Sharla. Wheat Ridge, Colorado. Computer channeling.

Jennifer Shepherd. Princeton, New Jersey. Tarot, palmistry, clairvoyance, channeling.

Johanna Gargiulo-Sherman. Brooklyn, New York. Psychometry, numerology, Sacred Rose Tarot (creator). Author.

Marc Sky. Tarot, astrology, palmistry, aura readings.

Carol Skylark, M.F.A. Fort Collins. Colorado. Clairvoyance, clairaudience, healings, aura portraits.

Jay Solomon. Whitehall, Pennsylvania. Satanic rites and ceremonies.

Joelle Steele. Santa Monica, California. Astrology.

Laura Steele. New York City, New York. Finding location of objects and personal relocation.

T

Shirlee Teabo. Federal Way, Washington. Tarot, psychic detection. Author.

Noel Tyl. Fountain Hills, Arizona. Astrology. Author.

V

Alan Vaughan, Ph.D. Los Angeles, California. Intuitive clairvoyance, precognitive and channeled readings, psychic archeology, psychic dreaming, recognition research. Author.

Louise Vernon, D.D., D.S. Honolulu, Hawaii. Exorcism, past lives, etheric healings. astronomology, numerology, biorhythms. Author.

Vija Virgo. Denver, Colorado. Astrology, cards, clairvoyance, clairaudience, palmistry, numerology, past lives, tea leaves, psychometry, automatic writing.

W

Ron Warmoth, M.A. Los Angeles, California. Personal and professional mineral dowsing. Newsletter author. (Deceased.)

Ronald L. Watson, C.C.H. St. George, Utah. Compatibility and natal readings by computer, hypnosis.

Richard Webster. Auckland, New Zealand. Feng Shui, auras, Chinese numerology, ogham, oracles. Author.

Charles Whitehouse, D.C. Arkansas. Psychotronics, radionics, entity clearing, geomancy, chakra balancing.

Jyoti Wind. Boulder, Colorado. Astrology, shamanic readings, Hakomi psychotherapy.

George Withers. Denver, Pennsylvania. Candle readings through crystal balls, crystal ball tarot.

Stacey Anne Wolf. New York City, New York. Tarot, psychic readings, past lives, entity clearing. Author.

Lois Wolfsong. Port Angeles, Washington. Portraits of past lives, spirit guides and angels, soul logos (persona symbols) with messages.

Ms. Lou Wright. Bayard Park, Delaware. General psychic readings, psychic detection, angelic communication.

BIBLIOGRAPHY

BOOKS

Anderson, Mary. *Divination: How to Use Unusual Methods.* York Beach, ME: Samuel Weiser, Inc., 1974.

Are You Mediumistic? A pamphlet. U.S.A.: Stanray Industries, Inc. 1971.

Ashby, Robert H. *The Ashby Guidebook for Study of the Paranormal.* Rev. ed. edited by Frank C. Tribbe. York Beach, ME: Samuel Weiser, 1987.

Bardon, Franz. *The Practice of Magical Evocation: Instructions for Invoking Spirits from the Spheres Surrounding Us.* Trans. Peter Dimai. Wuppertal, Germany: Dieter Ruggeberg/Wuppertal, 1975.

Brent, Peter. *Past, Present and Future: How to Read and Interpret Dreams, Handwriting, Palms, Cards, Tea Leaves, Dice, Doodles, Numbers.* Indianapolis and New York: The Bobbs-Merrill Company, Inc., 1975.

Burke, Adam. *Pocket Guide to Self-Hypnosis.* Freedom, California: Crossing Press, 1997.

Burns, Litany. *Develop Your Psychic Abilities: And Get Them to Work for You in Your Daily Life.* New York: Prentice Hall, 1985.

Butler, W. E. *How to Read the Aura, Practice Psychometry, Telepathy and Clairvoyance.* 1968, 1971, 1975. Reprint, New York: Destiny Books, 1978.

Carrington, Hereward. *Your Psychic Powers and How to Develop Them.* Van Nuys, California: Newcatle Publishing Company, Inc., 1975.

Carrington, Hereward and Willis Whitehead. *Keys to the Occult: Two Guides to Hidden Wisdom.* North Hollywood, California: Newcastle Publishing Company, Inc., 1977.

Cavendish, Richard. *A History of Magic.* London: Arkana, 1990.

Crow, W. B. *History of Witchcraft, Magic, and Occultism.* 1968. Reprint, North Hollywood, California: Wilshire Book Company, 1971.

Crowley, Aleister. *Magick Without Tears.* 1973. Reprint, Tempe, Arizona: New Falcon Publications, 1994.

Douglas, Alfred. *Extra-Sensory Powers: A Century of Psychical Research.* Woodstock, New York: Overlook Press, 1977.

Drury, Nevill. *Dictionary of Mysticism and the Occult.* New York: Harper and Row, Inc., 1985.

Ebon, Martin, ed. *The Signet Handbook of Parapsychology.* New York: New American Library, 1978.

Editors. *Dictionary of the Occult.* London: Brockhampton Press, 1996.

Editors. *Encyclopedia of Magic and Superstition.* London: Octopus Books Ltd., 1974.

Editors. *Psychic Powers.* Alexandria, VA: Time-Life Books, 1987.

Editors. *Webster's New Universal Unabridged Dictionary.* Deluxe second ed. New York: Simon and Schuster, 1985.

Farrar, Janet, and Stewart Farrar. *The Witches' Way.* London: Robert Hale, 1984.

Fodor, Nandor. *An Encyclopedia of Psychic Science.* Secaucus: Citadel Press, 1966.

Givry, Grillot de. *Witchcraft, Magic and Alchemy.* Trans. J. Courtenay Locke. New York: Frederick Publications, 1954.

Hall, Angus. *The Supernatural: Signs of Things to Come.* London: Aldus Books Ltd., 1975.

Hansel, C. E. M. *ESP and Parapsychology: A Critical Reevaluation.* New York: Prometheus Books, 1980.

Hipskind, Judith. *Palmistry: The Whole View.* St. Paul, MN: Llewellyn Worldwide, 1983.

Huson, Paul. *Mastering Witchcraft: A Practical Guide for Witches, Warlocks and Covens.* New York: Perigree Books, 1970.

Jaegers, Beverly C. *Beyond Palmistry: The Art and Science of Modern Hand Analysis.* New York: Berkley Books, 1992.

————. *You and Your Hand: A Textbook of Modern Hand Analysis.* Creve Coeur, MO: Aries Productions, 1974.

Klimo, Jon. *Channeling: Investigations on Receiving Information from Paranormal Sources.* Los Angeles: Jeremy P. Tarcher, Inc., 1987.

Liaros, Carol Ann. *Practical ESP: A Step-By-Step Guide for Developing Your Intuitive Potential.* 1985. Reprint, Buffalo, NY: Liaros, Polvino and Associates, 1989.

Logan, Jo and Lindsy Hodson. *The Prediction Book of Divination.* England: Blandford Press, 1984.

Maple, Eric. *Superstition and the Superstitious.* 1971. Reprint, North Hollywood, California: Wilshire Book Company, 1973.

Mayne, Ra. *Six Lessons in Crystal Gazing.* Los Angeles: International Imports, 1992.

Mischell, Patricia L. *Beyond Positive Thinking: Mind Power Techniques for Discovering How Extraordinary You Really Are.* 1985. Reprint, Cincinnati: Twin Lakes Publishing, 1993.

Montgomery, Ruth. *A Gift of Prophecy.* New York: William Morrow and Company, 1965.

Morwyn. *Green Magic: Healing Powers of Herbs, Talismans and Stones.* Atglen, Pennsylvania: Schiffer Publishing, 1994.

————. *Secrets of a Witch's Coven.* Atglen, Pennsylvania: Schiffer Publishing, 1988.

————. *Web of Light: Rites for Witches in the New Age.* Atglen, Pennsylvania: Schiffer Publishing, 1993.

————. *Witch's Brew: Secrets of Scents.* Atglen, Pennsylvania: Schiffer Publishing, 1995.

Nicholas, Margaret. *The World's Greatest Psychics and Mystics.* England: Octopus Books, Ltd., 1986.

Poinsot, M. C. *The Encyclopedia of Occult Sciences.* 1939. Reprint, New York: Tudor Publishing Company, 1968.

Potter, Carole. *Knock on Wood and Other Superstitions.* New York: Bonanza Books, 1984.

Riva, Anna. *How to Conduct a Seance.* Los Angeles: International Imports, 1994.

Rhine, Louisa E. *Psi What is It?: The Story of ESP and PK.* 1975. Reprint, New York: Harper and Row, 1976.

Rueckert, Carla L. *A Channeling Handbook.* Louisville, Kentucky: L/L Research, 1987.

Sepharial. *Second Sight.* 1911. Reprint, Santa Fe, New Mexico: Sun Publishing Company, 1992.

Spence, Lewis. *The Magic Arts in Celtic Britain.* New York: Dorset Press, 1992.

Squire, Elizabeth. *Fortune in Your Hand.* New York: Fleet Publishing Corporation, 1960.

Underwood, Peter. *Into the Occult.* London: George C. Harrop and Company, Ltd., 1972.

Valiente, Doreen. *An ABC of Witchcraft, Past and Present.* New York: St. Martin's Press Inc., 1973.

———— *Natural Magic.* New York: St. Martin's Press, 1975.

Verner, Alexr. *Practical Psychometry. A short handbook,* np, nd.

Walker, Charles. *The Encyclopedia of Secret Knowledge.* London: Limited Editions, 1995.

Ward, Bernie. *Nostradamus: The Man Who Saw Tomorrow.* Boca Raton, FL: Globe Communications Corporation, 1997.

Westen, Robin. *Channelers: A New Age Directory.* New York: Perigree Books, 1988.

Wilson, Joyce. *The Complete Book of Palmistry.* New York: Bantam Books, 1971.

ARTICLES, VIDEOS, PAMPHLETS

Begley, Sharon. "Is There Anything to It? Evidence, Please." *Newsweek,* July 9, 1996, pp. 54–55.

Collins, Matthew, writer, producer, director, and Kate Southall, associate producer. *Telegrams from the Dead: The Rise and Fall of Spiritualism in America.* Video, part of *The American Experience* series. Narrated by Ellen Burstyn. Boston: WGBH Educational Foundation, 1994. Distributed by Shanachie Entertainment Corp, 1994.

Cowley, Geoffrey. "Is There a Sixth Sense?" *Newsweek,* October 13, 1997, p. 67.

Feldman, Gayle. "Power of 'Do-It-Yourself' Book Publicity." *The New York Times,* Monday, February 16, 1998, p. C-7.

Leland John, and Carla Power. "Deepak's Instant Karma." *Newsweek,* October 20, 1997, pp. 52–58.

Muir, Andrew. "The End Is Nigh—But When Exactly Is Nigh?" *Newsweek,* September 8, 1997, p. 12.

Norwich, Julia. "Body and Soul: Psychics." *Elle,* no. 30, April, 1996, pp. 132–136.

Weekly World News. "The Third Prophecy of Fatima!" November 11, 1997, pp. 8–9.

Walton, Susan. "Fingering Disease." (rpt) *Boulder Daily Camera.* Boulder, Colorado, December 5, 1985.

Woodward, Kenneth L. "The Spiritual Surfer." *Newsweek,* April 1, 1996, p. 68.

INDEX

REACH FOR THE MOON

Llewellyn publishes hundreds of books on your favorite subjects! To get these exciting books, including the ones on the following pages, check your local bookstore or order them directly from Llewellyn.

ORDER BY PHONE
- Call toll-free within the U.S. and Canada, 1-800-THE MOON
- In Minnesota, call (651) 291-1970
- We accept VISA, MasterCard, and American Express

ORDER BY MAIL
- Send the full price of your order (MN residents add 7% sales tax) in U.S. funds, plus postage & handling to:

  Llewellyn Worldwide
  P.O. Box 64383, Dept. K236-4
  St. Paul, MN 55164–0383, U.S.A.

POSTAGE & HANDLING
(For the U.S., Canada, and Mexico)
- $4.00 for orders $15.00 and under
- $5.00 for orders over $15.00
- No charge for orders over $100.00

We ship UPS in the continental United States. We ship standard mail to P.O. boxes. Orders shipped to Alaska, Hawaii, The Virgin Islands, and Puerto Rico are sent first-class mail. Orders shipped to Canada and Mexico are sent surface mail.

International orders: Airmail—add freight equal to price of each book to the total price of order, plus $5.00 for each non-book item (audio tapes, etc.).

Surface mail—Add $1.00 per item.

Allow 2 weeks for delivery on all orders.
Postage and handling rates subject to change.

DISCOUNTS
We offer a 20% discount to group leaders or agents. You must order a minimum of 5 copies of the same book to get our special quantity price.

FREE CATALOG
Get a free copy of our color catalog, *New Worlds of Mind and Spirit*. Subscribe for just $10.00 in the United States and Canada ($30.00 overseas, airmail). Many bookstores carry *New Worlds*—ask for it!

Visit our web site at www.llewellyn.com for more information.

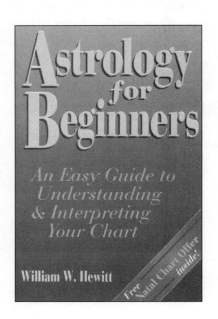

ASTROLOGY FOR BEGINNERS

An Easy Guide to Understanding and Interpreting Your Chart

William W. Hewitt

Anyone who is interested in astrology will enjoy *Astrology for Beginners*. This book makes astrology easy and exciting by presenting all of the basics in an orderly sequence while focusing on the natal chart. Llewellyn even includes a coupon for a free computerized natal chart so you can begin interpretations almost immediately without complicated mathematics.

Astrology for Beginners covers all of the basics. Learn exactly what astrology is and how it works. Explore signs, planets, houses and aspects. Learn how to interpret a birth chart. Discover the meaning of transits, predictive astrology and progressions. Determine your horoscope chart in minutes without using math.

Whether you want to practice astrology for a hobby or aspire to become a professional astrologer, *Astrology for Beginners* is the book you need to get started on the right track.

0-87542-307-8, 5¼ x 8, 288 pp.   **$9.95**

Instant Palm Reader

A Roadmap to Life

Linda Domin

Etched upon your palm is an aerial view of all the scenes you will travel in the course of your lifetime. Your characteristics, skills and abilities are imprinted in your mind and transferred as images onto your hand. Now, with this simple, flip-through pictorial guide, you can assemble your own personal palm reading, like a professional, almost instantly.

The Instant Palm Reader shows you how your hands contain the picture of the real you—physically, emotionally and mentally. More than 500 easy-to-read diagrams will provide you with candid, uplifting revelations about yourself: personality, childhood, career, finances, family, love life, talents and destiny.

With the sensitive information artfully contained within each interpretation, you will also be able to uncover your hidden feelings and unconscious needs as you learn the secrets of this 3,000-year-old science.

1-56718-232-1, 6 x 9, 288 pp., 500 illus.   **$14.95**

Omens, Oghams & Oracles

Divination in the Druidic Tradition

Richard Webster

Although hundreds of books have been written about the Celts and the druids, no book has focused exclusively on Celtic divination—until now. *Omens, Oghams & Oracles* covers the most important and practical methods of divination in the Celtic and druidic traditions, two of which have never before been published: an original system of divining using the druidic Ogham characters, and "Arthurian divination," which employs a geomantic oracle called druid sticks.

Even if you have no knowledge or experience with any form of divination, this book will show you how to create and use the 25 Ogham fews and the druid sticks immediately to gain accurate and helpful insights into your life. This book covers divination through sky stones, touchstones, bodhran drums and other means, with details on how to make these objects and sample readings to supplement the text.

Many Celtic divinatory methods are as useful today as they were 2,000 years ago—make modern forms of these ancient oracles work for you!

1–56718–800–1, 7 x 10, 224 pp., softcover   **$12.95**

PSYCHIC DEVELOPMENT
FOR BEGINNERS

*An Easy Guide to Releasing and
Developing Your Psychic Abilities*

William W. Hewitt

Psychic Development for Beginners provides detailed instruction on developing your sixth sense, or psychic ability. Improve your sense of worth, your sense of responsibility and therefore your ability to make a difference in the world. Innovative exercises like "The Skyscraper" allow beginning students of psychic development to quickly realize personal and material gain through their own natural talent.

Benefits range from the practical to spiritual. Find a parking space anywhere, handle a difficult salesperson, choose a compatible partner, and even access different time periods! Practice psychic healing on pets or humans—and be pleasantly surprised by your results. Use psychic commands to prevent dozing while driving. Preview out-of-body travel, cosmic consciousness and other alternative realities. Instruction in *Psychic Development for Beginners* is supported by personal anecdotes, 44 psychic development exercises, and 28 related psychic case studies to help students gain a comprehensive understanding of the psychic realm.

1-56718-360-3, 5¼ x 8, 216 pp.   **$9.95**

to order, call 1–800–THE MOON
prices subject to change without notice

TAROT PLAIN AND SIMPLE

Anthony Louis
with illustrations by Robin Wood

The tarot is an excellent method for turning experience into wisdom. At its essence the Tarot deals with archetypal symbols of the human situation. By studying the Tarot, we connect ourselves with the mythical underpinnings of our lives; we contact the gods within. As a tool, the Tarot helps to awaken our intuitive self. This book presents a thoroughly tested, reliable and user-friendly self-study program for those who want to do readings for themselves and others. It is written by a psychiatrist who brings a profound understanding of human nature and psychological conflict to the study of the Tarot. Tarot enthusiasts will find that his Jungian approach to the card descriptions will transport them to an even deeper level of personal transformation.

1-56718-400-6, 6 x 9, 336 pp., illus.   **$14.95**